INTRODUCTION

THIS BOOK WAS CHANNEL WRITTEN ~~~~~~~~~~~~ OM SOURCE. I USED MY OWN WAY OF W~~~~~~~~~~~ INFORMATION I WAS GIVEN. THE REASON I HAVE WRITTEN ALL CAPITAL LETTERS, IS NOT TO SHOUT AT YOU, BUT TO SHOW EVERYTHING WRITTEN IS IMPORTANT FOR YOU (THE READER) TO CONSIDER EVERYTHING YOU READ AND WRITE. I AM ACTUALLY EXCITED FOR THE OUTCOME OF THIS BOOK IN THE LONG-TERM!

THE BEAUTY OF THIS BOOK, IS THAT ALL READERS GET TO WRITE THEIR OWN BOOK OF TRUTH AND COMPARE IT TO THE INFORMATION THAT THEY HAVE BEEN PROGRAMMED WITH, THEREFORE BECOMING MORE AWARE AND POWERFUL WITHIN. IT IS THEN A CHOICE FOR THE READER TO LIVE FREELY.

WE LIVE IN A VERY UNSTABLE, IF NOT VOLATILE SOCIETY, THIS IS DUE TO SO MANY DIVISIONS IN HUMANITY...

THIS BOOK WILL TOUCH ON DIFFERENT TOPICS THAT CAUSE PEOPLE TO BE DIVIDED. NO JUDGEMENT SHALL BE PASSED, I HAVE BEEN THE SUBJECT OF JUDGEMENT MYSELF, I HAVE ALSO JUDGED, SOME MAY EVEN JUDGE ME ON WHAT IS WRITTEN IN THIS BOOK AND THAT'S OK IF THEY TOO ENJOY BEING JUDGED. IT IS TIME FOR CHANGE.

MY AIM IS TO ALLOW EVERYONE WHO READS THIS BOOK TO SEE LIFE FROM A DIFFERENT ANGLE WITHIN THEIR OWN MIND AND ASK QUESTIONS OF THEMSELVES, UNDERSTANDING THAT THERE IS ONLY ONE TRUTH, BUT MANY DIFFERENT VISIONS OR OPINIONS.

I DEDICATE THIS BOOK TO MY LATE GRANDMOTHERS CATHY AND MARGERY, ALSO MY LATE FATHER TREVOR. I ALSO DEDICATE IT TO EVERY MAN, WOMAN AND CHILD WHO HAVE UNWITTINGLY BEEN PROGRAMMED BY A SYSTEM SO BIG AND CLEVER, THAT THEY DON'T KNOW WHAT TRUTH IS ANYMORE.

WARNING

ONCE YOU (THE READER) BEGIN TO WRITE YOUR TRUTH, IT CANNOT BE DELETED FROM YOUR BRAIN, IT CANNOT BE FORGOTTEN AND IF YOU CHOOSE A LIFE TO LIVE, AGAINST YOUR TRUTH (WHICH YOU'LL ALL WRITE), YOU WILL LOSE ENERGY QUICKLY. IF YOU LIVE EXACTLY AS YOU WRITE, FROM THE QUESTIONS YOU WILL BE ANSWERING AND YOU WILL GAIN ENERGY. BUT ALSO CHANGE MANY PROGRAMS THAT HAVE BEEN EMBEDDED IN TO YOUR MIND AND BRAIN FROM SCHOOL, TV, STORIES THAT YOU HAVE HEARD, INHERITED BEHAVIOURS FROM FAMILY AND MORE!

THIS IS A DISCLAIMER, THAT YOUR LIFE WILL BECOME BETTER WHEN YOU LIVE WHAT YOU WRITE AS ANSWERS TO THE QUESTIONS YOU ARE ASKED. (SHOULD YOU BE WILLING TO TAKE PART) YOU'LL NEED A LINED PAD OT LAPTOP SO THAT YOU CAN WRITE YOUR OWN BOOK, BASED ON YOUR ANSWERS FROM THE QUESTIONS THAT YOU WILL BE ASKED. PLEASE REMEMBER, IN ORDER TO DO THIS PROPERLY, PLEASE WRITE YOUR REASONING FOR YOUR ANSWERS. YES OR NO ANSWERS WILL NOT ALLOW YOU TO UNDERSTAND WHENEVER YOU READ BACK WHAT YOU HAVE WRITTEN.

THE INSTRUCTIONS ARE EASY:

READ THE BOOK LIKE A STORY OR LISTEN TO THE AUDIO BOOK WITH AN OPEN MIND, READ THE BOOK AGAIN AND ANSWER EVERY QUESTION OUT LOUD AND WRITE YOUR TRUTH. THIS MEANS YOU WILL WRITE YOUR OWN BOOK, BASED- ON YOUR BELIEFS AND NOBODY ELSE'S. I'D ADVISE BUYING A LINED BOOK OF SOME DESCRIPTION TO WRITE YOUR OWN BOOK, BASED-ON THE QUESTIONS YOU'VE LISTENED TO OR READ.

GOOD LUCK AND GODSPEED!

CHAPTER 1: SOCIETY CONFLICTS

TO THINK ONE PERSON'S OPINION OR THEORY IS A UNIVERSAL TRUTH WOULD BE ABSOLUTELY RIDICULOUS WOULDN'T IT?

WE, AS HUMAN BEINGS ARE DIVIDED IN JUST ABOUT EVERY WAY POSSIBLE AND I'M SURE A LOT OF PEOPLE WILL AGREE WITH ME ON THIS. DIVIDED INTO CATEGORIES, SUB-CATEGORIES AND BEYOND! SO THAT LITTLE ME AND LITTLE YOU DO NOT UNDERSTAND THAT WE ARE PART OF SOMETHING MUCH BIGGER!

SO, WHO DECIDES ON WHAT SOCIETY IS? WHY IS IT DIFFERENT AGAIN IN DIFFERENT COUNTRIES? WHY DOES OUR SKIN COLOUR DETERMINE ANYTHING?

LET'S HAVE A LOOK INTO SOME OF THE CATEGORIES THAT DIVIDE US...

RELIGION:

IT'S PRETTY WILD TO THINK THAT DIFFERENT FAITHS CAN DIVIDE US, WITH WARS AND CONFLICTS. I AM A BELIEVER IN A HIGHER POWER (GOD) BUT NOT OF THE STAUNCH FOLLOWING OR CULT TYPE. THERE ARE MANY RELIGIONS, WE CAN EVEN MAKE OUR OWN IF WE GET ENOUGH FOLLOWERS!! CRAZY, HUH?

WHO GAVE US THE CHOICE WHEN WE WERE YOUNGER? WERE WE GIVEN AN ALTERNATIVE? WE LEARN FROM THE ADULTS AND PEERS WE ARE BROUGHT UP AROUND AND THEY LEARNED THE SAME WAY, AS DID THE PEOPLE WHO PRECEDED THEM. THERE WAS NOT MUCH OF A CHOICE REALLY. A BELIEF IS JUST A THOUGHT WE THINK OVER AND OVER AGAIN, SO WHEN WE LISTEN, READ AND SEE CERTAIN THINGS, WE LIVE OUR LIVES BY IT FROM A YOUNG AGE. CAN YOU THINK OF ANYTHING THAT YOU HAVE BEEN MADE TO BELIEVE, THAT YOU DIDN'T HAVE A CHOICE? WHAT WOULD YOU HAVE LIKED MORE FREEDOM OF THOUGHT ON WHEN YOU WERE YOUNGER?

I REMEMBER I WAS AGED 6 AND MY MOTHER AND SOON TO BE STEP FATHER AT THE TIME, MOVED UP TO THE ISLE OF LEWIS WITH MY THREE YOUNGER SIBLINGS. WE DIDN'T COME FROM A RELIGIOUS BACKGROUND PER SE, HOWEVER MY MUM KNEW OF A HIGHER POWER AND USED TO SAY HER PRAYERS. WE ARRIVED ON THIS BEAUTIFUL SCOTTISH ISLAND AND WE HAD FRESH AIR, RELATIVELY QUIET ROADS... IT WAS GREAT TO BRING UP YOUNG CHILDREN! WE STAYED A YEAR IN AN OLD HOUSE, NUMBER 1 LAXDALE LANE. SOME MORNINGS WOULD WAKE UP TO SHEEP IN THE HOUSE, AS THE DOORS WERE NEVER LOCKED IN THOSE DAYS!! WE WENT TO SCHOOL NEARBY AND NEVER REALLY BOTHERED WITH ANYONE OTHER THAN OUR FRIENDS WE HAD MADE, LIFE WAS EASY.

IT WASN'T UNTIL WE MOVED TO SEAVIEW, CNOC, ON THE ISLE OF LEWIS THAT OUR EYES OPENED FULLY. WE MOVED HOUSE ON THE SATURDAY, HAD DINNER AND WENT TO BED. SUNDAY MORNING WE WERE UP, WASHED, CHANGED AND OUT TO THE PARK, TO FIND THE SWINGS CHAINED AND PADLOCKED UP!! WE DID OUR BEST AND USED THEM AS A CLIMBING FRAME AND MESSED AROUND TO BE CHASED OUT OF THE PARK WITH TWO ELDERLY WOMAN YIELDING BROOMS... SHOUTING "THE LORD WILL PUNISH YOU" AND "SHOO! THIS IS THE SABBATH DAY!" ONE OF US WAS WHACKED WITH A BROOM. WE WERE ONLY LITTLE AND WE FROZE.

MY MOTHER WAS AT THEIR DOOR LIKE A WOMAN POSSESSED TO READ THE RIOT ACT! THE RULES IN SEAVIEW WERE.. ON THE LORD'S DAY, WE WERE NOT ALLOWED IN THE PARK, WE HAD TO GO TO CHURCH AND SUNDAY SCHOOL, NO MATTER WHAT! SURE ENOUGH IT HAPPENED AND WE HAD NO CHOICE WITH THE SOCIAL PRESSURE FROM THE NEIGHBOURS. IT WAS MADE FUN, WE SANG, READ, PLAYED AND LEARNED ABOUT THE BIBLE. WE WERE THREATENED WITHIN AN INCH OF OUR LIVES, IF WE DID ANYTHING WRONG, GOD WAS GOING TO PUNISH US AND HE WAS WATCHING AND KNEW OUR THOUGHTS... WAS A LITTLE TRAUMATIC AT TIMES WHEN I THINK BACK BUT SEEMED NORMAL WHEN I WAS YOUNG, I WOULDN'T PUT MY OWN CHILDREN THROUGH IT.

THAT WAS MY FIRST EXPERIENCE WITH RELIGION, IT WAS FORCED ON TO MY WHOLE FAMILY BECAUSE OF WHERE WE LIVED. WE HAD A GREAT TIME AS KIDS AS WE HAD THE COUNTRYSIDE ALL AROUND US AND WERE NEVER BORED.

IT MAKES ME WONDER WHAT LIFE WOULD BE LIKE WITHOUT RELIGION, OR A UNIVERSAL RELIGION TO BRING EVERYONE TOGETHER. WOULD PEOPLE HAVE THEIR RELIGION IF THEY HAD THEIR CHOICE? WOULD YOU?

WHO MADE IT A THING THAT WE FIGHT BECAUSE OF DIFFERENT BELIEFS ALSO?

RACE:

I BELIEVE IT'S PRETTY DISGUSTING THAT PEOPLE ARE TREATED DIFFERENTLY ACCORDING TO THEIR RACE, WHAT MAKES IT EVEN MORE MENTAL IS THAT A FEW DIFFERENT RACES SHARE THE SAME RELIGION BUT STILL HAVE CONFLICT! AGAIN, IT ALL GOES BACK TO THAT PROGRAMMING PEOPLE GET GROWING UP!

IS IT HISTORY LESSONS THAT KEEP IT UP SO THAT HUMANS ARE UNCONSCIOUSLY MADE RACIST THROUGH THEIR EDUCATION GROWING UP? I BELIEVE IT IS... FOR INSTANCE; WHITE PEOPLE USED BLACK PEOPLE AS SLAVES FOR MANY YEARS. THERE IS NO JUSTIFICATION TO THIS BEHAVIOUR IN MY HUMBLE BELIEF. WHY SHOULD THIS BE TAUGHT IN HISTORY CLASS?? MAYBE SO THAT THE SEED IS PLANTED AND IT SETS PEOPLE UP FOR WHEN THEY ARE OLDER... SOME WHITE PEOPLE BELIEVE THAT THEY ARE ABOVE BLACK PEOPLE AND SOME BLACK PEOPLE WANT JUSTICE AGAINST THE WHITE PEOPLE. AS I MENTIONED EARLIER, A BELIEF IS JUST A THOUGHT THAT WE THINK OVER AND OVER OR A PROGRAM THAT IS PLAYED TO US OVER AND OVER... WHAT IF RACISM WERE TAKEN OUT OF SCHOOLS AND MOVIES? WOULD PEOPLE FIGHT THE SAME? CAN WE MOVE ON AND DO WHAT WE WANT TO DO, RATHER THAN FIGHT FOR WHAT OUR ANCESTORS WANTED TO FIGHT OVER? WOULD THIS NOT BE THE ONLY WAY TO DISSOLVE IT?

SEXUALITY:

SEXUALITY IS UP THERE WITH RACE AND RELIGION, AS FAR AS DIVISION OF HUMANITY IS CONCERNED.

MAINSTREAM MEDIA SCAREMONGERING PEOPLE INTO FEELING LIKE THEY ARE VICTIMS BECAUSE A VERY, VERY SMALL PERCENTAGE OF THE POPULATION DOES NOT LIKE PEOPLE OF A CERTAIN GENDER OR SEXUAL PREFERENCE. DOES THIS MEAN THAT IF PEOPLE LIVE A LIFE AS A CERTAIN GENDER OR HAVE SEXUAL RELATIONS WITH A SPECIFIC PERSON OF THEIR CHOICE, THAT THEY INSTANTLY FEEL THAT THEY CANNOT FEEL POWERFUL?

PERSONALLY, I FEEL PEOPLE CAN DO WHAT THEY LIKE, HAVE SEX WITH CONSENTING ADULTS AS MUCH AS THEY LIKE. THIS DOESN'T CHANGE THE INDIVIDUAL. WHAT DOES CHANGE THE INDIVIDUAL, IS WHEN ONE HORRENDOUS STORY IS PUT ON THE NEWS AND THEY USE THE PROPAGANDA METHOD TO SCARE THE REST OF THE POPULATION WHO ARE LIVING BY THEIR OWN SEXUALITY, TO NOW LIVE IN FEAR. THIS CAUSES THEM TO BE SCARED TO BE THEMSELVES, ON THE BACK FOOT... OR ON THE FRONT FOOT, READY TO FIGHT, BEING ALL DEFENSIVE, WHEN IT DOESN'T ACTUALLY MATTER WHAT THEY DO AS THEY ARE STILL HUMAN BEINGS! DOES YOUR SEXUALITY MATTER IN THE GRAND SCALE OF LIFE? IF IT CHANGED, WOULD THE WORLD CHANGE? SO THE WORLD DOESN'T REVOLVE ROUND SEXUALITY EITHER THEN DOES IT?

SEXUALITY HAS BEEN USED TO SYSTEMATICALLY SPLIT PEOPLE FROM BEING TOGETHER FOR THE SAKE OF CONTROL. IT IS A CHOICE FOR EVERYONE, HOW THEY ACT OR REACT TO SOMEONE, REGARDLESS OF THEIR FEELINGS... I HAVE FAMILY AND FRIENDS WHO HAVE A DIFFERENT CHOICE OF SEXUALITY THAN ME AND I WELCOME THEM AS I DO, EVERY OTHER HUMAN THAT HAS A CONSENTING ADULT WITH A DIFFERENT SEXUAL PREFERENCE. IF SOMEONE WEREN'T TO AGREE WITH THE OTHER INDIVIDUAL'S CHOICE, SHOULD THEY HAVE THE RIGHT TO A FREE SPEECH OPINION? OR ASK QUESTIONS TO UNDERSTAND? (AS LONG AS IT WAS NOT

HATE SPEECH OR BULLYING)

WHY IS IT PROMOTED, THAT PEOPLE WITH DIFFERENT SEXUAL PREFERENCES/BEING SHOULD THEN LABELED IN GROUPS? IF YOU ARE A MEMBER OR ARE PART OF A SMALLER GROUP, WOULD YOU NOT NOW BE MADE VULNERABLE BY THE ONES WHO MADE UP THE TERMINOLOGY? AFTER ALL, THE TERMINOLOGY IS DROPPED INTO SOCIETY AS A CHOICE, NOT MADE UP BY THE PEOPLE NO? IF I WANTED TO BE POWERFUL AND WAS DIFFERENT TO ONE HUNDRED PEOPLE, WOULD I HAVE MORE OF A CHANCE NOT LOOKING AT THE DIFFERENCES OR DIVIDING US WITH DIFFERENCES? DO YOU UNDERSTAND HOW LABELING SEXUALITY IS ACTUALLY HARMFUL?

WHY ARE PEOPLE TREATED LIKE VICTIMS, BECAUSE OF THEIR GENDER OR SEXUALITY? WHAT IS A VICTIM? IF SOMETHING HAPPENS TO 10 PEOPLE OUT OF 100,000 ARE THEY ALL VICTIMS?

IMAGINE THERE WERE LAWS PUT IN PLACE, WHERE EVERYONE WAS TREATED THE SAME, NO MATTER THEIR GENDER OR SEXUALITY... WHERE PEOPLE COULD BE FREE AND NOT BE MANIPULATED IN TO FEELING JUDGED OR INSECURE... THIS COULD BE CREATED IF PEOPLE BELIEVED THAT THEY WERE MORE THAN A LABEL. PEOPLE KNOWING WHO THEY ARE WOULD ALLOW ACCEPTANCE AND GROWTH TO FLOOD THEIR LIVES, RATHER THAN LIVE LIFE ACCORDING TO THEIR LABELS AND OTHER PEOPLE'S EXPECTATIONS. WHY DO PEOPLE FOCUS ON LABELS SO MUCH? DEROGATORY COMMENTS ARE BAD, BUT IT'S HOW WE PROCESS THEM THAT IS DAMAGING. IF YOU ARE GAY OR STRAIGHT, DOES IT CHANGE WHO YOU ARE OR WHAT YOU DO?

WHY HAS SEXUALITY, GENDER AND OTHER DIVISIONS BECOME MORE POPULAR WHEN THERE ARE NEW POWERS WANTING TO CONTROL A WORLD OF UNHAPPY PEOPLE? WHY USE SEXUALITY? IS IT BECAUSE ITS LINKED TO HAPPINESS/DISTRACTION OR DOPAMINE HITS SO IT FEELS NORMAL TO DO SO?

AGE:

IF I WERE PAID A PENNY EVERY TIME I HEARD "THOSE MILLENNIALS" OR "GENERATION X/Z ARE STUPID" OR EVEN "THEY ARE JUST OLD, THEY DON'T HAVE A CLUE" I'D BE A FINANCIALLY WEALTHY PERSON, IT'S ALL CRAZY!! PEOPLE ARE JUDGED ON THEIR AGE SO MUCH AND IN SO MANY WAYS!

PUTTING PEOPLE INTO AN AGE BRACKET AND ADDING A LABEL WOULD BE LIKE TARRING PEOPLE WITH THE SAME BRUSH, MEANING THEY LACK INDIVIDUALITY, NO? ARE THEY INDIVIDUAL PEOPLE OR ARE THEY AN AGE?

I, BY SOCIETY'S STANDARDS WOULD BE A MILLENNIAL BECAUSE I WAS BORN IN 1983, I DON'T FEEL THE SAME AS EVERYONE ELSE, I DON'T FOLLOW TRENDS. IT WOULD APPEAR MY GENERATION IS THE BRIDGE BETWEEN 'OLD SCHOOL' AND 'NEW AGE'. IN MY BELIEF IT IS THE BEST AND TOUGHEST PLACE TO BE AS WE CAN ADHERE TO THE OLDER GENERATIONS WAY OF WORKING, WHILE UNDERSTANDING HOW THE YOUNGER ONES ARE BEING PROGRAMMED DIFFERENTLY. THE GAP BETWEEN THE OLDER GENERATION AND GENERATION 'X' AND GENERATION 'Z' IS HUUUGE !AS FAR AS SOCIETY HAS BEEN TAUGHT THROUGH ALL GENERATIONS, IT IS THE SAME METHOD WITH DIFFERENT INFORMATION. CHANGE THE RULES, CHANGE THE PEOPLE, PREDICT AND CONTROL THE PEOPLE AND THE OUTCOME OF LIVING.

BEING IN THAT 'MIDDLE GROUND' ALLOWS IT TO BE EASIER FOR MY GENERATION TO UNDERSTAND ALL OF THE GENERATIONS BETTER. WHY IS NOTHING BEING DONE TO BRING EVERYONE TOGETHER?? WHY ARE PEOPLE JUDGING OTHERS FROM DIFFERENT GENERATIONS AND NOT UNDERSTANDING THAT THERE IS STILL A HEART AND SOUL IN THE OTHER INDIVIDUAL? MORE TO THE POINT, WHY ARE WE ALLOWING IT? WE CAN BE THAT CHANGE!!!

CLASS:

THE CLASS SYSTEM... WHERE DO YOU BELONG? IS SOMEONE BETTER THAN YOU BECAUSE THEY HAVE AN INDOCTRINATED EDUCATION? ARE YOU BETTER THAN OTHERS IF YOU HAVE MORE MONEY THAN THEY DO?

I HAVE A HABIT OF PASSING HOMELESS PEOPLE IN THE STREET AND GIVING THEM SOME MONEY, A HOT DRINK OR A SANDWICH. MOST PEOPLE DON'T EVEN THINK THAT THIS IS A HUMAN BEING WITH A HEART, A SOUL AND MOST IMPORTANTLY; A STORY TO TELL! THEY ARE NO BETTER OR WORSE THAN YOU OR I, THEY JUST HAVE A DIFFERENT STORY. IN THE 2020s... YOU WOULD THINK, THE FACT THEY CAN PUNCH NUMBERS IN TO A SUPER BANKING COMPUTER AND CREATE FINANCIAL WEALTH, THAT THEY ARE ACTUALLY ABLE TO DISSOLVE WORLD HOMELESSNESS AND HUNGER WOULDN'T YOU? SO WHY ARE THEY CHOOSING NOT TO? WHY DO US, THE PEOPLE HAVE TO START A CHARITY, REGULATED BY THE GOVERNMENT TO HELP THEM BUT GOVERNMENT (WHICH IS NOTHING BUT A CORPORATION) COULD CHANGE A DECISION OVERNIGHT AND ERADICATE ALL HOMELESSNESS AND POVERTY?

HOMELESS PEOPLE HAVE TO BEG, STEAL AND DO WHAT THEY CAN TO SURVIVE. WE RELY ON CHARITIES TO HELP BY FUND RAISING ON CASH THAT HAS ALREADY BEEN TAXED TO GIVE SERVICES, WHICH WILL BE TAXED AGAIN, IS THIS RIGHT? THERE ARE MANY WAYS THE STREETS COULD BE CLEARED IN A VERY SHORT SPACE OF TIME AND YET, OUR DEAR AND SO-CALLED LEADERS SEEM TO LIKE TO SPEND IT ON DIVIDING THE PEOPLE AND SPENDING MORE TO ACCUMULATE MORE. WHEN WAS THE LAST TIME YOU STOPPED TO SPEAK TO A HOMELESS PERSON AND ASKED THEIR STORY? TRUST ME, THAT WOULD MAKE THEIR DAY MORE THAN GIVING THEM A SHINY COIN IN A CUP!

THEN WE HAVE THE WORKING CLASS, THE SALT OF THE EARTH (THIS WOULD BE MY SOCIAL CLASS IN SOCIETY'S STANDARDS) THEY WORK FOR MOST THINGS, HAVE HAD THEIR FINANCIAL STRUGGLES AND BELIEVE THEY HAVE TO STRUGGLE TO GET WHAT THEY WANT/NEED BUT DON'T

FEEL THEY ARE MUCH AS THEY SEE MANY OTHERS DOING WELL WHICH KNOCKS THEIR CONFIDENCE AND THEY FEEL WORTHLESS OR NOT AS ENTITLED... ITS THE ENTITLEMENT OF HUMAN BEINGS TO LIVE FREE AND HAPPY AND AGAIN... THEY HAVE A HEART AND A SOUL, LIKE YOU OR I. BECAUSE A LOT OF THE WORKING CLASS USUALLY DO NOT HAVE HIGHER EDUCATION, THIS PUTS THEM ON THE LOWER HALF OF THE CLASS SYSTEM. DO YOU THINK THIS IS RIGHT? DO YOU THINK ITS RIGHT THAT IF PEOPLE CANNOT AFFORD AN EDUCATION TO DO FINANCIALLY BETTER FOR THEM AND THEIR FAMILY, THAT THEY SHOULDN'T GET ONE? WHY ARE YOU COMPLICIT IN THIS SYSTEM?

MIDDLE CLASS IS A BIT OF A MIX, WORKING CLASS THAT HAS DONE WELL IN BUSINESS, PEOPLE THAT HAVE STEPPED UP AND HAVE AN INSECURITY AND A FEAR THAT THEY MIGHT END UP BACK IN THE WORKING CLASS BRACKET (SOME NOT ALL) MANY TRY HARDER TO EARN MORE AND FORGET WHERE THEY CAME FROM AND LITERALLY BELIEVE THEY ARE BETTER THAN WORKING CLASS AND HOMELESS PEOPLE. (SOME NOT ALL) IS THIS YOU? LACK OF IDENTITY, BECAUSE YOUR IDENTITY IS WHAT YOU'VE ACHIEVED?

LASTLY, IN MY SHORT GENERALISED LIST, WE HAVE THE UPPER CLASS... HIGHER EDUCATION, INHERITANCES, EXPLOITATION OF MIDDLE, LOWER AND HOMELESS CLASS PEOPLE TO ALLOW THEM TO FEEL SUPERIOR (SOME NOT ALL). CLICKING FINGERS IN RESTAURANTS, NOSES IN THE AIR, ONLY ASSOCIATING WITH PEOPLE OF SIMILAR STATUS SO THAT THEY DON'T CATCH A DISEASE OR HURT THEIR POOR EARS WITH BAD LITERACY. (AGAIN, SOME, NOT ALL)

DO YOU BELIEVE YOU ARE IN A CLASS?

DO YOU BELIEVE ANY HUMAN LIFE IS WORTH ANY LESS THAN YOURS?

I BELIEVE, IF SOMEONE PUTS THEMSELVES IN A CLASS, THERE NEEDS TO BE SOME INNER WORK TO BE DONE.

LOWER CLASS... WORK ON CONFIDENCE AND SELF ACCEPTANCE.

MIDDLE CLASS... WORKING ON CONFIDENCE AND SELF ACCEPTANCE, ALSO WORK ON BEING HUMBLE IN LIFE.

UPPER CLASS FOLKS... WORKING ON SELF ACCEPTANCE, CONFIDENCE, BEING HUMBLE AND ALSO EMPATHY. (AGAIN, SOME, NOT ALL, WE CAN ALL BE BETTER THOUGH)

A DECENT HUMAN BEING, IN MY BELIEF IS LOVE AND CAN HAVE OPINIONS, FREEDOM WITHIN THE REALMS OF SOCIETY AND THE WORLD ESTABLISHMENTS, BUT UNDERSTAND WE ARE ALL THE SAME, REGARDLESS OF FINANCIAL WEALTH OR WHERE SOCIETY WOULD HAVE YOU PLACED. WOULD YOU AGREE?

WOULD YOU BE A HAPPIER PERSON IF THESE LABELS WERE REMOVED? DO YOU FEEL YOU ARE THE BEST LOVING VERSION OF YOURSELF?

THERE ARE SO MANY QUESTIONS WE DON'T ASK OURSELVES DAILY. LIVING MINDFULLY AND PRESENT, WITH LESS DISTRACTIONS, WILL ALLOW US TO SEE THE BIGGER PICTURE OF WHAT IS REALLY GOING ON IN THE WORLD. WE REALLY CAN BE THE CHANGE WE WANT TO SEE, IF WE CHOOSE TO BE. WHAT COULD YOU DO DAILY TO MAKE YOUR LIFE AND THE LIVES OF OTHERS BETTER, WITH MINIMAL EFFORT?

WHAT IS STOPPING YOU FROM REMOVING LABELS, JUDGEMENTS AND DIVISIONS SO THAT THE WORLD CAN BE A PEACEFUL PLACE TO LIVE?

CHAPTER 2: CONSPIRACIES

WHEN IT COMES TO INFORMATION, EVERYONE CAN BE PLACED INTO FOUR CATEGORIES BASED ON THEIR RESPONSE. WHICH ONE ARE YOU?

CONSPIRACY THEORIST: EVERYONE IS OUT TO GET US. EVERYTHING IS A CONSPIRACY.

CONSPIRACY REJECTOR: ONE TRACK MIND PROGRAMMED BY THE SYSTEM TO REJECT CONSPIRACY THEORIES WITHOUT QUESTION.

CONSPIRACY ANALYST: IS THERE ANY TRUTH IN THIS? CAN I PROVE THEM WRONG?

TRUTH SEEKER: CAN I PROVE MYSELF WRONG, BEFORE TRYING TO PROVE OTHERS WRONG? CAN I SEE THE OTHER THREE PERSPECTIVES?

THE TERM CONSPIRACY THEORIST WAS INVENTED (AS FAR AS I'M LEAD TO BELIEVE) IN 1967 BY THE C.I.A TO PUT DOWN ANYONE WHO QUESTIONED THE 'OFFICIAL NARRATIVE' WHEN PRESIDENT JFK WAS SHOT.

THE CENTRAL INTELLIGENCE AGENCY (C.I.A) IS SHOWN IN MOVIES AND ON TV AS THE POLICE TYPE, SPIES AND THE HUB OF INFORMATION, BASED ON GATHERING OF EVIDENCE AND INFORMATION. IMAGINE IT WAS THE OPPOSITE! COULD IT BE TO PROGRAM PEOPLE WITH INFORMATION, TO CAUSE FEAR, TO GAIN CONTROL, TO REALLY PUT HUMAN BEINGS THROUGH MENTAL TORTURE BY NOT SHOWING THEM THE TRUTH? WHO MAKES THE PROGRAMS THEN? SOME EVEN SAY THAT THE TELEVISION WAS INVENTED BY THE C.I.A AS A HYPNOSIS TOOL TO PROGRAM PEOPLE, THROUGH NEWS, SHOWS AND MOVIES, COULD YOU BELIEVE THAT? I KNOW I CAN!

WHY IS IT CALLED A TELEVISION PROGRAM? IS IT BECAUSE THE PEOPLE WATCHING ARE BEING PROGRAMMED?

WHY IS IT CALLED TELEVISION?

TELL-LIE-VISION?

TELE – DISTANT VISION – VIEWING... VIA PROGRAMMING?

IT'S ALL A LOT TO TAKE IN, AS MOST PEOPLE ARE PROGRAMMED TO THINK

A CERTAIN WAY AND THIS COMES FROM SCHOOL, I WILL EXPLAIN THIS WITHIN THE EDUCATION CHAPTER LATER, IT SHOULD RAISE A FEW EYEBROWS AND OPEN SOME EYES! ARE YOU READY?

COGNITIVE DISSONANCE IS A THEORY, BUT AN INTERESTING ONE! I WON'T GIVE YOU THE DICTIONARY TERMINOLOGY, HOWEVER I'LL EXPLAIN THROUGH A SHORT STORY.

BEN IS THREE YEARS OLD AND HAS HIS FIRST CHRISTMAS WHERE HE HAS LEARNED SANTA CLAUS GIVES HIM HIS PRESENTS. HE IS PART OF A CHRISTIAN FAMILY AND SEES HIS FAMILY COME TOGETHER AND ENJOYS THE EXPERIENCE. AS BEN GETS OLDER, HE BECOMES MORE AND MORE IMMERSED IN THE FESTIVITIES AND THE BELIEF THAT A FAT MAN IN A RED SUIT, WITH A WHITE BEARD DELIVERS A PRESENT TO EVERY WELL BEHAVED CHILD IN THE WORLD. BEN ALSO LOVES HOW THE FAMILY COME TOGETHER AND CELEBRATES.

AS AN ADULT... WOULD YOU RENDER CHRISTMAS A CONSPIRACY?

BEN JUST HAD HIS 10TH BIRTHDAY, GOES TO ALICE'S HOUSE WITH ANOTHER FEW FRIENDS TO CELEBRATE HER 10TH BIRTHDAY. ALICE'S FAMILY ARE ATHEIST AND DON'T CELEBRATE CHRISTMAS. NEW TO THE AREA AND THE SCHOOL, THEY INVITE THE CLASSMATES OVER FOR A PARTY. IT'S THE MIDDLE OF JUNE AND SANTA HAS NEVER BEEN SPOKEN ABOUT. ALICE IS A LITTLE UNGRATEFUL AND WANTED TWO DIFFERENT COLOURS IN THE DRESS STYLE SHE ASKED FOR. BEN SAID, "ITS NEARLY CHRISTMAS AND SANTA CLAUS WILL BRING YOU ANOTHER IN A DIFFERENT COLOUR!"

ALICE BEGINS TO LAUGH AND POINT AT BEN; SHE STARTS SHOUTING THAT SANTA ISN'T REAL! BEN BEGINS TO SHOUT THAT SANTA IS REAL AND THE TWO OF THEM ARE ARGUING. BEN FREAKING OUT THAT HIS BELIEFS AND PROGRAMMING ARE BEING QUESTIONED, HE IS TOO YOUNG AND IMMATURE TO ASK WHY ALICE SAID THIS. ALICE'S MOTHER RUNS OVER AS SHE HEARD THE COMMOTION... "WHAT IS GOING ON OVER HERE?" SHE

ASKS! ALICE REPLIED, "BEN STILL BELIEVES IN SANTA CLAUS AND GOT MAD WHEN I SAID HE WAS FAKE!" ALICE'S MOTHER TOLD ALICE THAT IT WASN'T NICE TO JUDGE OTHER PEOPLE'S BELIEFS, TO WHICH BEN ASKED, "IS SANTA CLAUS FAKE?" TO WHICH THE REPLY WAS, "IF YOU BELIEVE HE IS REAL, HE IS REAL" AND THINGS SIMMERED DOWN AND PARTY WAS IN FULL SWING.

NOTHING ELSE WAS SAID UNTIL NOVEMBER WHEN BEN WAS BEING ASKED WHAT HE WANTED FROM SANTA, HE ASKED HIS PARENTS, "IS SANTA REAL? LIKE REALLY REAL?" "ALICE SAID HE'S NOT AND WAS LAUGHING AT ME WHEN I WAS AT HER PARTY." HIS PARENTS LOOKED AT EACH OTHER AND BEN'S FATHER EXPLAINED THE TRUTH. BEN SMASHED HIS PLATE ON THE FLOOR AS HE WAS AT THE DINNER TABLE, HE RAN UP THE STAIRS AND CRIED TILL HE CAME TO TERMS WITH THE INFORMATION.

COGNITIVE DISSONANCE IS WHEN LEARNED INFORMATION AND PROGRAMMED INFORMATION IS MET WITH NEW INFORMATION. THE BRAIN CANNOT COMPUTE IT AND THERE IS NOT USUALLY AN INITIAL POSITIVE OUTCOME, EVEN WHEN PROOF IS PRESENTED.

WOULD YOU BLAME BEN FOR HIS ACTIONS AND SMASHING THE PLATE? I WOULDN'T FOR THE FOLLOWING REASONS: HIS PARENTS (WHO HE'S MEANT TO TRUST THE MOST) HAVE LIED TO HIM HIS WHOLE LIFE, HIS BRAIN CANNOT TAKE IN THE NEW INFORMATION, SANTA NOT BEING REAL HAS CAUSED PROPER PAIN, TRAUMA AND INTERNAL TENSION! WELCOME TO ADULTHOOD LITTLE BEN, THE WORLD IS NOT ALL SUNSHINE AND RAINBOWS, EH?

CAN YOU SEE WHAT DAMAGE LIES CAN CAUSE? CAN YOU SEE HOW COGNITIVE DISSONANCE WORKS AND HOW WE'VE ALL BEEN BRAINWASHED INTO BELIEVING NONSENSE SINCE BEING VERY YOUNG?

SANTA AND THE BABY JESUS IN A MANGER DO NOT HAVE ANYTHING IN COMMON, APART FROM THE TIME OF YEAR THAT THEY ARE CELEBRATED! A MASSIVE DRINKS COMPANY CHANGED SANTA FROM GREEN TO RED AS

PART OF A HUGE ADVERTISING AGENDA IN 1931! IF YOU TRACE BACK SANTA'S ORIGINS, THESE AREN'T AS PURE AS THEY LOOK, I SUPPOSE LIES USUALLY AREN'T, ARE THEY?

WE ARE IN THE 2020S, THE YEARS OF DISINFORMATION AND DIVISION OF THE PEOPLE ON EARTH, WHERE THE TRUTH IS LIES AND LIES ARE THE TRUTH! PEOPLE DOWN RABBIT HOLES SO DEEP THAT THEY ACTUALLY BELIEVE THEY ARE A RABBIT IN A RABBIT HOLE, AS IN DIGGING DEEP FOR INFORMATION, ON THE INTERNET AND BOOKS USUALLY, THEY COULD BE LIVING HAPPY AND NOT GIVING A SH*T... HAVE YOU BEEN CAUGHT IN THE RABBIT HOLES OF NEW INFORMATION? DO YOU THINK IT'S BEST TO STAY BACK FROM THE BAD STUFF? I BELIEVE ITS GOOD TO KNOW WHAT IS TRUTH AND WHAT IS LIES SO WE CAN PRACTICE DISCERNMENT. HOW MUCH OF THE BAD STUFF IS ACTUALLY REAL THOUGH?

WE HAVE THE COGNITIVE DISSONANCE PEOPLE WHO SHOOT THE INFORMATION DOWN WITHOUT THINKING, AS IT HURTS THEIR PROGRAMMED BRAINS (CONSPIRACY REJECTOR). WE HAVE THE PEOPLE WHO JUST WANT EVERYTHING TO BECOME BETTER IN THE WORLD AND ARE HURT BY THE WAY IT FUNCTIONS, THEREFORE WILL BELIEVE ANYTHING JUST TO BLAME THEIR PAIN ON IT (CONSPIRACY THEORIST). THEN THERE ARE THE CRITICAL THINKERS (RARE BREED NOWADAYS) THAT THEY WILL ANALYSE ALL INFORMATION AND SEE HOW IT MATCHES UP TO DIFFERENT SOURCES, CONSISTENCY AND THE AMOUNT OF PEOPLE WHO ARE JUMPING ON THE BANDWAGON (CONSPIRACY ANALYST). FINALLY, THERE ARE THE TRUTH SEEKERS, THEY LOOK PAST THE DRAMA, THEY LOOK AT WHO'S BEING HURT AND DIVIDED WITH ALL THE INFORMATION AND THEN MAKE AN INFORMED DECISION ON WHAT IS TRUE, BY PROVING THEMSELVES WRONG FIRST, BEFORE THEY EVEN QUESTION ANOTHER! THIS MEANS THAT THEY CAN SEE AND EVEN ARGUE FOR THE OTHER THREE PERSPECTIVES.

WHICH CATEGORY DO YOU FIT INTO?

HAVE YOU PUT SOMEONE DOWN FOR HAVING DIFFERENT BELIEFS

WITHOUT CONSIDERING THEIR EXPLANATION? (CONSPIRACY REJECTOR)

DO YOU BELIEVE EVERYTHING YOU HAVE BEEN TAUGHT IS TRUTH? (CONSPIRACY THEORIST)

DO YOU BELIEVE YOU HAVE WHAT IT TAKES TO RESEARCH NEW INFORMATION? (CONSPIRACY ANALYST)

I CANNOT TELL YOU IF ANY ARE REAL. I'D LOVE YOU TO WANT TO GROW THE SYNAPSES IN YOUR BRAIN AND EXPAND THE INFORMATION HIGHWAYS BY TRAINING YOUR BRAIN INTO LOOKING AT WHAT MIGHT BE POSSIBLE. (TRUTH SEEKER)

WHAT IS COMING NOW IS A LIST OF INFORMATION THAT IS CLASSED AS A CONSPIRACY WHICH IS, IN ESSENCE, A THEORY. TRY TO SEE IF YOU CAN REJECT IT, BELIEVE IT, AND DETERMINE WHAT RESEARCH WOULD NEED TO BE DONE BEFORE YOU CAN MAKE A DECISION.

WHAT DO YOU THINK PSYCHOLOGY IS BASED ON? YOU KNOW IT... THEORY!!! GAME CHANGER!!! YOU WILL LISTEN TO PEOPLE IN A SYSTEM THAT IS USED TO CONTROL PEOPLE, BECAUSE YOU HAVE BEEN TOLD TO TRUST THEM WITHOUT QUESTION. IS THIS HEALTHY? TRUST A THEORY WITHOUT QUESTION REALLY? WILL YOU CONSIDER NEW TRUTH?

IF PARENTS CAN LIE TO THEIR KIDS FOR MOST OF THEIR YOUNG LIFE, CAUSE THEM SUBCONSCIOUS TRUST ISSUES, BECAUSE THE SYSTEM SAID... SURELY THE SYSTEM CAN LIE TO PEOPLE TO 'EDUCATE' THE MASSES SO THAT THEY ALL THINK THE SAME WAY? THE DIVERGENT ONES BECOME OUTCASTS BY THE MEDIA AND THEIR FAMILY MEMBERS. IS THIS FAIR? I HAVE QUESTIONED EVERYTHING SINCE I WAS A CHILD AND HAVE BEEN ALIENATED BY MANY. MAYBE HALF OF YOU READING THIS BOOK MIGHT FEEL TENSION ALREADY AND WE ARE ONLY ON CHAPTER 2! AS I SAID, I DON'T WISH ANY PAIN ON ANY OF YOU, ONLY FOR YOU TO THINK DEEPER AND WRITE DOWN YOUR THOUGHTS FOR YOU.

RESEARCH, WHEN YOU HAVE TIME AND TRY TO LOOK IN FROM THE

OUTSIDE PLEASE. IT IS EASY TO TURN A BLIND EYE AND SHUT THINGS DOWN, BUT WHEN YOU KNOW, YOU CAN'T NOT KNOW!

LOOK IN TO THE BELOW SUBJECTS WHEN YOU HAVE COMPLETED YOUR BOOK   AND IT WILL ABSOLUTELY OPEN YOUR MIND WHEN YOU TRY TO SEE IT FROM ALL THREE PERSPECTIVES. WHAT HAVE YOU GOT TO LOSE?

THE MOON LANDING FAKED; PRESIDENT NIXON CALLED THE SPACE SHUTTLE, 270,000 MILES AWAY FROM A LAND LINE TELEPHONE IN 1969, BUT WE CANNOT GET A MOBILE RECEPTION IN OUR HOMES FROM A MAST 1 MILE UP THE STREET IN THE 2020S?

FLAT EARTH; WE LIVE ON A SPINNING BALL... SPINNING AT 1000 MPH BUT GRAVITY KEEPS THE WATER ON THE BALL, WHEN WE THROW A WET BALL (IN THE SAME GRAVITY, THE WATER COMES OFF?) HOW ABOUT PLANES LANDING UPSIDE DOWN ON AUSTRALIA? WATER 'LEVEL' ON A BALL?

ADRENOCHROME; SECRET SOCIETIES SACRIFICING CHILDREN AS PART OF SATANIC RITUALS AND DRINKING THEIR BLOOD, THAT BLOOD HAS BEEN FLOODED WITH ADRENALINE, AFTER THE CHILDREN BEING TORTURED. IT IS SUPPOSEDLY HARVESTED AND IS A MIRACLE DRUG IN WITH THE ELITES TO KEEP THEM YOUNG, WHILE THEY GAIN AN ADDICTIVE BUZZ FROM THE ADRENALINE.

9/11 WAS AN INSIDE JOB; JET FUEL CAN'T MELT AND DISINTEGRATE STEEL BEAMS, WHERE DID THE PLANES DISAPPEAR TO ALSO? THE INSURANCE THAT WAS TAKEN OUT ON THE TWIN TOWERS PRIOR TO THEM COLLAPSING. THE VIDEO OF PRESIDENT BUSH HELPING TEACH A KINDERGARTEN CLASS HOW TO READ THE WORDS; KITE, HIT, STEEL, PLANE AND MUST, JUST AS THE BUILDINGS WERE ABOUT TO GO DOWN.

TITANIC WAS AN INSIDE JOB; THERE WERE MEANT TO BE SIX BANKERS ON THE TITANIC. THREE OF THEM DIDN'T MAKE IT AS THEY WANTED A CENTRAL BANKING SYSTEM AND THE THREE THAT WERE ON THE SHIP THAT SANK DID NOT, THIS IS WHY WE HAVE THE DEBT-BASED FINANCIAL

SYSTEM THAT WE USE TODAY! TITANIC WAS A TURNING POINT IN HISTORY, DO THE CURRENT BANKERS CELEBRATE THE CONTROL WHILE WE THE PEOPLE MOURN THE DEAD? DO YOU KNOW THERE ARE LIES IN THE HISTORY WE ARE TAUGHT?

CHILDREN SEX TRAFFICKING (CHILD RAPE) THE BIGGEST UNDERGROUND EXPORT IN THE WORLD. ELITES INVOLVED, HOLLYWOOD INVOLVED AND COVER UPS! EPSTEIN... DID HE REALLY KILL HIMSELF? THERE IS NO FOOTAGE OF HIM KILLING HIMSELF IN A CAMERA VIEWED HIGH SECURITY CELL.. IS HE PROTECTED OR IS HE WHISTLE BLOWING? WHY WAS THE EAR ON THE NEWS PAPER (CLAIMING TO BE EPSTEINS) PRINTED, LOOK DIFFERENT FROM EPSTEINS REAL EAR?

COVID 19 VACCINATIONS AND OTHER VACCINATIONS; ARE THEY WORKING TOWARDS TRANSHUMANISM BY CHANGING CHROMOSOMES AT CELLULAR LEVEL? POPULATION CONTROL? DEPOPULATION? THERE IS SO MUCH TO READ ON THIS AND IT WOULDN'T BE HARD TO FIND THE TRUTH.

GOVT SECRET OPERATIONS; THESE ARE INTERESTING TO READ ALSO AND HAVE BEEN PUBLISHED IN THE MAINSTREAM! PROJECT SUNSHINE, PROJECT MOCKINGBIRD, OPERATION NORTHWOODS, OPERATION PAPERCLIP, PROJECT GREEK ISLAND, OPERATION CHAOS, OPERATION MERLIN, PROJECT BLUE BEAM, DIRECT ENERGY WEAPONS, STARGATE PROJECT. PLEASE READ THESE... ACTUALLY MIND-BLOWING!

IF YOU HAVE THE ABILITY, THAT MANY DON'T TO LOOK THESE UP TO TRY TO UNDERSTAND THEM, YOU ARE BEST USING AN UNCENSORED SEARCH ENGINE. HOW MANY OF YOU REJECTED THESE LISTS BEFORE RESEARCHING AND PROVED YOU HAVE A PROGRAMMED BRAIN THAT ISN'T FREE? DO YOU NOT REALLY WANT TO FREE YOUR MIND? WILL YOU TRY AND UNDERSTAND THEM? WILL YOU EVER CONSIDER LOOKING AT ANY OTHER WAY TO GAIN INFORMATION?

CHAPTER 3: WHERE IS THE LOVE?

THE NON-CONTRADICTORY DEFINITION OF LOVE, 'GIVING VALUE WITHOUT EXPECTING ANYTHING IN RETURN', IS NOT THE DEFINITION THAT THE MAJORITY OF THE WORLD'S POPULATION USE UNFORTUNATELY. WHO DO YOU LOVE AND EXPECT NOTHING FROM? DO YOU EXPECT YOUR CHILD TO BEHAVE AND BE GRATEFUL? YOUR PARTNER TO SHOW YOU AFFECTION OR GRATITUDE? MOST PEOPLE EXPECT SOMETHING IN RETURN FOR THEIR LOVE OR KIND ACTS.

DOES YOUR FAMILY ACCEPT YOU AS YOU ARE, OR DO THEY HAVE AN OPINION ON EVERYTHING AND WANT YOU TO BE MORE LIKE THEM OR FOR YOU TO BE MORE TRADITIONAL? IS THAT LOVE? DO YOU DO THE SAME TO YOUR FAMILY MEMBERS OR FRIENDS?

WHAT ABOUT ON A GRANDER SCALE? DOES YOUR GOVERNMENT LOVE YOU? DO THEY EXPECT NO COMPLIANCE AFTER GIVING YOU WHAT THEY CLASS AS EVERYTHING TO LIVE A FREE AND HEALTHY LIFE?

DO CORPORATIONS GIVE YOU THINGS AS A CUSTOMER BUT RESPECT YOU AS A HUMAN BEING? OR DO THEY JUST SEND OUT PROGRAMMING ADVERTS AND REALLY EXPECT YOU TO JUST CONSUME, THEN KEEP ON CONSUMING? IS THAT LOVE?

DO PEOPLE ACCEPT EACH OTHER AS HUMAN BEINGS OR JUDGE EACH OTHER AS A LABEL? IS THIS LOVE?

THE WORD LOVE ACTUALLY CAN MAKE SO MANY PEOPLE CRINGE, FEEL UPTIGHT OR EVEN CAUSE SOME PEOPLE TO SHUT DOWN. WHY DO YOU THINK THIS IS? I BELIEVE IT IS BECAUSE THEY ALL HAD A DIFFERENT DEFINITION FOR LOVE GROWING UP (WHETHER THEY WERE CONSCIOUS OF IT OR NOT) AND IT WAS NEVER MET IN ANY OF THEIR EXPECTATIONS AND THIS MADE THEM FEEL LIKE IT WASN'T POSSIBLE.

MEN VERY RARELY TALK ABOUT LOVE OPENLY, WHY IS THIS? ARE MEN

AND WOMEN PROGRAMMED THROUGH SOCIETY THAT LOVE IS DIFFERENT FOR MEN AND WOMEN? I BELIEVE IT TO BE UNIVERSAL, AS LONG AS IT IS LIVED IN A NON-CONTRADICTORY MANNER, AS MENTIONED IN THE DEFINITION ABOVE.

WHAT HAS BEEN YOUR DEFINITION OF LOVE FOR THE MAJORITY OF YOUR LIFE?

LET'S LOOK INTO WHAT SOCIETY DEFINES AS DIFFERENT KINDS OF LOVE AND GO A LITTLE DEEPER WITH THESE PROGRAMS.

SELF LOVE:

IS THERE SUCH A THING? I DON'T BELIEVE THERE IS. BEFORE YOU SHOOT ME DOWN, PLEASE LET ME EXPLAIN... LOVE IS 'GIVING' WITHOUT EXPECTING ANYTHING IN RETURN... CAN YOU GIVE TO YOURSELF? WOULD THAT NOT BE THE DEFINITION OF TAKING FOR SELF FULFILLMENT? THIS IS, IN MY BELIEF, WHY SO MANY PEOPLE ARE NOT ABLE TO LOVE THEMSELVES... BECAUSE THEY CAN'T!! WE CAN SELF ACCEPT, THAT MEANS WE WOULDN'T WANT TO CHANGE ANYTHING AND JUST BE. THIS IS WHY IN A WORLD OF CONSUMERISM AND STRIVING FOR PERFECTION, THAT THE MAJORITY OF PEOPLE WILL NEVER GET TO A POINT OF SELF ACCEPTANCE, BUT CONSUME AND CHANGE THINGS TO HELP THEM LOVE THEMSELVES, OR CHANGE THINGS SO THAT THEY CAN BE LOVED BY OTHERS. CAN YOU EARN LOVE? THIS IS LITERALLY KILLING PEOPLE IN SO MANY WAYS, SENDING THE GENERAL POPULATION ON A WILD GOOSE CHASE FOR SELF LOVE... IT WILL BE LIKE LOOKING FOR HEN'S TEETH! HAVE YOU EVER FOUND A HEN'S TOOTH? IF I YOU LOVE SOMEONE, ARE YOU ALLOWED TO TAKE ANYTHING YOU WISH FROM THEM? WHY WOULD WE NEVER BE TAUGHT WHAT LOVE REALLY IS FROM A YOUNG AGE?

UNCONDITIONAL LOVE:

ANOTHER WILD GOOSE CHASE FOR UNCONDITIONAL LOVE? I BELIEVE SO! UNCONDITIONAL MEANS YOU TELL A PERSON UP FRONT THAT NO MATTER WHAT YOU WILL LOVE THEM AND THEY WILL LOVE YOU... NO MATTER WHAT! IS THAT POSSIBLE?

WOULD YOU LOVE SOMEONE AND STAY WITH THEM IF THEY WERE OUT SLEEPING WITH WHOEVER THEY WISHED, OUTSIDE YOUR RELATIONSHIP? WOULD YOU LOVE AND REMAIN WITH SOMEONE THAT WAS OUT ABUSING CHILDREN AND ELDERLY PEOPLE FOR FUN? WOULD YOU LOVE AND REMAIN WITH SOMEONE WHO HAD PHYSICAL RELATIONS WITH ANIMALS?

I KNOW IT SOUNDS RIDICULOUS ASKING THESE QUESTIONS, BUT THERE WILL ALWAYS BE SOMETHING THAT PUTS YOU OFF SOMEONE. THIS MEANS THAT THERE IS NO UNCONDITIONAL LOVE RELATIONSHIPS THEN DOESN'T IT? WE LOOK OVER THE WAY RELATIONSHIPS WERE YEARS AGO, SO MANY PEOPLE STAYED WITH THEIR PARTNERS, NO MATTER WHAT... THIS WAS LIKE SELF SABOTAGE! BUT AT THE SAME TIME WHAT MOST CRAVE NOWADAYS!

NOWADAYS THE MAJORITY DON'T HAVE ANY LONGEVITY AND MOST HAVE ATTACHMENT OR DETACHMENT ISSUES! I BELIEVE THIS IS BECAUSE THE EXPECTATION OF UNCONDITIONAL LOVE CANNOT BE MET, OR MANY PUT TOO MANY CONDITIONS IN PLACE, SO IT IS CONTROL AND NOT LOVE!

THE ISSUE IS THAT LOVE IS UNCONDITIONAL IN PRACTICE AND NOT AS A GOAL. YOU CAN GIVE TO SOMEONE IN THE MOMENT AND NOT EXPECT ANYTHING IN RETURN AND YOUR BRAIN WILL RELEASE PLEASURE CHEMICALS! SOMEONE CAN GIVE TO YOU WITHOUT EXPECTING ANYTHING IN RETURN AND YOUR BRAIN WILL RELEASE PLEASURE CHEMICALS! THAT IS WHAT EVERYONE WANTS, BUT MAKING A CONTRACT OR LAW BEFORE HAND ACTUALLY PREVENTS YOUR BRAIN FROM RELEASING PLEASURE CHEMICALS! NOW WHEN THEY LOVE YOU, YOU DON'T KNOW IF THEY DID IT BECAUSE THEY HAD TO OR WANTED TO.

WILL YOU STOP LOOKING FOR UNCONDITIONAL LOVE?

LOVE IS LOVE:

IS LOVE REALLY JUST LOVE THOUGH? LET'S LOOK AT WHO CAME UP WITH THE SLOGAN? IT'S BEEN THE TITLES OF FILMS, A COMIC, AN ALBUM AND SONGS... WHAT DO FILMS, COMICS, SONGS AND ALBUMS HAVE IN COMMON? THEY ARE ALL OPEN TO INTERPRETATION AND FOR ENTERTAINMENT PURPOSES. ENTERTAINMENT IS QUITE REAL, HOWEVER, SOME OF THE CONTENT IS NOT! PROGRAMMING CAN COME THROUGH ENTERTAINMENT AND IT'S HARD TO SHAKE OFF A PROGRAM, UNLESS YOU SEE TRUTH! HOW CAN LOVE BE LOVE IF PEOPLE DO NOT HAVE A NON-CONTRADICTORY DEFINITION FOR THE WORD LOVE? UNCONDITIONAL LOVE WAS REVERSING THE DEFINITION BY MAKING THE APPLICATION THE CAUSE. LOVE IS LOVE IS WORSE! IT ISN'T A DEFINITION, SO ANYTHING IS ALLOWED.

IF AN ADULT IS TO BE PHYSICALLY ATTRACTED TO A MINOR AND DECIDED TO BE PHYSICAL WITH THEM IN ANY WAY IS THIS LOVE? LOVE IS LOVE COULD RESULT IN A SLOW PROCESS WHERE THE SO CALLED WORLD LEADERS WISH TO LOWER THE AGE OF CONSENT, WHICH WILL ALLOW ADULTS TO ABUSE MINORS BECAUSE THEY 'LOVE THEM'. IS THIS OK?

LOVE IS NOT LOVE, LOVE IS GIVING (VALUE) WITHOUT EXPECTING ANYTHING IN RETURN. HAVING SEX IS NOT LOVE, IT IS HAVING SEX. KISSING SOMEONE IS NOT LOVE, IT'S KISSING SOMEONE. SOME PEOPLE SAY THAT THEY SHOW LOVE DIFFERENTLY TOO. IF YOU ARE GIVING SOMEONE WHAT THEY NEED AND WANT AND DON'T EXPECT ANYTHING IN RETURN, YOU HAVE NAILED IT! IF YOU GIVE SOMEONE SOMETHING THAT YOU WANT TO GIVE THEM, IS THIS THE SAME? THAT SOUNDS MORE LIKE AGENDA NO? OR ONE NOT UNDERSTANDING THE OTHER...

THERE HAS BEEN A LOT OF THE LOVE IS LOVE ON THE PROMOTION OF

PRIDE AND THE LGBTQIA+ PLATFORMS (THERE WILL PROBABLY BE MORE LETTERS ADDED BY THE TIME YOU READ THIS BOOK). DOES LOVE CHANGE WITH SAME SEX RELATIONSHIPS? NO! DOES LOVE CHANGE IN RELATIONSHIPS WHEN PEOPLE CHOOSE NOT TO BE IDENTIFIED AS A GENDER? NO! DOES LOVE CHANGE WHEN SOMEONE HAS A DIFFERENT RACE OR RELIGION? NO! IT IS ALWAYS GIVING VALUE AND NOT EXPECTING ANYTHING IN RETURN. VALUE, WHEN GIVEN WILL ALWAYS BENEFIT THE OTHER PARTY OR ITS NOT LOVE. CAN YOU UNDERSTAND THIS TRUTH?

A RELATIONSHIP IS WHEN BOTH OR MORE PARTIES ADD VALUE (GIVE) TO EACH OTHER IN ORDER TO KEEP THINGS BALANCED AND FULFILLED. SO WHY IS LOVE IS LOVE USED IN THESE CATEGORIES? LGBTQIA+ DO YOU KNOW WHAT IT STANDS FOR? LESBIAN, GAY, BI-SEXUAL, TRAN-SEXUAL, TRANS, TRANS-GENDER, QUEER, INTER-SEXUAL, A-SEXUAL AND ALLIES. IS THERE ANYTHING STOPPING ANYONE FROM THIS GROUP FROM LOVING ANYONE AND EVERYONE? NO! IS THERE ANYTHING WRONG WITH ANYONE BEING PART OF THIS GROUP? I BELIEVE NOT. IS IT KEEPING PEOPLE FROM BEING PART OF EVERYTHING ELSE AND CREATING BARRIERS WITH OTHER PEOPLE WHO DON'T UNDERSTAND? I BELIEVE YES, BECAUSE MOST PEOPLE ARE JUDGEMENTAL. DOES THIS MEAN PEOPLE SHOULD PUSH HARDER TO MAKE PEOPLE SEE THE SAME AS THEM? IS THIS NOT THE OPPOSITE OF LOVE? WHO CREATED THE MOVEMENT? WHAT WAS THEIR AGENDA?

NOW YOU PROBABLY WONDER WHY I WAS SPEAKING ABOUT THIS AND WHERE IT IS GOING? I HAVE FRIENDS AND FAMILY WHO ARE MEMBERS OF THIS GLOBAL GROUP AND I HAVE NO JUDGEMENT OR OPINION, AS IT HAS NOTHING TO DO WITH ME WHAT OTHER PEOPLE DO, AS LONG AS ITS CONSENTING ADULTS GIVING EACH OTHER VALUE!

I DIGRESS... THERE HAVE BEEN A SPECIFIC GROUP OF PEOPLE TRYING TO BREAK INTO THE LGBTQIA+ AND THAT IS PEOPLE WHO DEFINE THEMSELVES AS 'MAPS'. A MAP IS A 'MINOR ATTRACTED PERSON' AND THEY EVEN HAVE THEIR OWN FLAG, THAT IS IN THE STYLE OF THE

LBGTQIA+ FLAG AND AS FAR AS I HAVE BEEN LED TO BELIEVE, THE COLOURS ON THE FLAG MATCH THE TYPE OF MINORS THAT THEY ARE ATTRACTED TO. WOULD THIS NOT BE CLASSED AS TRYING TO LEGALISE PAEDOPHILIA? SUPPOSEDLY NOT AS THERE ARE A LOT OF MAPS WHO ARE ON BOARDS TO PROTECT CHILDREN, BUT DON'T TOUCH THEM AND HAVE THEIR FEELINGS UNDER CONTROL, SO IT DOESN'T BECOME PHYSICAL.

IS A MAP THINKING ABOUT GIVING A CHILD (AS YOUNG AS A BABY) SOME SEXUAL TOUCHING OR KISSING CONSIDERED LOVE??? WOULD YOU LIKE A MAP TO BE TEACHING YOUR CHILDREN IN A SCHOOL? HOW WOULD YOU THEN KNOW IF A MAP WAS TRYING TO HELP, NURTURE OR GROOM YOUR CHILD? THEY DON'T EVEN HAVE TO TELL THEIR ORIENTATION WHEN THEY APPLY FOR JOBS ECT, BECAUSE THEY "ARE SCARED PEOPLE MIGHT DISAPPROVE". WHAT IS THE WORLD COMING TO? WHY ARE THE WORLD LEADERS ALLOWING THIS? RE GROWTH AND UNDERSTANDING IS NEEDED!

IF YOU ARE A PARENT YOU HAVE A CHOICE TO BE AWARE THAT THIS IS GOING ON. EVEN IF YOU ARE NOT A PARENT, YOU ARE STILL ENTITLED TO KNOW. FULLY FLEDGED ADULTS ARE BEING PROTECTED FOR HAVING SEXUAL OR SENSUAL FEELINGS TOWARDS A CHILD... THIS IS NOT AND WILL NEVER BE LOVE! THE DIFFERENCE BETWEEN A PEADOPHILE AND A MAP IS THAT A PEADOPHILE WILL OR HAS TOUCHED A CHILD. IS THIS LOVE? WHERE IS THE LAST PLACE YOU'D WANT A MAP OR PEADOPHILE TO WORK? WITH CHILDREN MAYBE? HOW LONG BEFORE A VAMPIRE CAN CONTROL THEMSELVES BEFORE THEY HAVE TO FEED? HOW LONG BEFORE PARENTS START TO ASK QUESTIONS TO PROTECT THEIR CHILDREN FROM PREDATORS? HOW LONG BEFORE PEOPLE UNDERSTAND THAT LOVE IS NOT LOVE, ITS GIVING (VALUE) WITHOUT EXPECTING ANYTHING IN RETURN!

IF YOU HADN'T EATEN FOR A WEEK AND WERE STARVING, YOU WERE CRAVING FOOD SO BAD AND I GAVE YOU A JOB IN A KITCHEN WITH THE FINEST FOOD, HOW HARD WOULD IT BE TO REFRAIN? THIS IS THE

FEELING A MAP HAS WHEN TEACHING THE CHILDREN... ALL IT TAKES IS ONE WRONG 'DECISION' AND A POOR CHILD'S LIFE IS RUINED. WHY IS IT THAT THESE PEOPLE CAN TEACH IN SCHOOLS OR LIVE IN OR AROUND CHILDREN? IS IT AN ILLNESS OR A CHOICE?

IF I GIVE THE HOMELESS MAN/WOMAN IN THE STREET MONEY, IS IT AN ACT OF LOVE WHEN THERE IS A CHANCE I KNOW THAT THEY COULD GO AND BUY SOMETHING TO ABUSE THEIR BODY OR THOUGHTS IN SOME WAY? WHAT IF I FIND OUT WHAT THEY LIKE TO EAT AND DRINK AND I PURCHASE IT FOR THEM, SO THEY DON'T GO HUNGRY AND I CHAT TO THEM? THIS SOUNDS LIKE AN ACT OF LOVE MORE TO ME. WHAT IF THEY DON'T SAY THANK YOU AND I FEEL ANGRY, DID I DO IT OUT OF LOVE (GIVING) OR DID I DO IT FOR THE THANK YOU (EXPECTATION)? THEY MIGHT BE EMBARRASSED OR SHY TO SAY THANK YOU.

I CAN ASK A MAN/WOMAN IF THEY LOVE THEIR PARTNER AND THEY SAY YES. WHEN I ASK THEM WHAT THEIR PARTNER NEEDS, THEY LOOK AT ME WITH A BLANK LOOK. THIS IS EVEN WORSE WHEN IT'S BEEN SEVERAL YEARS OR EVEN DECADES IN A RELATIONSHIP TOGETHER! TO KNOW WHAT YOUR PARTNER NEEDS FROM YOU IS THE SECOND MOST IMPORTANT PART OF YOUR RELATIONSHIP. THE FIRST IS BEING ABLE TO COMMUNICATE IT.

IF TWO PEOPLE ARE TOGETHER AND CLAIM THEIR LOVE IN WORDS ALL OVER SOCIAL MEDIA FOR OTHERS TO SEE, BUT CANNOT COMMUNICATE OR TELL WHAT THE OTHER NEEDS IN A RELATIONSHIP, THEN I CAN SAFELY SAY THAT IT IS NOT REAL LOVE. IN A REAL LOVE RELATIONSHIP (REGARDLESS OF TIME TOGETHER) THE PEOPLE SHOULD WANT TO ENERGISE EACH OTHER DAILY, BUT THE MAJORITY OF THE BEAUTIFUL POPULATION CANNOT GET THEIR HEAD ROUND THIS. RELATIONSHIPS BREAK DOWN WHEN ONE SIDE STOPS GIVING THE VALUE, NEEDS OR WANTS (BECAUSE THEY FEEL OWED), THEN THE OTHER RETALIATES WITH THE SAME. NOW ITS A CIVIL RELATIONSHIP, WITH LESS FUN THAN WHAT BOTH PARTIES DESERVE AND BY STAYING IN IT, BOTH ARE

SABOTAGING THEIR OWN LIVES. WHAT DO YOU EXPECT FROM A RELATIONSHIP? WHAT DO YOU WISH YOU COULD HAVE IN A PARTNER? DO YOU HAVE IT NOW? HAVE YOU ASKED FOR IT?

I MADE A GAME UP FOR MY CLIENTS TO PLAY WHEN THEY FELT THINGS WERE GOING STALE OR THEY WANTED TO GROW TOGETHER AND BE UNDERSTOOD MORE. THE BEST THING ABOUT THIS GAME IS THAT IT CAN BE PLAYED AT ANY POINT IN A RELATIONSHIP! ARE YOU WILLING TO FRESHEN THINGS UP, OR ARE YOU WILLING TO START THE WAY YOU MEAN TO GO ON IN FUTURE RELATIONSHIPS FROM NOW ON?

MOST RELATIONSHIPS BEGIN WITH ATTRACTION, THEN BASED ON PAST EXPERIENCE, PEOPLE TRY TO LIVE A NEW EXPERIENCE. IS THIS THE MOST SENSIBLE WAY TO BEGIN A RELATIONSHIP? WHERE DO YOU SEE THE LOVE HERE? THE ATTRACTION HAS TO BE THERE. SOMETIMES IT CAN GROW OVER TIME THOUGH, SO WE REALLY SHOULDN'T WRITE PEOPLE OFF BECAUSE THEY DON'T MEET OUR PHYSICAL EXPECTATIONS. THEN WE BEGIN TO GROW THROUGH LEARNING ABOUT EACH OTHER... NOT ABOUT PAST RELATIONSHIPS OR HARDSHIPS, BUT WHAT REALLY ENERGISES OUR PARTNER, ONLY THEN ARE WE BEGINNING TO SHOW LOVE, THE REAL LOVE IS WHEN WE PUT WHAT WE HAVE LEARNED INTO ACTION TO HELP OTHERS GAIN ENERGY WITH EVERY INTERACTION. LET'S LOOK AT THE COOKIE JAR GAME!

WHAT YOU NEED:

2 COOKIE JARS, BLANK PAPER, A PEN, AN OPEN MIND AND THE WILLINGNESS TO MAKE THE RELATIONSHIP BE THE BEST IT CAN BE.

THE METHOD:

BOTH PEOPLE CUT THE SHEETS OF BLANK PAPER INTO 21 EVEN-SIZED

PIECES AND WRITE ON THEM SOMETHING THAT THEY WISH THEIR PARTNER TO FULFILL WITHIN THE DAY (SAME 24 HOURS). THIS CAN RANGE FROM RUNNING A ROSE PETAL BATH, TO A MASSAGE OR BOOKING A WEEKEND AWAY, TO HAVE A FULL EVENING WITH NO PHONES. IT IS DOWN TO THE NEEDS AND DESIRES OF THE INDIVIDUAL. THE 21 PIECES OF PAPER ARE FOLDED AND PUT INTO THE COOKIE JAR AND THEN SWAP COOKIE JARS AND HAVE YOUR PARTNER'S AT YOUR BEDSIDE.

THE FIRST THING MOST PEOPLE LOOK AT IN THE MORNING IS THEIR PHONES. IF YOU WAKE UP BESIDE YOUR PARTNER AND THEY LOOK AT THEIR PHONE BEFORE YOU, HOW WOULD THAT MAKE YOU FEEL? HOW WOULD YOU THINK THEY FEEL IF YOU DID IT TO THEM?

WE BEGIN THE MORNING WITH THE MUTUAL AGREEMENT THAT BOTH PEOPLE DO NOT LOOK AT THEIR PHONES, AT LEAST UNTIL THEY HAVE SAID GOOD MORNING AND EXCHANGED ENERGY WITH A CUDDLE (TO SHOW EACH OTHER THEY ARE IMPORTANT). THIS IS STARTING THE DAY WITH A POSITIVE BEHAVIOUR.

THE SECOND STAGE IS TO GO INTO YOUR PARTNER'S COOKIE JAR AT YOUR SIDE OF THE BED AND RANDOMLY TAKE OUT ONE PIECE OF PAPER, READ IT, BUT DON'T SHOW YOUR PARTNER AS IT'S A SURPRISE!

THE THIRD STAGE IS THE FUN PART! YOU BOTH HAVE TO FIND TIME BEFORE YOU FALL ASLEEP, TO FULFIL WHATEVER IS ON THE PAPER WITHOUT COMPROMISE!

MOST RELATIONSHIPS WILL STRUGGLE BECAUSE PEOPLE WILL GIVE WHAT THEY WANT AND NOT WHAT THE OTHER NEEDS. THIS IS WHY IT IS BEST THAT PEOPLE ARE BEST FRIENDS BEFORE THEY START SERIOUSLY TOGETHER, NOT BECAUSE OF THE SHALLOW REASONS THAT LIFE IS BUILT ON AT THE MOMENT. WOULD YOU LIKE TO SEE A BETTER FUTURE FOR RELATIONSHIPS? THIS GAME IS THE BEST STARTING POINT I KNOW OF AND THAT IS WHY I CREATED IT.

BOTH INDIVIDUALS WILL GAIN 21 PIECES OF KNOWLEDGE OF WHAT THEIR PARTNER LIKES, WITHOUT THE AWKWARD CONVERSATIONS, OR PRETENDING TO KNOW. THESE CAN BE KEPT AND REUSED AT RANDOM TO SHOW THAT THEIR PARTNER IS IN THEIR THOUGHTS AND NOT JUST FOR THE GAME. THE RELATIONSHIP CAN HAVE ITS TENSIONS (AS ALL RELATIONSHIPS DO) BUT THAT JUST SHOWS WHERE MOST PEOPLE FAIL.

EVERYONE'S UNCONSCIOUS KNOWS THAT LOVE IS GIVING WITHOUT EXPECTING ANYTHING IN RETURN, SO WHY DON'T WE ALL START? WOULD IT BE BETTER IF EVERYTHING WAS GIVING RATHER THAN TAKING SO THAT TWO PEOPLE BOTH GIVE AND GET PLEASURE CHEMICALS FROM THEIR BRAIN? IT'S BALANCE AND THAT IS HOW BALANCE IS MAINTAINED.

LOVE CAN BE PAYING IT FORWARD TO A STRANGER, HELPING A FAMILY MEMBER, FEEDING THE HOMELESS, SHARING INFORMATION... IT'S NOT ABOUT HAVING A PARTNER. IT'S A WAY OF LIFE AND WHEN YOU LIVE A LIFE OF LOVE, IT COMES BACK WITHOUT EXPECTATION.

WHERE WOULD YOU LIKE TO SEE MORE LOVE IN THE WORLD?

CHAPTER 4: SEX SELLS

WHAT IS SEX? IS IT FOR PLEASURE? MAKING BABIES? A CRUTCH/HABIT? TO TRY TO SHOW LOVE PHYSICALLY? A SALES TOOL? A JOB?

THE WAY WE LIVE HAS CHANGED THE MEANING OF SEX FOR SO MANY PEOPLE. SO MUCH ACTUALLY, THAT SO MANY PEOPLE FEEL THAT THEY 'NEED' IT IN THEIR LIVES TO BE HAPPY!!!

WE NEED CLEAN AIR, FOOD, WATER AND WARMTH THE LAST TIME I CHECKED, FOR US TO BE HEALTHY AND HAPPY. I WILL GO INTO THE DATING SIDE OF SEX IN THE NEXT CHAPTER. FOR NOW, WE WILL

CONCENTRATE ON THE FACT SEX SELLS AND IS A HUGE MONEY MAKER, EVEN FOR PRODUCTS THAT HAVE ABSOLUTELY NOTHING TO DO WITH SEX. DO YOU REMEMBER WHEN A PRODUCT WAS SOLD FOR IT'S FEATURES AND BENEFITS? ME TOO! I EVEN REMEMBER THE DAYS WHEN PEOPLE USED TO RESPECT THEMSELVES AND OTHERS BY BEING HUMBLE.

THE EARLIEST KNOWN SEX SELLING WAS IN 1871 BY 'PEARL TOBACCO'. THEY PUT TRADING CARDS IN PACKETS, SO THAT BUYERS COULD TRADE THEM! I REMEMBER AS A CHILD, TENNENTS LAGER (SCOTLAND) HAVING SCANTILY CLAD LADIES ON THEIR CANS, WITH THEIR 'GIRL NEXT DOOR' NAMES TO MAKE THEM FEEL MORE ATTAINABLE TO THE TYPICAL WORKING MAN DRINKING IT. BECAUSE THEY GET A DOUBLE HIT AT THE MAN... ALCOHOL FOR DISTRACTION AND THE STIMULATION TO THE NUCLEUS ACCUMBENS (LITERALLY THE PRIMAL INSTINCT OF A MAN WHO IS VERY BASIC) TO MAKE HIM WANT TO CONSUME BOTH THE WOMAN AND THE ALCOHOL! THE BIOLOGICAL WOMAN'S NUCLEUS ACCUMBENS DOES NOT WORK IN THE SAME WAY AND THIS IS WHY I ONLY MENTIONED MEN.

IN ALL HONESTY, I DON'T SEE MANY SEMI-NAKED MEN SELLING PRODUCTS TO WOMEN. IT SEEMS THAT THEY RESPECT THE FELLOW FEMALE FORM OR WANT TO LOOK LIKE THE WOMAN SELLING THE PRODUCT. STRANGE EH? ARE THE SEMI-NAKED MEN IN UNDERWEAR SELLING THE UNDERWEAR OR AFTERSHAVE SO THAT MEN BUY IT, BECAUSE THIS WILL MAKE THEM FEEL LIKE THE MODEL? OR SO THE PERSON BUYING THE PRODUCT CAN PERVE IN THE HOUSE AFTER THEY GIVE IT AS A PRESENT?

SEX GIVES US A RUSH WITH DOPAMINE (TENSION CHEMICALS) AND RELEASES ENDORPHINS (SATISFYING CHEMICALS), ALMOST LIKE A BAR OF CHOCOLATE WHEN CRAVING SOMETHING SWEET... ONLY MUCH BIGGER! ADVERTISERS HAVE CAREFULLY MANIPULATED PEOPLE INTO THINKING THEY DON'T JUST WANT THE PRODUCT; THEY NEED THE PRODUCT, LIKE THEY FEEL THAT THEY NEED SEX. DO YOU FEEL LIKE YOU NEED SEX IN ORDER TO BE SATISFIED? WHAT WOULD HAPPEN IF YOU COULD NEVER

HAVE SEX AGAIN? WOULD LIFE BE OVER?

A WHILE BACK (COUPLE OF DECADES AND BEFORE), MOST PEOPLE USED TO LIVE THEIR LIVES WITH A STEADY SUPPLY OF A BRAIN CHEMICAL CALLED SEROTONIN (LONG-TERM HAPPINESS/CONFIDENT FEELING). THEY DIDN'T CHASE VERY MUCH AND FELT QUITE CONTENT WITH LIFE. YES, THERE WERE SEX MAGAZINES, TV CHANNELS AND MOVIES, ALTHOUGH THIS WAS NOT PARADED ALL OVER THE PLACE, DUE TO RESPECT OF SELF, FAMILY, FRIENDS AND YOUNG PEOPLE'S EYES AS THEY WERE KEPT INNOCENT. QVC TELEVISION CHANNEL WAS A HUGE HIT, AS WELL AS CATALOGUES AND OTHER OUTLETS, FOR CONSUMERS TO SEE THE PRODUCT THAT THEY WISHED TO PURCHASE. IT WAS VERY TAME AS THE CONSUMERISM ERA HADN'T REALLY STARTED PROPERLY. NOW CONSUMERISM IS IN FULL SWING, PEOPLE FEEL LIKE THEY NEED EVERYTHING... THEY NEED A NEW BAG, NEED A PAIR OF SHOES, NEED LIP FILLERS OR THAT NEW CAR!

WHERE AM I GOING WITH ALL THIS? WELL... NOWADAYS, SO MANY PEOPLE LIVE THEIR LIFE WITH LESS SEROTONIN (LONG-TERM HAPPINESS), DUE TO CHEMICALS IN FOOD, CHEMICALS IN MEDICINE AND BELIEVE IT OR NOT, THEIR THOUGHT PROCESSES. THOSE CHEMICALS CAN CAUSE THE SEROTONIN RECEPTORS IN THE BRAIN TO BECOME DORMANT OR UNABLE TO WORK THE WAY INTENDED BY DESIGN. ESPECIALLY IF PEOPLE HABITUATE TO SHORT-TERM HAPPINESS BURSTS, THIS IS HOW THEY WILL LIVE AND NEVER BE FULFILLED.

VITAMIN B6, B2 AND IRON HAVE TO BE PRESENT, ACCORDING TO HEALTH EXPERTS, TO SYNTHESISE THE TRYPTOPHAN INTO SEROTONIN. TRYPTOPHAN IS FOUND IN CHEESE, MILK, TURKEY, EGGS, TOFU, NUTS, CHICKEN, SEEDS AND FISH. PEOPLE WHO ARE VEGAN, WILL NOT EAT THE MAJORITY OF THESE FOODS. THEY CAN BUY TRYPTOPHAN SUPPLEMENTS TO BOOST SEROTONIN LEVELS. AMAZING WHAT WE ARE NOT TOLD ISN'T IT? WE ARE TOLD BEING VEGAN IS HEALTHIER, KINDER TO ANIMALS, BUT NOT HOW TO HELP KEEP US HAPPY IN THE LONG TERM.

PEOPLE ARE NOW CALLED CONSUMERS, MORE THAN CUSTOMERS IN MY OWN HUMBLE BELIEF. (THERE WILL BE A LOT OF HUMBLE BELIEFS IN THIS BOOK.) WHAT WOULD YOU SAY YOU WERE? DO YOU KNOW THE DIFFERENCE? PURCHASES ARE MADE, BECAUSE THEY PRODUCE A CHEMICAL CALLED DOPAMINE (SHORT-TERM BUZZ/TENSION) THAT LIKE ENDORPHINS ARE RELEASED BEFORE, DURING AND AFTER SEX. IF PEOPLE ARE NOT LIVING LIFE ON THE LONG-TERM HAPPY (SEROTONIN) SCALE, THEY ARE GOING TO HAVE TO CHASE THE DOPAMINE AREN'T THEY? CHASING SEX AND CHASING THAT ULTIMATE PURCHASE TO FULFIL THAT DESIRE! DO YOU THINK ADVERTISING PSYCHOLOGISTS KNOW THIS? OF COURSE, THEY DO!!! PUT THE TWO TOGETHER AND YOU HAVE QUITE THE FIERCE PAIR EH?

SO... THE PROCESS KINDA LOOKS LIKE THIS; FEELING UNHAPPY- HAVE SEX/MAKE PURCHASE- RELEASE DOPAMINE- FEEL ENERGISED (SHORT TERM) AND THEN THE ENDORPHINS LEAVE YOU WITH A SATISFYING FEELING. REPEAT OVER AND OVER UNTIL A HABIT IS CREATED. THIS HABIT WILL MEAN, WE ARE ALWAYS ON THE LOOKOUT FOR THE NEXT 'HIT' OF DOPAMINE OR THAT BUZZ AND WILL LITERALLY BE PRETTY INSATIABLE. BAD NEWS FOR CONSUMERS, GREAT NEWS FOR CLEVER COMPANIES GETTING RICH AND GOVERNMENT REAPING IN THE TAX!!! DOES THIS SOUND LIKE A SIMILAR PROCESS TO WHAT YOU DO CURRENTLY OR SOMEONE YOU KNOW?

LOOKING AT A SCANTILY CLAD PERSON, WILL RAISE THE BLOOD PRESSURE OF MOST OF THE POPULATION (AS LONG AS THEY RESONATE IN SOME WAY). THAT SPARKS THE THOUGHT, THE THOUGHT SPARKS THE HABIT AND THE HABIT MAKES THE PURCHASE, ALL TO GET THAT BUZZ!

I'M NOT JUDGING ANYONE THAT DOES THIS, I DID IT MYSELF FOR LONG ENOUGH AND REALISED IT WASN'T HELPING MY LIFE. I ASKED MYSELF "WHAT WOULD LIFE BE LIKE IF I WASN'T ALWAYS CHASING?" SO... I STOPPED CHASING! MY NEW PROGRAM WAS TO TELL MYSELF "I'M CONTENT" EVERY TIME I WAS LOOKING TO MAKE AN UNNECESSARY

PURCHASE OR USE SEX TO GIVE MYSELF THAT DOPAMINE HIT. I TOLD MYSELF, I WAS CONTENT, WHILE USING MY SELF TAPPING THERAPY AND BROKE THE CYCLE.

TAPPING THERAPY IS AN EMOTIONAL FREEDOM TECHNIQUE AND I HIGHLY RECOMMEND EVERYONE LEARNING HOW TO PRACTICE THIS ON THEMSELVES. YOU HAVE THE POWER, THE DISCIPLINE AND LOVE TO SEE YOURSELF THROUGH TO FEELING CONTENT AND BALANCED, WITHOUT ANY CRUTCHES.

I STARTED THIS WHEN I WAS SERVING IN THE ARMY AND WAS STRUGGLING WITH MENTAL AND PHYSICAL HEALTH PROBLEMS. ALL I WAS OFFERED WAS TABLETS AND COUNSELING. I WAS IN THE HABIT OF THE SEX/PURCHASE = EMOTIONAL FULFILLMENT. IT WAS UP TO ME TO CHANGE IT AND I FOUND EFT... LIFE CHANGING! WOULD IT BE HARMFUL TO TRY IT? WOULD YOU BE UPSET IF THIS COULD HELP YOU AND YOU WERE TOO LAZY TO TRY?

HERE IS A LINK:

WWW.HEALTHLINE.COM/HEALTH/EFT-TAPPING

THIS WILL HELP EXPLAIN HOW IT WORKS IN MORE DETAIL AND GIVES YOU INSTRUCTIONS AS TO HOW TO DO IT. MORE INFORMATION WILL BE ABLE TO BE FOUND ON THE INTERNET.

I BELIEVE SEX IS SOMETHING THAT SHOULD BE HAD BECAUSE SOMEONE IS ALREADY HAPPY AND WANTS TO DO IT. HOWEVER, COMPANIES LOOKING TO MAKE A PROFIT KNOW HOW TO CREATE ADDICTS AND HAVE USED SEX TO BEGIN THE PROCESS OF REWIRING OUR BRAINS TO BECOME ADDICTED TO CONSUMING AS OUR PLAN FOR HAPPINESS. IN THE PROCESS, THEY HAVE REWIRED OUR BRAIN TO THINK THAT WE NEED SEX, WHICH UNDERCUTS OUR BRAIN'S ABILITY TO ENJOY SEX.

CONSUMING IS NOT HAPPINESS AND WE NEED NOTHING BUT NECESSITIES.

WOULD YOU LIKE TO FEEL MORE CONTENT? WOULD YOU LIKE TO CHASE LESS AND JUST BE? YOU CAN!! IT'S A CHOICE AND ABOUT CREATING NEW HABITS. DON'T THINK ABOUT THE OLD ONE, JUST CONCENTRATE ON THE NEW ONE YOU'D LIKE TO CREATE! IF THIS APPLIES TO YOU, KEEP READING!

CHAPTER 5: ONLINE DATING

SO... WE'VE ALMOST SEEN THE DEMISE OF COMMUNITY IN THE WORLD OVER THE LAST 30 YEARS OR SO. IT'S BEEN RAMPED UP CONSIDERABLY IN THE LAST 10 YEARS! THIS STARTED WITH THE SELF, THEN PERSONAL RELATIONSHIPS AND FAMILY. THEN WE HAVE SEEN THE DEMISE OF THE BIGGER COMMUNITIES IN NEIGHBORHOODS, CITIES, COUNTRIES AND THE WORLD! IT'S BEEN LIKE THE BIGGEST RIPPLE EFFECT EVER. WHAT IS YOUR DEFINITION OF COMMUNITY? MY DEFINITION WOULD BE "A COLLECTIVE COMING TOGETHER IN HARMONY".

IF WE ARE NOT IN HARMONY WITH OURSELVES, HOW ARE WE MEANT TO HAVE COMMUNITY IN RELATIONSHIPS OF ANY KIND? WE JUST SAW HOW CORPORATIONS HAVE TURNED SEX FROM A HEALTHY WANT TO AN ADDICTIVE NEED. HOW DO YOU THINK THAT HAS AFFECTED DATING?

I SPENT A FEW YEARS OF MY LIFE ON DATING APPS LOOKING FOR THE PERFECT PARTNER, WHILE CHIPPING AWAY AT MY SOUL, EVERY TIME I SENT AN ICE BREAKER MESSAGE OR SWIPED IN THE DIRECTION, BASED ON MY OWN JUDGEMENT. HOW MANY TIMES DO YOU HAVE TO DO SOMETHING BEFORE YOU REALISE IT IS WRONG? DO YOU GO THROUGH ALL THE SHALLOW-BASED RELATIONSHIPS AND LEARN? OR DO YOU GO THROUGH THE MOTIONS AND BLAME?

WHAT DO YOU FEEL THE BENEFITS ARE TO ONLINE DATING? DO YOU FEEL

IT HAS REALLY HELPED SOCIETY AND IS BRINGING PEOPLE TOGETHER? DO YOU BELIEVE IT IS HEALTHY?

THE FIRST THING WE FEEL AS HUMAN BEINGS IS ENERGY, THE CONNECTION AND THEN WE MAKE A CHOICE ON HOW TO ACT ON THE FEELING. SO... WE ARE ONLINE DATING, WHAT IS THE REASON FOR IT? IS IT TO FIND OUR OTHER HALF WHO IS MEANT FOR US? OR IS IT TO FIND SOMEONE ELSE WHO IS UNCOMFORTABLE BEING THEMSELVES, SO WE CAN CREATE A CODEPENDENT RELATIONSHIP, BASED ON LOOKS AND USING OUR CONSCIOUS CHOICE TO MAKE THE WRONG DECISION?

HOW MUCH CAN YOU ACTUALLY TELL ABOUT SOMEONE VIA AN IMAGE? ARE YOU SO IN TUNE, YOU CAN FEEL EVERYONE'S ENERGY OVER A SCREEN, WHEN THEIR INTENTION IS TO PUT THEIR BEST FOOT FORWARD TO LURE YOU IN... JUST LIKE A CONSUMER TARGETED BUSINESS?

STARTING THE WAY YOU MEAN TO GO ON IN LIFE IS ALWAYS A CHOICE. THE ISSUE WITH THE WORLD IS THAT THE CHOICES HAVE BEEN MADE FOR MOST PEOPLE IN A WAY OF PROGRAMMING AND MAKING PEOPLE BELIEVE THERE ARE LACK OF CHOICES! IF YOU SEE SOMETHING AS A NEED, THEN YOU DO LACK CHOICES AND THE ONLY CHOICE YOU HAVE IS CONVENIENCE. MAKING THINGS CONVENIENT, SUCH AS ONLINE DATING WILL CAUSE PEOPLE TO BE LAZY, ALLOW THEM TO SHOW WHAT THEY WANT OTHERS TO SEE, BECAUSE THEY DESPERATELY THINK THEY NEED IT, RATHER THAN WHO THEY ARE. THAT SOUNDS TO ME A LITTLE LIKE MANIPULATION, TO GET WHAT ONE'S SELF WANTS, RATHER THAN BEING HONEST FROM THE BEGINNING. CAN WE EXPECT A LOVING RELATIONSHIP TO BE CREATED WHEN IT DOESN'T BEGIN WITH LOVE?

WHAT'S YOUR DEFINITION OF A PERSONAL RELATIONSHIP?

MINE IS: "TWO PEOPLE COMING TOGETHER ENERGETICALLY, TO ADD VALUE TO EACH OTHER THROUGH LOVE (GIVING VALUE WITHOUT EXPECTING ANYTHING IN RETURN)"

WHAT I HAVE FOUND WITH MY EXTENSIVE EXPERIENCE OF 'MAKING THE WRONG DECISION' IS THAT IT WASN'T MY CHOICES THAT WERE ALWAYS WRONG PER SE, IT WAS WHY I WAS MAKING THE CHOICES. THAT WAS BEING ONLINE FISHING AND NOT DOING ME, UNTIL I FOUND WHAT WAS GOING TO COME TO ME ANYWAY. THERE IS SOMEONE FOR EVERYONE, BUT EVERYONE IS NOT FOR EVERYONE, UNLESS THEY LIVE THEIR LIVES AS THEMSELVES AND NOT FROM EXPERIENCES OF THE PAST.

LET'S LOOK AT THE PROCESS:

FEELING EMPTY, ALONE, BORED, RESTLESS, UNFULFILLED, SOMETHING MISSING.

GO ONLINE WITH A SMÖRGÅSBORD OF INDIVIDUALS, ALL LOOKING FOR SELF FULFILMENT, EXPECTING TO 'FIND LOVE'.

MATCH, GET TALKING WITH INTENTION OF PUTTING THE BEST FOOT FORWARD, IN ORDER NOT TO BE JUDGED OR SHOW INSECURITY.

ARRANGE A SELF GRATIFICATION/SATISFACTION DATE TO FEEL BETTER, OR DISTRACT FROM CURRENT FEELINGS, DON'T BE WHO YOU ARE AT ESSENCE, IN ORDER TO CONTROL THE OUTCOME. (SOUNDS KINDA NARCISSISTIC TO ME.)

UNDERSTAND THE BAR HAS BEEN SET AND MOST INTERACTIONS WILL NOW BE BASED ON WHAT HAS BEEN PUT OUT, THEREFORE INTERACTING AS A PROJECTION OF SELF (ON BOTH SIDES) NOT UNDERSTANDING WHO THE OTHER REALLY IS.

EITHER USE THE OTHER PERSON VIA EMPTY INTERACTIONS UNTIL SOMETHING COMES ALONG THAT IS BETTER, OR GET SERIOUSLY INVOLVED WITHOUT REAL LOVE AND UNDERSTANDING (ATTACHMENT- THIS IS NOT LOVE).

REALISE AFTER A CERTAIN LENGTH OF TIME, THE RELATIONSHIP/ ATTACHMENT IS NOT REAL, SET BLAME, LOOK FOR EXCUSES AND GET

OUT, TRY TO CHANGE THE OTHER TO SUIT, USUALLY NEGATIVE INTERACTIONS TO FINISH AND THIS USUALLY CAUSES HURT, NOT ALWAYS INTENTIONALLY.

REPEAT THE PROCESS, BASED IN FEELING THE SAME AS BEFORE AND NOW HAVING ENERGETIC BARRIERS/THOUGHTS TO ADD TO THE ONES PREVIOUSLY AND HAVE LESS CHANCE OF FINDING A REAL CONNECTION. DESPERATION INCREASES!

WHAT PARTS DO YOU NOT AGREE WITH IN THIS PROCESS?

EVEN IF YOU HAVE NEVER HAD THE DISPLEASURE OF HAVING TO GO THROUGH THE ONLINE DATING PROCESS, DOES IT SOUND LIKE A NICE, FULFILLING PROCESS THAT BUILDS COMMUNITY?

I WAS TOLD BEFORE, "GIVE A MAN A FISH, HE CAN EAT FOR THE NIGHT, SHOW HIM HOW TO CATCH FISH AND HE CAN EAT FOR A LIFETIME". TELL HIM TO GO ONTO PLENTY OF FISH AND HE MIGHT CHANGE CAREER TO BEING A PRIEST. HAHA!

THERE ARE LOTS OF PEOPLE, TELLING OTHER PEOPLE WHAT TO DO, ALSO WHAT NOT TO DO ON THE ONLINE DATING SCENE, WHICH MEANS OTHERS WILL DO WHAT OTHERS HAVE LEARNED, WHILE NOT DOING WHAT THEY NEED TO BE DOING FOR HAPPINESS. THEY WON'T GET TO FEEL FULL FROM THEIR FISH FOR THE NIGHT AND THEY DEFINITELY ARE NOT BEING SHOWN HOW TO CATCH THE RIGHT FISH. THIS MEANS CONSTANT HUNGER FOR LIFE, AS IT ALL STARTS WITH SELF! MEANING THE REASON FOR BEING ON THE DATING APP WAS TO DISTRACT FROM SELF AND SEARCH FOR EXTERNAL FULFILLMENT.

THE PICTURES YOU SHOW WILL DETERMINE THE CONNECTION YOU RECEIVE (KARMA). THE CONVERSATIONS YOU GET INVOLVED IN WILL BE A MIRROR OF SELF (WHAT YOU PUT OUT) AND THIS CAN SHOW WHAT NEEDS UNDERSTOOD WITHIN... EG: ALWAYS FIND YOURSELF TALKING ABOUT SEX AND NO REAL CONNECTION? THIS CAN BE

THE MISINTERPRETATION OF THE PICTURES USED ON THE PROFILE, ALL DOWN TO DEFINITIONS AND INTERPRETATIONS... A BIKINI/ UNDERWEAR PICTURE WILL BE USED TO SHOW CONFIDENCE, MAYBE THE FACT THAT LIFE IS EXCITING FROM SPENDING TIME ON HOLIDAY OR EVEN THAT THE OUTSIDE IS ALL THAT IS AVAILABLE TO SHOW, AS THE INSIDE IS EMPTY. THIS CAN BE INTERPRETED AS EASY ACCESS, WILLING TO TAKE CLOTHES OFF EASY, A SEXUAL PERSON FOR SHOWING SKIN OR EVEN SOMEONE THAT IS INSECURE, LOOKING FOR ATTENTION BY PUTTING IT OUT THERE (OPEN TO PREDATORY BEHAVIOUR). HOW IMPORTANT DO YOU THINK DEFINITIONS AND INTENTIONS ARE? WHY DO PEOPLE ALMOST NEVER ASK AND JUST ASSUME?

THIS MIRROR WE LOOK INTO AS WE LIVE OUR LIFE IS NOT A PHYSICAL ONE, BUT IT WILL ALWAYS SHOW US A TRUE REPRESENTATION OF HOW WE ARE LIVING IF WE REALLY LOOK. THE EGO WILL ALWAYS GIVE BLAME, RATHER THAN ACCEPT WHAT WE NEED TO ACCEPT OR CHANGE. HOW DO YOU LOOK AT YOURSELF? HOW DO OTHERS LOOK AT YOU? REMEMBER, WHAT YOU SHOW, IS ALWAYS WHAT YOU ARE TRYING TO HIDE, UNLESS YOU ARE BEING YOUR TRUE SELF IN ALL SITUATIONS.

LET'S NOW LOOK AT WHY ONLINE DATING IS ACTUALLY UNHEALTHY, OVER AND ABOVE WHAT YOU HAVE JUST READ.

HOW DO YOU BUILD A HEALTHY RELATIONSHIP?

THE PROCESS:

INITIAL ATTRACTION- LOOKS + INTERESTS.

ASK QUESTIONS- ICEBREAKER + UNDERSTANDING.

GIVE- BE OURSELVES + GIVE ACCEPTANCE TO THE OTHER.

GROWTH- ADD VALUE AND DON'T TRY TO CONTROL + OFFER SUPPORT.

REMAIN TRUE- CONSISTENT COMMUNICATION + UNDERSTANDING +

ACCEPTING + BE LOVE.

NOTICE, EVERY STEP AFTER INITIAL ATTRACTION RESULTS IN OUR BRAIN RELEASING DOPAMINE (TENSION), ENDORPHIN (SATISFYING), AND SEROTONIN (CONFIDENCE/CONTENTMENT) CHEMICALS! NO WONDER THIS RESULTS IN HAPPINESS!

THESE STEPS ALL LEAD TO A PLACE OF SAFETY AND MUTUAL HAPPINESS FOR THE OTHER, IF BOTH PARTIES ARE DOING THE SAME, IN THEIR OWN WAY, ON PURPOSE... THERE IS NO SUCH THING AS AN IDEAL PARTNER, AS YOU ARE WORKING FOR EACH OTHER FOR THEIR FULFILLMENT. LITERALLY LIVING LOVE.

CHOICE! WHAT WE ALL WANT BUT CAN LEAD TO GREED! HOW CAN BOTH PEOPLE GET THEIR BRAINS TO RELEASE PLEASURE CHEMICALS WITH ONLINE DATING? THE SMÖRGÅSBORD I SPOKE OF EARLIER, WITH ONLINE DATING IS NOT A GOOD MIX AND WILL IN LOTS OF CASES LEAD TO LACK OF COMMITMENT AND PEOPLE FEELING LIKE DISPOSABLE SACKS OF SH*T. (BLUNT YES, BUT YOU DON'T RESPECT A SACK OF SH*T AND YOU WON'T RESPECT SOMETHING YOU HAVE TOO MUCH OF)

THE CHOICE YOU UNCONSCIOUSLY MAKE ON DATING SITES IS: YOU FULFILL DIFFERENT SIDES OF YOU, THROUGH A VARIETY OF DIFFERENT PEOPLE. YOU CAN FLIRT WITH ONE, BE NAUGHTY WITH ANOTHER, BE INTELLECTUAL WITH ONE, BUT EMOTIONAL WITH ANOTHER. DOES THIS SOUND LIKE A FOCUSED AND FULFILLED LIFE? NOT ONLY ARE YOU REWIRING YOUR BRAIN TOWARDS A SHORT-TERM FIX WITH THESE PEOPLE, BUT YOU ARE ALSO PICKING UP THEIR TRAITS THAT DON'T RESONATE WITH YOU, BY ONLY TAKING WHAT YOU WANT, WHICH MEANS THERE IS NO REAL RESPECT, NO REAL LOVE.

THE CONTROL FROM THE BIGGER SYSTEM COMES FROM THE BREAKDOWN OF THE SMALLER SYSTEM. MENTAL HEALTH IS BAD, SO RELATIONSHIPS AREN'T GOING TO BE AS HEALTHY AS THEY COULD BE. THE FUNNIEST PART OF THIS IS THAT THERE IS ALWAYS SOMEONE

CASHING IN ON THE MISFORTUNE OF OTHERS. IF YOU LOOK AT THE MONEY THAT IS BEING MADE BY THESE ONLINE DATING COMPANIES, YOU'D BE SURPRISED!

IF ONLINE DATING WAS SO GOOD AND HEALTHY, WHY WOULD THERE BE A CONSTANT MOVING TURNSTILE OF PEOPLE GOING THROUGH THE MOTIONS AND THEN COMING BACK FOR MORE? WOULD THESE COMPANIES STAY IN BUSINESS IF THEY FACILITATED HEALTHY FOCUSED RELATIONSHIPS?

PEOPLE BROKEN DOWN SO BAD, THAT THEY FEEL THAT THEY 'NEED' A SIGNIFICANT OTHER TO BE WHOLE, THEY THEN ACCEPT ANYTHING, BASED ON A PICTURE AND SHALLOW MINDSET FOR A DOPAMINE HIT, THIS PUTS A BAND AID OVER THE CRACKS TO TAKE THEM ONE STEP FORWARD, BUT EVENTUALLY TWO STEPS BACK AND NOW THERE IS MORE RESENTMENT AND LACK OF SELF BELIEF ADDED EVERY TIME.

WHAT NEEDS TO BE DONE TO CHANGE THIS?

CHOICES ARE ALWAYS PRESENTED TO PEOPLE AND USUALLY THE EASIEST AND MORE CONVENIENT CHOICES ARE TAKEN, A SHORTCUT IF YOU WILL. DO YOU PREFER A SHORTCUT?

IF YOU ARE OR HAVE ONLINE DATED, IS IT ALWAYS THE OTHER PERSON WHO IS TO BLAME WHEN YOU BREAK UP?

WHY NOT JUST WAIT UNTIL YOUR TIME COMES?

WHERE DID WE GET THESE IDEAS?

CHAPTER 6: MUSIC AND MOVIES

MUSIC:

DID YOU KNOW, LISTENING TO CERTAIN MUSIC CAN LEAVE US FEELING UNEASY DUE TO THE FREQUENCY? BE AWARE OF YOURSELF AND WATCH YOUR NEAREST AND DEAREST AND LOOK HOW MOODS CAN CHANGE WITH MUSIC AND HOW MUSIC CHANGES THE AMBIENCE IN YOUR SURROUNDINGS!

I GAVE SOME OF MY CLIENTS A CHALLENGE; TO LISTEN TO REIKI MUSIC AND OTHER HEALING/SPIRITUAL FREQUENCY MUSIC FOR A WEEK, NOTHING ELSE AND SEE HOW THEY FELT AFTER IT. AFTER TRYING THIS MYSELF, I COULDN'T BELIEVE HOW MUCH MOOD MANIPULATION COMES THROUGH MUSIC! WOULD YOU EVER SUSPECT, THAT THE THING THAT IS MEANT TO MAKE US FREE, ACTUALLY HAS US TRAPPED AND TRIGGERED?

IN 1953, THE INTERNATIONAL STANDARD ORGANISATION (ISO) CHANGED THE FREQUENCY FOR MOST OF THE MUSIC IN THE WORLD FROM 432 HZ TO 440 HZ FREQUENCY. THIS FREQUENCY HAS BEEN KNOWN TO GENERATE ANTISOCIAL BEHAVIOUR IN PEOPLE AND HAS AN UNHEALTHY EFFECT ON THE CONSCIOUSNESS OF PEOPLE! 432HZ IS A NATURAL HEALING FREQUENCY THAT BENEFITS GROWTH, ACCORDING TO THE UNIVERSE. 440HZ IS A STANDARD TUNING THAT DECLARED A CONSCIOUSNESS WAR ON THE WESTERN HUMAN BEING, WITHOUT THEM EVEN KNOWING IT.

IF YOU ARE ASKING HOW THIS IS POSSIBLE... OUR BODIES ARE MADE UP OF AROUND 70% WATER. WATER ITSELF IS A FREQUENCY OF ITS OWN, IT IS ALSO EASILY MANIPULATED BY OTHER FREQUENCIES AND THIS CAUSES THE WATER IN OUR BODIES AND BRAINS TO REACT. 432HZ WILL ALLOW US TO FEEL BALANCED AND CALM, THIS IS SUPPOSEDLY CALLED THE UNIVERSAL FREQUENCY AND ANYTHING ELSE WILL HAVE A DIFFERENT AFFECT.

REPETITION PROGRAMS AND REPROGRAMS THE BRAIN, LIKE AN ADDICTION, WE HAVE BEHAVIOURS THAT PRODUCE PLEASURE CHEMICALS SO THAT WE KEEP DOING THEM! HOW OFTEN DO YOU ESCAPE TO MUSIC? ARE YOU AWARE OF WHERE YOU ESCAPE TO AND WHAT FREQUENCY IT IS?

WHY DO WE USE/HAVE MUSIC? TO DANCE, TO DISTRACT US FROM THOUGHT, TO ENHANCE OUR EMOTIONS, TO SING TO/ALONG WITH, TO RELAX? WHILE WE ARE LOOKING TO EXPRESS FEELING OR EMOTION, LOOKING FOR INSPIRATION... MUSIC HAS TRANCE LIKE CAPABILITIES AND WHEN WE ARE 'TUNED IN' WE ARE OPEN TO PROGRAMMING AND MANIPULATION. DOES MUSIC REALLY ALLOW US TO BE FREE?

NOW WE HAVE THE FREQUENCY AND REASONS FOR MUSIC TOUCHED ON, HOW DO YOU BELIEVE THE WORDS WORK WITH US? THIS IS REALLY SIMPLE, SO SIMPLE THAT MOST PEOPLE DON'T GRASP IT.

WHEN WE LISTEN TO MUSIC, WE ARE OPEN TO SUGGESTION/PROGRAMMING. FOR INSTANCE... WHAT WOULD YOU CLASS AS A LOVE SONG? MOST LOVE SONGS ARE USUALLY ABOUT LOSS OR BREAK UP WITH A PARTNER, CODEPENDENCY AND EVEN FIGHTING... PHYSICALLY OR VERBALLY. HOW MANY SONGS CAN YOU THINK OF THAT IS JUST ABOUT PURE LOVE? IF THE DEFINITION OF LOVE IS GIVING VALUE WITHOUT EXPECTING ANYTHING IN RETURN... THERE WON'T BE MANY SONGS WRITTEN ABOUT LOVE ITSELF!

MANY PEOPLE BELIEVE LOVE CAN BE MEASURED IN FREQUENCY AND THE FREQUENCY IS 528 HZ, AS SAID BY MANY. IF YOU ARE LOOKING TO LISTEN TO LOVE, IT IS ALWAYS GOING TO BE MORE RELAXING WHEN YOU LISTEN TO 528HZ AS IT ALLOWS THE BRAIN TO CALM ALSO.

I AM NOT GOING TO PROMOTE ANY SINGERS/SONGWRITERS THAT CLAIM TO BE MAINSTREAM LOVE SONG WRITERS, EVEN IF THEY ARE WRITING ABOUT LOVE, THE FREQUENCY IS OFF FOR THEM TO DELIVER IT IN A PROPER LOVING WAY, IN MY BELIEF. I LOVE LEARNING AND AFTER

READING THIS CHAPTER, YOU COULD ALWAYS RESEARCH THIS AND FIND OUT MORE. MY INTENTION IS NOT TO CHANGE YOUR MIND OR FOR YOU TO THINK LIKE ME, BUT FOR YOU TO HAVE A CHOICE OF THOUGHT AND LIVE YOUR TRUTH.

THE WORDS IN SONGS ARE VERY IMPORTANT, THEY EVEN HAVE GREATER SIGNIFICANCE THAN WHEN USED IN CONVERSATION. THIS IS BECAUSE OUR FREQUENCY IS BEING MANIPULATED AND OUR ACCEPTANCE OF THE SONG WITH THE LYRICS CONVINCES OUR UNCONSCIOUS BRAIN WE ARE IN AGREEMENT WITH THE LYRICS, EVEN IF WE AREN'T CONSCIOUS OF WHAT WE ARE HEARING. IMAGINE SONGS WERE WRITTEN AND GIVEN TO ARTISTS AND THE WORDS WERE BEING USED TO MANIPULATE THE THOUGHTS AND FEELINGS THROUGH THEIR AUDIENCE... CRAZY IF IT WERE TRUE RIGHT? MAYBE YOU'D LIKE TO CHECK THAT OUT?

HOW ARE HUMAN BEINGS PROGRAMMED? HYPNOSIS AND REPETITION. IF WE LISTEN TO MUSIC WHERE NEGATIVE WORDS ARE LINKED TO LOVE SONGS, OR ANY SONGS FOR THAT MATTER, HOW ARE WE GOING TO THINK? THE FREQUENCY AND WORDS ARE USED AS MANIPULATION, SORCERY OF THE HIGHEST ORDER, YET MOST PEOPLE WILL BELIEVE IT'S ALL HEALTHY. NOT FOR A MINUTE AM I SUGGESTING YOU STOP LISTENING TO MUSIC, JUST UNDERSTAND IT MORE AND DETACH YOUR FEELINGS FROM IT SO YOU CAN MAKE A CONSCIOUS DECISION ON WHAT YOU ARE ACCEPTING. PLEASE DON'T TAKE MY WORD FOR IT, RESEARCH IT ALL, IT'S PRETTY CLEVER AND AMAZING HOW IT'S DONE.

JUST FOR TALKING SAKE, THERE WAS A SONG CALLED 'WAP' BY A VERY WELL KNOWN ARTIST. 'WAP' STANDS FOR WET ASS P*SSY AND IS NOT PUT IN THE TITLE FOR OBVIOUS REASONS. VERY YOUNG KIDS ON SOCIAL MEDIA DOING DANCES WITH THEIR PARENTS TO THIS SONG (BECAUSE IT WAS POPULAR). IMAGINE THE UNCONSCIOUS PROGRAMMING IT IS HAVING ON THE KIDS AND EVEN THE PARENTS. HOW IS THIS GOING TO AFFECT WHAT THEY THINK IS LOVE AND WHAT THEY OUGHT TO LOOK FOR FROM ANOTHER IN ORDER TO BE HAPPY?

MUSIC CAN BE INCREDIBLY HARMFUL IN SO MANY WAYS, THE AWARENESS OF THE LISTENER IS THE ONLY THING THAT CAN KEEP THE MIND AND BRAIN SAFE. WHY DO PEOPLE LISTEN TO SONGS ABOUT HEARTBREAK WHEN THEY FEEL HEARTBROKEN? WHY SHOULD THAT BE AN OPTION? HEAVY METAL MUSIC WHEN ANGRY... IT'S LIKE THE PIED PIPER OF HAMELIN, LEADING EVERYONE AWAY, NOT JUST THE KIDS; WE ADULTS ARE HERE TO PROTECT THE KIDS. THINK ABOUT WHAT'S BEING SAID AND NORMALISED IN YOUR MUSIC. MOST OF ALL ITS IMPORTANT TO BE UNDERSTANDING HOW THE CHILDREN ARE BEING PROGRAMMED.

I WENT TO A PLANT MEDICINE MUSHROOM RETREAT IN PERTH, SCOTLAND A COUPLE OF YEARS AGO AND WAS BLESSED TO HAVE SOME AMAZING PEOPLE (FRIENDS AND STRANGERS) AROUND ME TO SHARE IT WITH. WE SHARED LAUGHS, TEARS AND INSIGHTS.. HONESTLY AN INCREDIBLE DAY AND THE PRACTITIONERS OF THE PLANT MEDICINE WERE TWO AMAZING WOMEN TO WHOM I LOVE WITH ALL MY HEART AND I'M GRATEFUL TO HAVE THEM AS FRIENDS. WHAT THEY DO DEFINITELY 'SQUARES YOU UP'

AFTER THE CEREMONY, ONE OF THE PARTICIPANTS BRIAN BENJI, FROM HOWTH, IRELAND BROUGHT OUT HIS GUITAR AND PLAYED A COVER OR TWO FOR US, BEFORE PLAYING US SOME ORIGINALS HE HAD WRITTEN. I CAN NOT BEGIN TO TELL YOU THE FEELING THAT WENT THROUGH MY BODY! I HAD MUSIC, TRUTH AND ENTERTAINMENT ALL IN ONE... BRIAN SANG ABOUT IMPORTANT THINGS LIKE LIFE, THE MIND, COMMUNITY, LOVE AND ALL THE OTHER GOOD STUFF! LISTENING TO HIS TRUE AND CONSCIOUS WORDS GAVE ME A DIFFERENT TYPE OF ENJOYMENT ALTOGETHER! IT SHOWED ME THE DIFFERENCE BETWEEN THE MUSIC WE ARE GIVEN IN THE MAINSTREAM, COMPARED TO THE MUSIC THAT IS ACTUALLY OUT THERE! I'D HIGHLY RECOMMEND SEARCHING BRIAN BENJI ON YOUTUBE AND SPOTIFY (NOT PAID PARTNERSHIP WITH THE ARTIST OR THE MEDIA PLATFORMS). CONSCIOUS MUSIC COULD BE A HUGE CATALYST IN TO RELEASING HUMANITY FROM A CERTAIN DARKNESS, BUT WE NEED TO LOOK FOR IT.

THERE WILL BE MORE FROM MEETING BRIAN IN THE 2ND BOOK IN THIS

TRILOGY 'TRUTH-BIGGER SYSTEMS AND INSTITUTIONS'

MOVIES:

FOR ANYONE WHO HAS OR HAS HAD A TV (TELL-LIE VISION) DO YOU KNOW THIS ACTUALLY PROGRAMS YOU MORE THAN MUSIC? NOT ONLY DOES IT USE SOUND FREQUENCIES AND WORDS, IT ALSO USES PICTURE FREQUENCIES AND CAN BE VERY HYPNOTIC, ESPECIALLY NOW WITH LED (LIGHT EMITTING DIODE) SCREENS! SOME MIGHT SAY IT IS LIKE PROGRAMMING HUMAN BEINGS TO BE ROBOTS! LED LIGHTING HAS BEEN FOUND TO STOP THE BRAIN PRODUCING AS MUCH MELATONIN TOO, THIS MAKES IT HARDER FOR PEOPLE TO SLEEP WHICH WOULD HELP REPAIR AND REST THE BRAIN. LED IS GOING EVERYWHERE AND PEOPLE ARE SLEEPING BADLY AND FEELING UNBALANCED AND THEIR BRAINS ARE LACKING REPAIR. COINCIDENCE? READ UP ON IT FOR YOURSELF! WHY WOULD THEY REPLACE ALL LIGHT BULBS? MOST WILL SAY TO SAVE ELECTRICITY, WOULD THAT BE TRUE IF PEOPLE USE EVEN MORE ELECTRICITY CHARGING CARS, POWER TOOLS AND ALL THE GADGETS CONSUMERS USE? AGAIN, RESEARCH INTO THIS IS ABSOLUTELY ASTOUNDING!! LIGHT IS FREQUENCY AND LED COMES AND MENTAL HEALTH/SLEEP GO DOWN HILL... WORTH LOOKING INTO BEFORE YOU CHOOSE NOT TO BELIEVE WHAT YOU ARE SEEING. MANY PHD STUDIES TOO!

HOW ARE WE PROGRAMMED? R-E-P-E-T-I-T-I-O-N!

ARE YOU GOING TO GROW, BE FREE AND BE BALANCED IF YOU ARE WATCHING BOX SETS, TV PROGRAMS AND MOVIES ALL THE TIME?

IF WE GET INTO THE HYPNOTIC TRANCE, IS IT EASY TO GET OUT OF? OUR FEELINGS, FREQUENCY AND BELIEFS ARE MANIPULATED BY THIS BOX WE STARE AT AND WE DON'T EVEN REALISE. FEELING LOW? WATCH A COMEDY! SPLIT UP WITH YOUR PARTNER? WATCH A LOVE STORY AND FEEL SORRY FOR YOURSELF! THERE IS SOMETHING FOR EVERYONE.

THERE ARE MINIMAL FEW WHO CAN SWITCH OFF AND DON'T LET IT CONTROL THEM WHEN THEY GET STARTED. HOW IS YOUR MOVIE CHOICE TO YOUR MOODS USUALLY? NEXT TIME THINK HOW YOU FEEL AND THEN SEE WHAT YOU FEEL LIKE WATCHING.

ANYWAY, WE ARE HERE TO TALK ABOUT MOVIES, BELIEFS, PROGRAMMING, MANIPULATION, LIES AND PRAISING FAMOUS PEOPLE WHO WE HOLD HIGHER THAN WE DO OURSELVES, SOME OF OUR FAMILY AND OUR PEERS. AGAIN, I WILL NOT GO IN TO PROMOTING INDIVIDUAL FILMS, BUT I WILL GO IN TO HOW I BELIEVE THEY WORK.

I WAS TOLD BY A VERY TALENTED WRITER ONCE "A BELIEF IS A THOUGHT WE THINK REPEATEDLY" IMAGINE WE BELIEVED EVERYTHING THE MOVIES TELL US, EVEN THOUGH WE KNOW IT'S ALL ACTORS AND WRITTEN SCRIPTS! YOUR BRAIN DOESN'T HAVE EYES, BUT HAS EVERYTHING YOU HAVE EVER SEEN, STORED AND READY TO BE TRIGGERED OR NORMALISED BASED ON YOUR INITIAL RESPONSE TO EXPERIENCING IT. IMAGINE MOVIES WERE TO NORMALISE TRAUMA, VIOLENCE AND CONTROL… IT'S ALREADY STORED IN THERE! WOULD THAT MAKE SENSE AS TO HOW F*CKED UP CERTAIN PARTS OF SOCIETY IS?

FIRSTLY, IN A WORLD WHERE EVERY HUMAN IS EQUAL, WHY WOULD WE GIVE OUR POWER AND WORSHIP AWAY TO AN ACTOR WE WILL MOST LIKELY NEVER MEET? SECONDLY, IF WE ARE PROGRAMMED WITH WORDS, OTHER SOUND FREQUENCIES AND PICTURES, WOULD THIS MEAN WE CAN ONLY CHOOSE WHAT WE SEE FROM A COLLECTION OF PURPOSELY CREATED MOVIES, SHOWS OR PROGRAMS? WHY ARE ONLY A CERTAIN GROUP OF PEOPLE ABLE TO WRITE AND PRODUCE SCRIPTS, WHEN WE HAVE SO MANY TALENTED HUMAN BEINGS IN THE WORLD?

WE ALL USE PATHWAYS IN OUR BRAINS DIFFERENTLY, WE LEARNED THIS FROM EXPERIENCE WHILE GROWING UP. SOME PEOPLE WILL BE MORE INCLINED TO WATCH CERTAIN GENRES; DEPENDING ON HOW THEIR LIFE HAS BEEN LIVED, HOW THEY ARE EMOTIONALLY, HOW THEY FIRST RESPONDED TO IT AND WHAT THOSE CLOSE TO THEM WATCH. ON A

LARGE SCALE, IT IS VERY CLEVER AND CAN STILL CONTROL THE MASSES IN SEVERAL WAYS; SUBLIMINAL MESSAGES, THOUGHT AND EMOTION TRIGGERS AND DISTRACTION.

CONFLICT... A HUGE PART OF FILM... THE PROBLEM, CONFLICT (REVENGE), RESOLUTION MODEL IS PRETTY STANDARD AND THIS TEACHES HUMAN BEINGS THAT IT IS OK TO FIGHT AND IT IS NORMAL TO FIGHT FIRE WITH FIRE AND HATE. THERE IS USUALLY A VICTIM IN THE FILM THAT PEOPLE WILL BECOME ATTACHED TO, OR A VILLAIN THAT THE VIEWER LIKES/DISLIKES... OR WANTS TO BE. THEN IN COMES THE HERO, THE BRAVE ONE! JUSTICE IS SERVED THROUGH LOVE, KARMA, VIOLENCE OR WHO WE DEPICT AS THE LAW. WHY WOULD WE NEED TO SEEK PUNISHMENT OR REVENGE TO FEEL GOOD WHEN GOOD AND NICE DOES NOT RELATE TO PUNISHMENT OR REVENGE? WOULD YOU AGREE THAT THIS IS AN INTERNAL CONFLICT? HOW ABOUT IF YOU'D NEVER BEEN TAUGHT RETALIATION OR REVENGE, WOULD YOU WANT IT SO BADLY IN REAL LIFE SITUATIONS?

WAR... ALSO A VERY POPULAR CHOICE IN THE MOVIE BUSINESS, THEY MAKE IT GLAMOROUS AND EXCITING SO THAT IT PROMOTES NECESSITY IN OUR SOCIETY. WHY SHOULD INNOCENTS DIE, COUNTRIES RANSACKED AND BULLIED? IS THIS NORMAL? I WAS TRAINED AS A SOLDIER AND I, ALONG WITH MANY, MANY OTHERS WAS TREATED WITH LITERALLY NO RESPECT AS A HUMAN BEING. I WAS MICROMANAGED WITHIN AN INCH OF MY LIFE. NOTHING LIKE WE SEE IN FILMS, BUT OUR SPIRIT IS BROKEN SO WE TAKE IT AND FOLLOW ORDERS. SOUND NICE? WAIT TILL YOU READ THE MILITARY CHAPTER.

THE GLAMOROUS WAR MOVIES ARE ALL LIES AND WE DO NOT NEED WAR. THE WORLD CAN DO WITHOUT IT. DO YOU BELIEVE TERRORISTS ARE CREATED FOR AN EXCUSE TO CAUSE WAR OR TO TRY AND STOP THE SYSTEM CAUSING WAR? IT DOESN'T MATTER HOW PRETTY THE ACTORS ARE OR HOW TOUGH THEY ARE, THE MESSAGE WILL ALWAYS BE THE SAME: "WAR IS OK AND NEEDED". SO THEN THE UNCONSCIOUS BRAIN

BELIEVES YOU HAVE ACCEPTED IT AND THEN IT'S ALL GOOD WHEN WE SEE THE SO-CALLED GLOBAL LEADERS DESTROYING COUNTRIES AND KILLING PEOPLE?

LOVE STORIES... IF THE MEANING OF LOVE IS 'TO GIVE WITHOUT EXPECTING ANYTHING IN RETURN' HAVE YOU EVER REALLY WATCHED A LOVE STORY? WHAT ABOUT A LOVE STORY WITHOUT ONE CONFLICT OR DISAGREEMENT? WHAT ABOUT A HAPPY BEGINNING, MIDDLE AND END? WE ARE TAUGHT WE NEED TO GO THROUGH BAD EXPERIENCES TO GET TO GOOD ONES. WE ARE TAUGHT THAT THERE IS NO LOVE WITHOUT CONFLICT AND THAT PEOPLE CANNOT BE HAPPY ALL THE TIME. I BELIEVE THAT THEY CAN, AS LONG AS THEY ARE BALANCED. HOWEVER, IF WE ARE CONSTANTLY WATCHING MOVIES ON PROMISCUITY, HURT, CONFLICT AND CODEPENDENT RELATIONSHIPS... EVEN PORN AND THEY ARE ALL CLASSED AS LOVE STORIES, WE ARE GOING TO RELATE ALL THAT I JUST MENTIONED TO LOVE AS WE LEARN FROM REPETITION AND THIS IS ALSO DESTROYING RELATIONSHIPS! REMEMBER THE OLD FILMS ON COURTING, GOING DANCING AND JUST BEING HAPPY? IT'S ALL THERE TO WATCH BUT NOWADAYS PEOPLE LOVE DRAMA SO THEY WILL BE BORED WITH REAL LOVE!

SUPERHERO MOVIES... PEOPLE WITH GIFTS AND TALENTS THAT THEY CAN USE TO SAVE THE WORLD/HUMANITY! HAVE YOU EVER SEEN A SUPERHERO AND THEIR SUPERPOWER IS LOVE? HOW MANY SUPERHEROES HAVE YOU SEEN, THAT AREN'T ABOUT TAKING INDIVIDUALS TO JUSTICE (GOVERNMENT OR OTHER), VIOLENCE, REVENGE OR SHOWING THAT HUMAN BEINGS ARE WEAK?

HUMAN BEINGS ACTUALLY HAVE GIFTS THAT CAN HEAL THE WORLD, THEY ARE IN NUMBERS GREATER THAN ANY ARMY OR SUPERPOWER FORCE OF ANY ESTABLISHMENT. HUMAN BEINGS CONTINUE TO ACCEPT THEY ARE WEAK AND THAT THEY CANNOT MAKE A DIFFERENCE. THERE IS NO POWER GREATER THAN THAT OF LOVE AND HUMAN COMMUNITY; IT WAS THE POWER WE ALL CAME IN TO THE WORLD WITH. WE ARE THE

REAL SUPERHEROES AND POSSESS THE REAL SUPERPOWER TO TAKE US TO BETTER TIMES.

GANG AND GANGSTER MOVIES... IF PEOPLE WERE GENUINELY HAPPY, LOVED THEMSELVES AND OTHERS, WOULD THEY REALLY WANT TO BULLY, HURT OR EXTORT OTHERS? I BELIEVE THE ANSWER IS NO. IF THESE MOVIES TEACH US ABOUT POWER COMING FROM CONFLICT, WHAT ARE CERTAIN INSECURE PEOPLE GOING TO DO TO FEEL POWERFUL? THEY DON'T HAVE TO BE A GANGSTER TO BULLY SOMEONE TO FEEL A SENSE OF POWER, DO THEY? YET THE SAME 'WINNING CONFLICT IS POWER'. THEN THERE IS THE FEAR SIDE OF IT: FEAR OF THEMSELVES, FEAR OF WHAT OTHERS THINK OF THEM, FEAR OF LOOKING WEAK. THIS COMES IN REAL LIFE FROM LACK OF SELF ACCEPTANCE AND APPRECIATION. LACK OF SELF ESTEEM THAT MAKES PEOPLE WANT TO HURT OTHERS IN MY BELIEF.

WHAT ABOUT THE ACTORS? WHAT ABOUT THE MAJORITY OF THEM BEING EXTREMELY PRETTY OR HANDSOME? (ACCORDING TO SOCIETY'S STANDARDS) PARADED ABOUT ON A SCREEN FOR ALL TO SEE, SPENDING THEIR LIVES PRETENDING TO BE SOMEONE ELSE, IS THIS A LIFE? THEN THEY HAVE THE PEOPLE WHO ARE WATCHING THEM, PUTTING THEM ON A PEDESTAL THINKING THEIR LIVES ARE GREAT, WHEN THEY ARE JUST AS CONTROLLED! USING SOCIETY STANDARD-PRETTY ACTORS ALSO CAUSES PEOPLE TO FEEL INSECURE OR BELIEVE THAT PRETTY IS A TALENT, IS IT? THIS ALSO CAUSES PEOPLE TO BE INSPIRED BY CHARACTERS AND PEOPLE WHO HAVE BEEN CREATED AND PROGRAMMED TO DO A JOB WHEN NONE OF IT IS REAL.

I KNOW FROM MY PERFORMING DAYS, I WAS TOO BUSY TRYING TO BE OTHER CHARACTERS, I FORGOT WHAT IT WAS LIKE TO BE ME. IT WAS NOT A LIFE, YET SO MANY PEOPLE ARE PRAISED FOR IT IN THE MOVIES. I AM NOT PUTTING THE ACTORS DOWN, THEY ARE USING THEIR EXPRESSION TO DO A JOB. THE DAMAGE IS BEING DONE ABOVE THEM, IN THE MASSIVE BILLION DOLLAR INDUSTRY THAT HAS MASSES AND MASSES OF PEOPLE UNDER CONTROL.

IF YOU THINK FOR A SECOND, I'M TRYING TO PUT YOU OFF FILM, TV OR ACTORS, I AM NOT. I STILL WATCH MOVIES AND DOCUMENTARIES BUT TAKE THEM AS A PINCH OF SALT. I AM A TRUTH SEEKER: I BELIEVE WHAT I FEEL AND NOT WHAT I AM TOLD. THIS COULD WORK FOR YOU TOO. LOOK OUT FOR THE MESSAGING IN FILMS, THE FEELINGS YOU GET WHILE WATCHING, THE RESPONSE YOUR UNCONSCIOUS BRAIN SEES YOU HAVING AND THE AMOUNT OF CONFLICT WE ARE PROGRAMMED WITH. IT'S CRAZY!!!

WHAT FILMS MAKE YOU FEEL HAPPY, SCARED, SAD, ANGRY? IS IT GOOD THAT FILMS ARE ABLE TO MANIPULATE YOUR EMOTIONS FOR SOMETHING THAT ISN'T REAL?

AS IF DEALING WITH MUSIC AND MOVIES HASN'T BECOME MORE CHALLENGING OVER THE YEARS, WE HAVE AN EVEN BIGGER INFLUENCE TO DEAL WITH TODAY... WHEN DO THE MASSES WAKE UP AND QUESTION?

CHAPTER 7: VANITY, INFLUENCERS AND ONLINE FAME

WHERE DO WE BEGIN? AT THE BEGINNING?

THE LAST DECADE HAS BEEN MEGA! PEOPLE BECOMING MORE SELF ABSORBED/ INSECURE, USUALLY DUE TO LACK OF SELF ESTEEM, SELF ACCEPTANCE AND TRYING TO KEEP UP WITH OTHERS. THERE ARE MANY PARTS TO THIS CHAPTER AND I WILL BREAK THEM DOWN AND PROMPT YOU TO ASK YOURSELF WHERE YOU FIT IN AND WHY.

VANITY:

VANITY IS A CONCEPT, LOOKED AT DIFFERENTLY BY MANY. IF YOU FEEL ATTACKED BY ANYTHING IN THIS CHAPTER, I'D ASK YOU TO BE A TRUTH

SEEKER AND LOOK A LITTLE DEEPER INSIDE, AS TO WHY.

LOOKING AT (ANTI)- SOCIAL MEDIA PLATFORMS AND WATCHING PEOPLE IN DAILY LIFE IS A FAVOURITE PASTIME OF MINE. I DON'T PARTICULARLY CARE MUCH FOR THE CONTENT. HOWEVER, I DO LIKE TO WATCH TRENDS, PEOPLE'S BEHAVIOUR AND MOVEMENTS SO THAT I CAN FEEL WHAT'S GOING ON IN THE WORLD.

WHAT DO YOU BELIEVE TO BE THE BEST THING ABOUT ONLINE PLATFORMS? DO YOU HAVE ANY PARTICULAR THING THAT ANNOYS YOU ONLINE?

SELFIES!! TAKE A SELFIE, LOOK AT MY SELFIE!!, HOLD ON TILL I TAKE A SELFIE!! THIS IS A MAJOR PART OF ONLINE LIFE. WHO IS YOUR WORST CRITIC? WHO WILL NOT GIVE YOU ANY FORGIVENESS IN THE WAY THAT YOU LOOK? YES, YOU GOT IT, YOU!! THE SELFIE CAMERA WAS THE BEGINNING OF A SEVERE DECLINE IN THE POPULATION'S MENTAL HEALTH IN MY BELIEF. IF YOU LOOK AT YOUR FLAWS, YOU WILL THINK OTHERS WILL TOO AND THIS BECOMES A BELIEF!   MASSES ARE JUDGING THEMSELVES, THEY ARE BECOMING POWERLESS IN SOCIETY AND ALWAYS STRIVE FOR PERFECTION... VERY CLEVER! SO WHY TAKE SELFIES WHEN PEOPLE DON'T ACTUALLY CARE FOR THEM? I THINK PEOPLE HAVE AN INNATE DESIRE TO UNDERSTAND WHO THEY ARE AND THEY HAVE BEEN MANIPULATED TO THINK IT IS THEIR BEHAVIOUR AND APPEARANCE, WHICH IS ONLY GOING TO LEAD TO DETERIORATING MENTAL HEALTH.

VANITY, IN MY PERSONAL BELIEF COMES FROM JUDGEMENT OF SELF, STRIVING TO LOOK THE BEST, SO THAT OTHER PEOPLE APPRECIATE YOU BECAUSE YOU THINK YOU ARE YOUR APPEARANCE. WE HEAR INDIVIDUALS SAY "I'M DOING IT FOR ME, SO I FEEL GOOD, NOT OTHERS" IN REALITY THOUGH, WE CAN'T SEE OURSELVES!! THERE IS A PROGRAM IN OUR BRAINS THAT ALLOWS US NOT TO SEE THE TRUTH SOMETIMES, THIS IS CREATED BY MEDIA OF ALL KINDS, TV AND FILM. WE WATCH, SAY OR THINK THINGS REPEATEDLY AND IT BECOMES EMBEDDED IN OUR UNCONSCIOUS BRAIN.

YOU CONSCIOUSLY TELL OTHERS "I DON'T CARE WHAT OTHERS THINK", HOWEVER YOUR ACTIONS SAY, "I HAVE SEEN, HEARD OR THOUGHT THIS REPEATEDLY AND IS WHAT I'M MEANT TO BE DOING SO I'LL DO THIS!" THIS MEANS THAT MOST OF THE POPULATION AREN'T DOING IT FOR THE BENEFIT OF OTHERS BUT TO GET RECOGNITION/ATTENTION! I WOULD LOVE TO BE ABLE TO TELL EVERYONE READING THIS BOOK THAT THEIR CONSCIOUS BRAIN HAS CONTROL OF THEIR LIFE, BUT IT CERTAINLY DOESN'T. THIS IS ALL UNCONSCIOUS MAGIC AND WHY IT'S SO POWERFUL!

THE CONSCIOUS BRAIN IS ONLY 10% (AWARENESS) AND THE UNCONSCIOUS (TRUTH) IS 90% AND IT IS WHERE ALL YOUR BEHAVIOUR AND ENERGY IS, WHICH MEANS IT CONTROLS YOUR WHOLE LIFE! WHEN IT SEES WHAT YOU REALLY VALUE, IT HELPS YOU ONLY FEEL SETTLED WHEN YOU PURSUE THIS AND IT MAKES YOU FEEL UNEASY AND DEPRESSES YOUR ENERGY WHEN YOU DON'T DO IT. IF YOU AREN'T A TRUTH SEEKER, 90% OF YOUR ACTIONS ARE OCCURRING WITHOUT YOU CONSCIOUSLY REALISING IT.

TRUST ME WHEN I SAY, YOUR PROGRAM IS NOT USUALLY YOUR OWN, UNLESS YOU ARE EXTREMELY CONSCIOUS OF WHO AND WHAT YOU ARE SURROUNDING YOURSELF WITH! SEARCH 'AUTO-SUGGESTION' THE NEXT TIME YOU ARE ON A SEARCH ENGINE! YOU HAVE ALL HAD A PREFERENCE ON WAYS OF LIVING DUE TO YOUR OWN CHOICES AND THIS WILL MEAN WHATEVER YOU HAVE BEEN SURROUNDING YOURSELF WITH HAS BEEN PROGRAMMING YOUR UNCONSCIOUS THROUGH REPETITION ESPECIALLY IF YOU HAVEN'T STATED YOU ARE AGAINST IT. REPETITION IS HOW WE LEARN EVERYTHING! FROM THE ALPHABET TO HOW TO DRIVE. IMAGINE FOR A SECOND YOU CAN LEARN INSECURITIES THE SAME WAY! WHAT DO YOU THINK WOULD HAPPEN? WHAT ABOUT BEHAVIOURS AND TRIGGERS?

AESTHETICS:

BOOM! COSMETIC SURGERY, IMPLANTS AND POOR MENTAL HEALTH ALL GO HAND IN HAND, EVEN THOUGH SOCIETY TEACHES THE PUBLIC THAT ITS NORMAL AND HEALTHY. THE CAUSE OF WANTING TO GET IT SHOULD

BE UNDERSTOOD, RATHER THAN MASKING THE EFFECTS OF THE CAUSE (INSECURITIES)   TO HELP IN THE SHORT TERM.

FOR INSTANCE, RESTORATIVE SURGERY FOR PEOPLE WHO HAVE BEEN INVOLVED IN AN ACCIDENT OR BEING BORN WITH SOMETHING UNIQUE THAT CAN CAUSE INSECURITIES OR UNWANTED ATTENTION, WOULD YOU SAY THIS WAS HEALTHY OR UNHEALTHY?

PEOPLE CHANGING THEIR PHYSICAL APPEARANCE IN THE NAME OF FASHION, TRENDS OR SOCIETY, FOR STATUS OR ATTENTION.. HEALTHY OR UNHEALTHY?

WHAT IF A PERSON WAS DOING IT TO FIT IN AS THEY DIDN'T KNOW THEIR UNIQUE SELF, HEALTHY OR UNHEALTHY? AND WHY?

WE KNOW THAT THERE IS NO SUCH THING AS NORMAL. THERE ARE MANY INDIVIDUALS WITH MANY DIFFERENT TASTES, IDEAS AND VISIONS OF BEAUTY AND PERFECTION. I AM NOT ACTUALLY SINGLING ANYONE OUT, I HAVE HAD MANY YEARS OBSERVING THE MOVEMENT OF HUMANITY AND THINGS HAVE SHIFTED SO MUCH IN THE LAST 20 YEARS, ESPECIALLY IN THE LAST 10.

OUR BODIES ARE BEAUTIFUL, THEY ARE FORMED DIFFERENTLY AND THAT IS JUST ONE WAY WE ARE UNIQUE BUT IT IS NOT WHO WE ARE. ITS GOT TO THE POINT WHERE VEGETABLES THAT ARE MISSHAPED ARE NOT ALLOWED IN THE BAG WITH THE STANDARD SHAPED VEGETABLES, WHAT DOES THAT SAY FOR PEOPLE? THERE ARE TALES OF DOPPELGANGERS, COULD THIS BE TRUE? DO YOU BELIEVE THERE IS SOMEONE SO SIMILAR TO YOU AMONGST 8 BILLION PEOPLE? DO YOU BELIEVE COMPARING YOURSELF TO SOMEONE WHO IS COMPLETELY DIFFERENT IS GOOD FOR YOUR MENTAL HEALTH?

THIS IS WHERE THE PLOT THICKENS... "I WANT HIS/HER HAIR"; "I WISH MY BOOBS WERE BIGGER LIKE HERS"; "I WISH I WAS SLIMMER SO I LOOKED LIKE..." SO MANY PEOPLE WITH 'MAINSTREAM THINKING' GIVE

THEMSELVES GOALS TO LOOK, ACT, DRESS OR SOUND LIKE SOMEONE ELSE!! THIS WILL NEVER MAKE ANYONE HAPPY LONG TERM... EVER!!! WHEN YOU GET THERE, YOU HAVE NOTHING TO STRIVE FOR, SO YOU WILL LITERALLY LOOK FOR FAULT AND REPEAT! WHAT WOULD BE THE BEST ALTERNATIVE?

GOING BACK TO WHEN I SAID "THERE IS NO SUCH THING AS NORMAL", WHAT I MEANT IS, EVERYONE IS UNIQUE AND THE ONES WHO I BELIEVE TO BE MOST INSECURE, FOLLOW THE CROWD AND TRENDS. IT'S LIKE A SAFETY IN NUMBERS AND THEY WILL BE NOTICED LESS, BUT NOT IN THEIR CONSCIOUS BRAIN. THE CONSCIOUS BRAIN WISHES TO BE NOTICED FOR WHAT THEY HAVE MADE AN EFFORT ON. THE UNCONSCIOUS BRAIN STILL SUFFERS THE INSECURITIES FROM BEFORE! IT SOUNDS MORE COMPLICATED BUT I'LL EXPLAIN MORE DURING THE MENTAL HEALTH CHAPTER AS YOU READ ON. HOWEVER, I WILL SAY THIS... IF YOU (FOR TALKING SAKE) HAVE SMALL BOOBS AND YOU ARE INSECURE ABOUT THEM, TRYING TO SOLVE THE INSECURITY BY CREATING THEM FROM IMPLANTS WON'T MAKE THE INSECURITIES GO AWAY. DISSOLVING THE INSECURITY BY ACCEPTING YOURSELF AND REALISING YOU ARE UNIQUE, AMAZING AND THERE IS NOBODY THE SAME AS YOU IN THE WORLD THE SAME AS YOU WILL ALLOW YOU TO GROW, RATHER THAN HIDE BEHIND FAKE BOOBS, LIPS, BUM, TEETH OR WHATEVER ELSE.

NATURAL IS A WORD WE USE A LOT ISN'T IT? WE WANT NATURAL FOOD, TOOTHPASTE, SKINCARE... BUT MANY, MANY PEOPLE WILL HAVE UNNATURAL PLASTIC PUT IN TO THEIR BODIES AS WELL AS BOTOX AND OTHER CHEMICALS (THAT ARE NOT NATURAL) AND THIS MAKES IT LOOK 'NORMAL' (WHEN THERE IS NO SUCH THING). SO WHERE IS THE LOGIC? HOW CAN YOU HAVE NATURAL LOOKING FAKE?

DO YOU BELIEVE YOU ARE AS HAPPY NOW AS YOU WERE WHEN YOU WERE AN INNOCENT CHILD WITH NO JUDGEMENT OF SELF OR OTHERS?

HAVE YOU FULLY ACCEPTED YOURSELF AND BELIEVE YOU ACCEPT YOURSELF FOR WHO YOU ARE AND WHAT YOU LOOK LIKE?

MAKING CHANGES TO YOURSELF WHEN YOU FULLY ACCEPT YOURSELF WILL ALWAYS BE SAFER THAN WHEN YOU DO NOT AND THAT IS FACT. WHAT I DON'T BELIEVE PEOPLE UNDERSTAND, IS THAT SO MANY INDUSTRIES GAIN SO MUCH WEALTH FROM INDIVIDUALS INSECURITIES AND IT PUTS THEM IN THE HABIT OF TRYING TO SOLVE AN INSECURITY BY CHANGING IT, RATHER THAN ACCEPT THEMSELVES AS BEING UNIQUE. AS LONG AS PEOPLE FEED THEM MONEY, THEY WILL KEEP TAKING. WHAT IS MORE IMPORTANT, HOW YOU LOOK? OR HOW YOU FEEL?

INFLUENCERS AND ONLINE FAME:

WHAT WOULD YOUR ANSWER BE IF I WAS TO ASK YOU: WHO IS MORE INSECURE, THE INFLUENCER OR THE INDIVIDUAL BEING INFLUENCED/MANIPULATED?

DO YOU BELIEVE BEING AN INFLUENCER IS A NOBLE TITLE? OR DO YOU BELIEVE IT IS SELFISH?

DO YOU BELIEVE AN INDIVIDUAL IS CORRECT TO THINK OTHERS SHOULD BE DOING AS THEY SAY AND DO SO THEY FEEL IMPORTANT OR TO GIVE THEM STATUS?

IS THIS BECAUSE THEY ARE SO INSECURE AND NEED YOUR VALIDATION?

IT'S A VERY MESSED UP WORLD WE LIVE IN AND SO MANY INDIVIDUALS ARE LOOKING FOR GUIDANCE AND WILL USUALLY TURN TO THE ONES WITH LARGE FOLLOWINGS OR SOCIETAL GOOD LOOKS 'INFLUENCERS' AND THIS LEADS THEM IN THE OPPOSITE DIRECTION FROM THEIR UNIQUENESS AND CAN CAUSE MUCH WORSE MENTAL HEALTH PROBLEMS, POOR HABITS, WHICH CAN LEAD TO DETERIORATION OF RELATIONSHIPS OF ALL KINDS AND THE FEELING OF BEING LOST OR UNFULFILLED. WHEN A PERSON WANTS TO BE SOMEONE ELSE, THEY ARE TELLING THEIR UNCONSCIOUS THEY DON'T WANT TO BE WHO THEY ARE. HOW DO YOU THINK THIS AFFECTS THEIR MENTAL HEALTH AND ABILITY TO BE HAPPY? DOES THIS SOUND LIKE ANYONE YOU KNOW? WHO? HOW CAN YOU HELP

THEM? WOULD THEY BENEFIT FROM READING THIS BOOK?

BEAUTY PRODUCTS AND CLOTHES ARE ONE THING... WHAT I FIND HARD TO GRASP IS THE LIFE COACHING AND MOTIVATIONAL COACHING INFLUENCERS! SAYING THINGS LIKE "I WILL SHOW YOU HOW TO CHANGE YOUR LIFE" OR WORSE... PUSHING AN AGENDA WHICH MAKES PEOPLE FEEL BAD SO THAT THEY FEEL THE NEED TO GO TO THEM! THE WORST PART IS, MANY INFLUENCERS OR COACHES ARE OFF BALANCE, EGOTISTICAL, INSECURE AND NEED TO BE HEARD! EVERY INDIVIDUAL IS UNIQUE AND THE ONLY WAY TO COACH OR INFLUENCE THEM IN A HEALTHY MANNER IS TO FIND OUT 'WHO' THE CLIENT IS AND TAILOR THEIR SERVICE TO THEM. ONE SIZE DOES NOT FIT ALL!!!

WHY ARE PEOPLE LOOKING FOR SO MUCH GUIDANCE?

SOCIETY HAS PROGRAMMED THE PEOPLE SO THAT FAMILIES ARE DIVIDED, PEOPLE ARE WEAK AND CARE WHAT OTHERS THINK, RATHER THAN HOW THEY FEEL ABOUT THEMSELVES! SAD STATE OF AFFAIRS REALLY ISN'T IT?

I MET A MAN, A HUMBLE MAN AND HIS NAME IS JOHN LENHART. JOHN HAS BEEN STUDYING THE MIND-BRAIN FOR 27 YEARS AND BECAUSE THERE IS NO ACTUAL MODEL FOR PSYCHOLOGY, JOHN HAS DEVELOPED A FULL MODEL FOR THE MIND-BRAIN. JOHN DOES NOT WANT TO BE FAMOUS OR TO INFLUENCE ANYONE AND MOST CERTAINLY DOES CARE ABOUT THE GENERAL MENTAL HEALTH OF THE WORLD'S POPULATION.

JOHN HAS SPENT THE LAST FOUR YEARS ASKING THE "BIGGEST" AND MOST "POPULAR" INFLUENCERS, THEIR DEFINITIONS FOR WORDS AND STATEMENTS THAT THEY USE... IN THAT TIME, HE HAS RECEIVED MAYBE 10-15 ANSWERS AND THIS WAS FROM ME AND OTHER CARING INDIVIDUALS... NOT THE INFLUENCERS!

JOHN HAS PROVED THAT EVEN SOME OF THE TOP INFLUENCERS ARE OPENING THEIR MOUTHS AND LETTING THEIR BELLIES RUMBLE FOR THE SAKE OF MONEY, FAME AND EGO, NOT TO MENTION LIVING THE LIVES

THAT THEY WANT THROUGH THEIR CLIENTS OR SUBJECTS (DEPENDS ON THEIR STYLE OF COACHING). I HAVE SEEN IT AND HAVE STARTED ASKING QUESTIONS, ONLY TO BE IGNORED, SO TRUTH MUST SCARE PEOPLE!

IMAGINE HAVING THE ONLY MODEL IN THE WORLD FOR THE MIND-BRAIN... I HEAR A 'REAL' NOBEL PRIZE NOMINATION! WE WILL DISCUSS MORE ABOUT JOHN AND FLOWCESS IN THE MENTAL HEALTH CHAPTER!

PEOPLE ARE NOW FAMOUS FOR HAVING LOTS OF LIKES AND FOLLOWERS, THEY CAN BUY LIKES AND FOLLOWERS WHICH MAKES THEM LOOK MORE POPULAR TOO! GONE ARE THE DAYS WHEN COMPANIES HAD A 'CELEBRITY' SELLING THEIR PRODUCTS FOR A FORTUNE. THEY CAN NOW GIVE THEIR PRODUCTS TO FAME HUNGRY PEOPLE FOR A FRACTION OF THE PRICE AND DO IT MANY TIMES OVER. ARE THESE PEOPLE GLORIFIED SALES PEOPLE, WHILE BELIEVING THAT THEY ARE A CUT ABOVE THE REST? DO THEY KNOW WHAT IT IS TO BE HUMBLE? DO YOU?

IF YOU ARE AN INFLUENCER AND YOU LOSE ALL YOUR FOLLOWERS, WOULD YOU STILL BE HAPPY AND FULFILLED? COULD YOU STILL INFLUENCE AS MANY PEOPLE? WHAT VALUE HAVE YOU GIVEN?

I'D LOVE TO GIVE EVERY HUMAN THE GIFT OF BEING ABLE TO RECOGNISE THEIR UNIQUENESS, HOW THEY CAN BE STRONG WITHIN THEMSELVES TO LIVE A FULFILLED LIFE AND GAIN ENERGY DAILY.

CHANGING YOUR THOUGHTS WILL CHANGE YOUR HABITS, THIS WILL CHANGE YOUR BELIEFS AND INEVITABLY CHANGE YOUR LIFE! EVERY ONE OF YOU ARE MORE THAN CAPABLE OF BEING HAPPY WITH NOTHING, IT MEANS ALL POSSESSIONS AND RELATIONSHIPS WILL BE A BONUS! INFLUENCE YOURSELF, IT'S THE WAY FORWARD TO HAPPINESS AND YOU CAN START TODAY, FROM NOW!!! WHAT'S STOPPING YOU?

CHAPTER 8: SOCIAL MEDIA

WE TOUCHED A LITTLE ON SOCIAL MEDIA IN THE LAST CHAPTER, TAKING THINGS A LITTLE DEEPER SO THAT WE CAN FEEL MORE.

DO YOU KNOW WHO YOU REALLY ARE? WHO DO YOU THINK YOU ARE?

DO YOU REMEMBER THE DAYS WHEN WE USED A CAMERA WITH A SPOOL TO TAKE A PICTURE OF OUR MEAL, TAKE IT TO THE LOCAL PHOTOGRAPHY SHOP, WAIT 2-7 DAYS TO GET IT DEVELOPED AND TAKE IT ROUND ALL OUR FRIENDS FAMILY AND THEY WERE REALLY INTERESTED?

DO YOU REMEMBER WHEN HOLIDAY SNAPS WERE ACTUAL SCENERY AND FULL LENGTH PICTURES OF PEOPLE?

WHAT ABOUT TAKING ONE PICTURE AND GETTING A SURPRISE AS TO HOW YOU LOOKED RATHER THAN TAKING 20 TO GET THAT PERFECT PICTURE? PEOPLE USED TO SEE THE PICTURES, EVEN IF WE DIDN'T LOOK OUR BEST AND WE PASSED COMMENT BUT DIDN'T CARE AS MUCH AS WE DO. WERE WE CLOSER TO VALUING OURSELVES FOR WHO WERE REALLY WERE? SINCE THE SELFIE CAMERA AND SELF OBSESSION STARTED IN THE LAST COUPLE OF DECADES, IT HAS CONVINCED US WE ARE OUR APPEARANCE AND MENTAL HEALTH CONTINUES TO WORSEN.

WHAT ABOUT WALKING 3 MILES TO YOUR FRIEND'S HOUSE, TO FIND THEY WEREN'T IN AND NOT BEING BOTHERED, YET NOW WHAT IS OUR RESPONSE IF THEY DON'T ANSWER THE PHONE OR GET BACK QUICKLY? THERE IS DRAMA MORE NOW BECAUSE OF EXPECTATION OF OTHERS DUE TO ANTISOCIAL MEDIA AND YET WE HAVE A CHOICE TO CHANGE OUR WAYS.

CONCERTS USED TO BE GREAT! LIVING IN THE MOMENT, WATCHING YOUR FAVOURITE BAND OR SINGER DO THEIR THING AND HANG ON TO THE MEMORIES FOREVER AS YOU WERE CONSCIOUSLY PRESENT! HOW MANY

PEOPLE HAVE YOU SEEN WATCHING THE CONCERT THROUGH THEIR PHONE SCREEN BECAUSE THEY CANT WAIT TO GET ATTENTION FROM POSTING ABOUT IT? DO YOU BELIEVE PEOPLE ACTUALLY SIT AND WATCH BACK EVERY RECORDING? IT ACTUALLY DEFEATS THE PURPOSE OF SPENDING A FORTUNE ON TICKETS! WANTING TO SHOW EVERYONE AT HOME VIA THEIR STORIES ON INTERNET PLATFORMS, NOT REALISING THEIR CONSCIOUSNESS IS WITH THE PEOPLE AT HOME AND NOT IN THE MOMENT. IT'S SO SAD TO WATCH! THINK ABOUT IT, MOST PEOPLE SKIP PAST THE STORIES ANYWAY. WHY? BECAUSE IT'S NOT THE SAME AS BEING THERE!! HAVE YOU DONE THIS AT A SHOW? IF SO, WHY? IS HAVING A MEMORY ON THE PHONE AS SPECIAL AS IN YOUR HEAD AND HEART?

SOCIAL MEDIA HAS A LOT TO ANSWER FOR IN THE SOCIETY WE LIVE IN. MANY, MANY PEOPLE BELIEVE IT'S THE BEST THING OR IT'S LIFE! PEOPLE ALLOW IT TO RUN THEIR LIVES AND DOCUMENT THEIR EVERY MOVE. AS MUCH AS IT HAS SOME AMAZING USES, THERE ARE A LOT OF QUESTIONABLE STIPULATIONS ALSO LIKE: TRACKING PEOPLES MOVEMENTS, DATA CAPTURE, FRAUD, CHILD ABUSE NETWORKS SHARING CONTENT, TO NAME BUT A FEW.

MISLEADING INFORMATION HAS BEEN ONE OF THE BIGGEST DIVIDES IN HUMANITY AND THE DESTRUCTION IT HAS CAUSED I BELIEVE TO BE IRREPARABLE IF NOT DEALT WITH ASAP. RACE, RELIGION, SEXISM, POLITICS... THE LIST CAN GO ON, I'M SURE YOU GET THE DRIFT!

ON THE PLUS SIDE, THERE ARE MANY PEOPLE 'WAKING UP' TO THE WAYS OF THE WORLD, THE CORRUPTION, THE CONTROL AND THE MANIPULATION. I TALKED ABOUT THIS IN THE CONSPIRACY CHAPTER.

WHAT'S YOUR DEFINITION OF SOCIAL MEDIA? COULD YOU LIVE WITHOUT IT?

SOCIAL USUALLY MEANS INTERACTION AND TOGETHERNESS OF SORTS... IS THIS THE CORRECT TERMINOLOGY FOR PEOPLE TO BE SITTING AT HOME, ON THEIR OWN CHATTING ON A DEVICE? WHAT IS THAT CALLED?

BETTY NO MATES? LONELY? DISTRACTED? WHAT IS YOUR TAKE ON IT?

HUMAN TOUCH AND INTERACTION SEEMS TO BE DWINDLING AND MOST INTERACTIONS ARE 'ONLINE' NOW. THIS IS WHY I CALL IT ANTI-SOCIAL MEDIA. LESS EFFORT IS PUT IN BECAUSE PEOPLE CAN TALK TO 10 GROUPS OF FRIENDS WITHOUT HAVING TO GET THEIR LAZY ASS OUT OF BED! YOU MIGHT THINK THIS IS A POSITIVE THING, I BELIEVE IT MAKES PEOPLE LAZY. FOR EXAMPLE, HAPPY BIRTHDAY VIA AN ONLINE MESSAGE WITH A MEME, DOES NOT SAY EFFORT LIKE A VISIT AND SPENDING TIME WITH SOMEONE. HUGGING SOMEONE IS BETTER THAN A MESSAGE OR A POSITIVITY MEME.

WHY WOULD SOMEONE WANT TO POST THEIR LIVES ONLINE?

SOME SAY TO SHOW FAMILY BECAUSE THEY DON'T HAVE TIME TO SEE THEM, OR THEY MIGHT LIVE IN A DIFFERENT COUNTRY. THAT IS VALID, BUT WHY NOT SEND THEM IT IN A PERSONAL MESSAGE? IS IT FOR LIKES, VALIDATION, ATTENTION FROM OTHERS? MAYBE EVEN TO SHOW OFF? SO MANY PERSONAL RELATIONSHIPS HAVE BROKEN DOWN BECAUSE IT IS TAKEN FOR GRANTED THAT PEOPLE POST ONLINE AND EXPECT OTHERS TO SEE IT. I HAVE SEEN PEOPLE DOING ALL SORTS OF ACTIVITIES AND HAVING EXPERIENCES. WHEN I SEND THEM A MESSAGE AND ASK THEM WHAT THEY HAVE BEEN UP TO... THEY SAY, "NOT MUCH, YOU?" I MEAN COME ON... DOES IT NOT FEEL LIKE PEOPLE ARE ON AUTOPILOT GOING THROUGH LIFE? PUTTING THINGS OUT IN PUBLIC MAKES INTERACTIONS LAZY FOR MANY PEOPLE. ONLINE FRIENDSHIPS ARE COMPLETELY DIFFERENT THAN IN-PERSON FRIENDSHIPS FOR ME. WE CAN HAVE PROPER FRIENDSHIPS ONLINE BY CHATTING, ASKING THE RIGHT QUESTIONS AND GETTING TO KNOW SOMEONE. ONLINE PLATFORMS ARE VERY OPINIONATED AND YOU WILL FIND PEOPLE WILL COME TOGETHER BECAUSE OF A GROUP OR OPINION ON A SUBJECT, THIS CAN ALSO BE FOR VALIDATION AND SAFETY IN NUMBERS. DOES THIS SOUND LIKE A TRUTH SEEKER?

I WAS TAUGHT THAT BEING MY UNIQUE SELF WOULD BE MORE

BENEFICIAL. YOU KNOW WHAT? IT WORKED AND MY HAPPINESS GREW, YOURS CAN TOO WHEN YOU MAKE THE CHOICE.

ONLINE BUSINESSES ARE GREAT, YOU CAN REACH LOTS OF PEOPLE. IMAGINE THE PLUG WAS PULLED ON THE INTERNET OR THE POWER FOR YOUR STREET, TOWN OR CITY... IS IT SOMETHING YOU CAN ADAPT QUICKLY VIA PHONE OR WOULD YOU BE STUCK? LOTS GOING ON IN THE WORLD AND SOME VOLATILE PEOPLE ABOUT, IN POWER AND VIGILANTE LIKES. THERE ARE POSSIBILITIES AT ANY POINT, THAT POWER AND/OR INTERNET CAN BE SHUT DOWN FOR PERIODS OF TIME. MAYBE GOOD IDEA HAVING A BACKUP OR A TANGIBLE CONTACT SYSTEM DON'T YOU THINK?

PEOPLE ARE LOSING THEIR RIGHTS LEFT, RIGHT AND CENTRE. FREEDOM OF SPEECH IS BEING TAKEN AWAY BY DISTRACTING THE PEOPLE WITH ONLINE NONSENSE AND THEY SOAK IT IN LIKE SPONGES! THE SAYING: "IF YOU READ IT ONLINE, IT MUST BE TRUE" COMES TO MIND!! WE HAVE MANY EXPERTS THAT HAVE LEARNED MISINFORMATION AND PREACH IT TO BECOME FAMOUS OR FOR 'CLICK BAIT' CLICK-BAIT IS WHEN DISINFORMATION IS PUT OUT TO DISTRACT, WE WILL TALK MORE OF THIS IN THE NEXT CHAPTER.

THE DESENSITISATION OF CHILDREN HAS GOT OUT OF HAND IN MY BELIEF. ADULT INFORMATION, SO EASILY ACCESSIBLE, WARPING THEIR YOUNG MINDS AND CAUSING POOR THOUGHT PROCESSES FROM VERY A YOUNG AGE MEANS THEY DON'T HAVE MUCH OF A CHANCE TO LIVE THEIR UNIQUE SELF, NOR ARE THEY ENCOURAGED TO IN MOST CASES. CHILDREN ARE ABLE TO ACCESS ALL TYPES OF SEXUAL CONTENT, VERY EASILY AND THERE IS NOT MUCH BEING DONE BY THE CHAIN OF COMMAND AND THIS IS WORRYING. MY FRIENDS AND I HAD TO PLAN A HUGE OPERATION WHEN I WAS YOUNGER TO LOOK AT A NAUGHTY MAGAZINE WITHOUT GETTING CAUGHT BECAUSE 25-30 YEARS AGO IT WAS MUCH HARDER FOR KIDS TO FIND THIS TYPE OF CONTENT, I KNOW, BECAUSE I LIVED THROUGH IT AND WAS AN 80'S BABY AND HAD A CHILDHOOD. THERE WAS LITTLE ADULT CONTENT PUSHED ONTO US VIA TELEVISION, CHILDREN WEREN'T

USUALLY DIAGNOSED WITH ANXIETY OR PANIC ATTACKS EITHER!

DO YOU BELIEVE THERE IS ENOUGH BEING DONE TO PROTECT CHILDREN'S MINDS WHEN IT COMES TO ONLINE CONTENT AND PROTECTING THEIR WELLBEING AS A WHOLE? CAN YOU MAKE IT BETTER FOR YOUR FAMILY OR FRIEND'S KIDS? WHAT CAN YOU DO? WILL YOU SEE IT THROUGH AFTER WRITING IT IN THIS BOOK?

I AM AWARE THAT THERE ARE CHILDREN BEING EXPLOITED IN THE NAME OF SOCIETY. TWERKING VIDEOS, SCANTILY CLAD AND OTHER PROVOCATIVE CONTENT... I WONDER IF THE PARENTS HAVE ASKED THEMSELVES IF THIS IS HEALTHY FOR THEIR KIDS? THE PRE-PROGRAMMING FOR A HYPER SEXUALISED NEXT GENERATION, HAS ALREADY STARTED, HORRIFIC WHAT IS GOING TO BE COMING SOON!

SHOULD A CHILD BE A CHILD OR BE MADE MORE MATURE EARLY? IS IT GOOD THAT THEY BECOME MENTALLY ILL EARLIER IN LIFE, WITH ADULT PROBLEMS IN A CHILD'S BRAIN? 95% OF ADULTS STRUGGLE WITH MENTAL HEALTH AS IT IS... MAYBE THEY ARE PUSHING FOR THE FULL 100% IN THE FUTURE? CHILDREN ARE LEARNING FROM THE OLDER PEOPLE AND ARE BEING DESTROYED THROUGH KNOWING TOO MUCH AND SEEKING ATTENTION ONLINE, I'LL TALK MORE ON THIS IN THE NEXT CHAPTER.

BE THE CHANGE YOU WISH TO SEE, UNDERSTAND WHAT IT IS AND HOW CHILDREN'S MINDS SHOULD BE PROTECTED! WOULD YOU BE WILLING TO LOOK AT THIS TO PROTECT YOUR OWN?

DISINFORMATION IS MASSIVE NOW AND WE WILL GO DEEPER IN THE NEXT CHAPTER!

WHO DO YOU BELIEVE? YOUR FRIENDS? FAMILY? GOOGLE? FACEBOOK? BROADCAST NEWS?   NEWSPAPERS/MAGAZINES?

ALL NEWS AND ALL INFORMATION IS NOT CORRECT OR REAL! THE POINT IN THIS BOOK IS TO GET ALL OF YOU READING, TO BEGIN THINKING FOR YOURSELF MORE, QUESTIONING EVERYTHING! BEING TRUTH SEEKERS!

THE INTERNET IS A CRAZY PLACE THAT PUTS CLICK-BAIT OUT THERE TO GAIN OR FILTER USER TRAFFIC TOWARDS ADVERTS, A PRODUCT OR PERSON. DO YOU CLICK ON THE FIRST PIECE OF POINTLESS NONSENSE YOU SEE AND FALL INTO THE TRAP?

SELF AWARENESS AND INTUITION ARE BECOMING SUPERPOWERS TO SUPERHEROES, RATHER THAN A NATURAL, HUMAN ABILITY THESE DAYS! HOW MANY TIMES HAS SOMEONE SAID SOMETHING OR YOU HAVE READ/HEARD SOMETHING AND THOUGHT "WHAT A LOT OF SH*#"? COULD YOU DO THIS ON PURPOSE MORE OFTEN? IF YOUR ANSWER IS YES... DO IT! IF YOUR ANSWER IS NO, PRACTICE MAKES BETTER! OUR BRAINS, IN MY BELIEF ARE BEING PROGRAMMED SO THAT WE CANNOT CRITICALLY THINK, THIS CAUSES LOTS OF TENSION FROM WITHIN (EXACTLY WHY PEOPLE WILL DISLIKE ME, AFTER READING THIS BOOK!) THINKING ISN'T NECESSARILY THE BEST WAY TO WORK. WE CAN THINK, OVER-THINK, RETHINK AND NOT THINK ENOUGH... NOT ONE OF THOSE OPTIONS WAS FEEL!

COULD YOU TRUST YOUR INTUITION MORE THAN YOUR BRAIN? CAN YOU IMAGINE, YOU CAN MAKE AT LEAST 50% BETTER CHOICES IN YOUR LIFE? HOW MANY TIMES HAVE YOU DONE SOMETHING, THAT YOU KNOW YOU SHOULDN'T HAVE AND IT DIDN'T WORK OUT? YOU MIGHT HAVE TALKED YOURSELF OUT OF SOMETHING THAT TURNED OUT AMAZING AND KICKED YOURSELF FOR IT?

WE WATCH MANY PEOPLE BEING PART OF THE HERD AND BEING TOO SCARED TO MAKE DECISIONS OR CHOOSE BELIEFS THAT GO AGAINST THE SOCIETY NARRATIVE. HAVE YOU GOT WHAT IT TAKES TO CONTRASTIVELY THINK AND SEE TRUTH? TO PROVE YOURSELF WRONG? TO LOOK AT BOTH SIDES OF THE COIN BEFORE JUDGEMENT?   GOING AGAINST THE NORM DOES NOT FEEL RIGHT INITIALLY, BUT ONCE YOU FIND YOUR PATH, ITS LIBERATING IN WAYS THAT CANNOT BE DESCRIBED. HOW DOES THAT SOUND?

REMEMBER, THERE ARE ONLY FOUR RESPONSES YOU CAN HAVE TO

INFORMATION.

CONSPIRACY REJECTOR: ONE TRACK MIND PROGRAMMED BY THE SYSTEM TO REJECT WITHOUT QUESTION.

CONSPIRACY THEORIST: EVERYONE IS OUT TO GET US. EVERYTHING IS A CONSPIRACY.

CONSPIRACY ANALYST: IS THERE ANY TRUTH IN THIS? CAN I PROVE THEM WRONG?

TRUTH SEEKER: CAN I PROVE MYSELF WRONG, BEFORE TRYING TO PROVE OTHERS WRONG? CAN I SEE THE OTHER THREE PERSPECTIVES?

WHICH ONE ARE YOU?

CHAPTER 9: MEDIA MANIPULATION

IS IT A SECRET THAT 6 COMPANIES OWN NEARLY ALL MEDIA OUTLETS IN THE WORLD? A JOINT NET-WORTH OF OVER 430 BILLION DOLLARS! THIS INFORMATION CAN BE FOUND ON ANY NON-CENSORED SEARCH ENGINE AND WILL POSSIBLY SURPRISE MANY OF YOU!

IS NEWS AND MEDIA, MOSTLY COMING FROM 6 CORPORATIONS REALLY NEWS? IS IT POSSIBLE THIS COULD BE AN AGENDA, FULL OF PROPAGANDA? LOOK AT BETWEEN 2020 UNTIL NOW... THE AMOUNT OF THINGS GOING ON IN THE WORLD IS LIKE WATCHING A DRAMA EVERY NIGHT FOR THOSE WHO WATCH THE NEWS AND YOUR UNCONSCIOUS HAS TAKEN EVERYTHING IN INCLUDING YOUR RESPONSE, CREATING THE INTERNAL TENSION... THIS IS HOW THEY MANAGE THE FEAR BASED CONTROL!

WE HAVE SEEN A MASSIVE SHIFT OVER THE LAST COUPLE OF DECADES, IT SHOWS THAT THE MAIN NEWS STATIONS LITERALLY HAVE THE SAME STORIES TO TELL ALL OVER THE WORLD, THEY JUST PUT LOCAL NEWS IN BETWEEN, TO MAKE SURE PEOPLE FEEL IT'S MORE PERSONALISED AND DIRECTED TO THEIR CITY OR TOWN, SO CLEVER AND WELL ORCHESTRATED.

HAVE YOU EVER WATCHED THE NEWS AND WHEN IT'S FINISHED THOUGHT, "WOW! I FEEL REFRESHED AND BETTER FOR WATCHING"? I HAVEN'T EITHER. THE HYPNOTIC WAYS OF THE TELEVISION FREQUENCIES AND SUBLIMINAL PROGRAMMING, OR OTHER VIEWING DEVICES HAVE PEOPLE GLUED, MANY PEOPLE LOVE A BIT OF DRAMA AND IT CAN BECOME A VERY BAD HABIT. DO YOU LIKE DRAMA? ARE YOU A FIXER? MOST THINGS ON THE NEWS CANNOT BE FIXED OR REPAIRED BY THOSE WATCHING IT, JUST BY MAKING THEM AWARE, THIS MEANS THAT THE VIEWERS ARE ONLY LEFT WITH THE TENSION AFTER WATCHING THE NEWS, WITH NO SOLUTION.

HOW DOES THE BRAIN LEARN? THROUGH REPETITION!!

IF YOU ARE REPEATEDLY FED INFORMATION (OF ANY SORT) FOR LONG ENOUGH, YOU MIGHT NOT BELIEVE IT, ALTHOUGH IT BECOMES NORMALISED IN THE BRAIN... COMFORTABLE, IF YOU WILL. THERE ARE CERTAIN AGENDAS AT PLAY AT THE MOMENT THAT HAVE BEEN PLANNED SINCE BEFORE THE 2020S AND THIS IS EASILY FOUND BY TYPING SOCIETY AGENDAS INTO A DECENT, UNCENSORED SEARCH ENGINE AND DIGGING A LITTLE! ONE COULD SAY THAT THE PROPAGANDA COULD BE TO INSTILL FEAR SO THAT THERE IS VERY LITTLE PUSH NEEDED TO CONTROL THE MASSES.

HOW OFTEN DOES THE NEWS REPORT ABOUT NEW WAYS TO KEEP PEOPLE HEALTHY?

HOW OFTEN DOES IT SHOW HAPPY PEOPLE, OR HOW TO LIVE HAPPY AND HEALTHY?

IF THE NEWS COULD MAKE YOU HAPPIER, WOULD THE ANSWER INVOLVE WATCHING MORE TELEVISION? WHY WOULD THE NEWS DO ANYTHING THAT CAUSED YOU TO WATCH THE NEWS LESS?

HAVE YOU EVER WATCHED THE LOCAL NEWS WITH 27 MINUTES OF SADNESS, FEAR, PROPAGANDA AND THEN A 2 MINUTE CLIP OF A PANDA OR A CHARITY TO TAKE YOUR MIND FROM WHAT YOU HAVE JUST BEEN PROGRAMMED WITH? ITS LIKE WE MOVE ON WITH THE LAST THING WE SEE!

FEAR IS THE EASIEST AND BEST WAY TO CONTROL A LIVING BEING WITH THE CAPABILITIES OF UNDERSTANDING WHAT IT IS TO BE SCARED. REPETITIVE FEAR WILL STOP THE HUMAN BRAIN FROM FUNCTIONING HEALTHILY AND THE NEURAL PATHWAYS WILL HABITUATE THERE! WHAT WOULD FREEDOM OF THOUGHT AND FREEDOM OF LIFE LOOK LIKE? DO YOU THINK WE WILL GET THERE WITHOUT MAKING CHANGES? I DON'T THINK SO!

WHAT ARE YOU AFRAID OF? HOW MUCH OF THAT FEAR HAS COME FROM EXPERIENCE AND HOW MUCH WAS LEARNED THROUGH MEDIA PROGRAMMING? HORROR FILMS, NEWS, ONLINE... ALL HAVE THEIR PART TO PLAY.

IF YOU COULD IMAGINE A WORLD OF MINIMAL DRAMA AND MINIMAL FEAR, HOW WOULD IT LOOK? WHAT'S STOPPING YOU FROM GETTING THERE? I WILL TAKE A STAB IN THE DARK AND SUGGEST IT'S YOU THAT'S STOPPING YOURSELF! NOT BECAUSE YOU AREN'T CAPABLE... BECAUSE SUBLIMINALLY, FROM A VERY YOUNG AGE, YOU HAVE BEEN TOLD NO AND THAT YOU CAN'T! ANYONE THAT GOES AGAINST THE NARRATIVE, IS SHOT DOWN WITH A CONSPIRACY LABEL, POOR MENTAL HEALTH LABEL... THEN WE FEEL WEAK AS A COLLECTIVE.

WHAT IF THE NUMBERS STOPPED WATCHING THE NEWS AND OTHER MEDIA, THEN LEARNED TO THINK FOR THEMSELVES?

I WATCH INTELLIGENT PEOPLE ALLOW THEMSELVES TO HABITUATE TO

THE THOUGHTS, RULES AND DECISIONS OF OTHERS. EVERYTHING FROM THE WORLD WARS, TO PANDEMICS, TERRORISM, MENTAL HEALTH... ALL ORCHESTRATED BY HUGE CORPORATIONS AND LIVING A REAL-LIFE GAME OF 'THE SIMS'. WHY AREN'T OUR SPIRITS ALLOWED TO BE FREE AND HAPPY?

WE ARE LED TO BELIEVE THAT WHAT WE SEE ON THE NEWS IS GOSPEL. THIS COMES THROUGH THE GENERATIONS OF OUR FAMILY AND OUR GUARDIANS: WE GO AGAINST WHAT THEY TEACH US, THEY FALL OUT, OR CHALLENGE US TOO! IT'S VERY DIFFICULT TO BREAK THE CYCLE, ALBEIT A CHOICE TO EVEN TRY. ARE YOU WILLING TO TRY?

THE PEOPLE WHO ARE THE TERM 'AWAKE' AND DON'T FOLLOW THE NEWS, TEND TO RESEARCH INTO MORE INDEPENDENT NEWS WHICH IS A MUCH HEALTHIER WAY TO USE THE BRAIN. THIS ALSO HAS ITS IMPLICATIONS, AS THERE ARE MANY RED HERRINGS (DISTRACTIONS) PUT OUT INTENTIONALLY, TO KEEP THESE PEOPLE AWAY FROM THE TRUTH, SO WE HAVE SLEEPING/PROGRAMMED, AWAKE AND TRUTH-SEEKING PEOPLE. THIS IS LIKE THE LEFT AND RIGHT-WING POLITICS. BOTH WINGS, MORE THAN LIKELY BELONG TO THE SAME BIRD!

WHO ARE YOU MOST LIKELY TO BELIEVE? WHO SHOULD YOU BELIEVE? IMAGINE THE INTERNET WAS SO CENSORED IT WAS MOSTLY LIES ON BOTH SIDES... IMAGINE FOR A SECOND, THAT THE INTERNET WAS MADE TO PROGRAM YOU AS THE MAIN SOURCE OF INFORMATION! WHERE IS THAT FEELING OF TRUTH GOING TO COME FROM?

WE ALL HAVE AN EARLY WARNING SYSTEM IN OUR BODIES, 5 YEARS AGO I WOULD HAVE LAUGHED AT SOMEONE TELLING ME THIS! NOW I'M THE ONE BEING LAUGHED AT, BY FRIENDS, FAMILY FOR BEING 'THE WOO WOO SPOOKY GUY'. IT SHOWS ME, EXACTLY WHERE I WAS AND HOW FAR I'VE COME INTERNALLY. I LEARNED THAT EVERYTHING IS ENERGY, EVERYTHING HAS A FREQUENCY IN OUR BODY WHEN WE THINK ABOUT IT. IF IT FEELS GOOD ENERGY, ITS USUALLY GOOD, IF IT DOESN'T... YOU GOT IT! IT USUALLY ISN'T!

WHEN WE UNDERSTAND ENERGY, WE UNDERSTAND THE WORLD AND NIKOLA TESLA SAID SOMETHING VERY SIMILAR! IF WE HEAR SOMETHING AND OUR INTUITIVE FEELING IS NOT MATCHING WHAT OUR BRAIN IS THINKING, WHAT SHOULD WE BE USING? THERE IS EVIDENCE TO SHOW THAT THE FIGHT OR FLIGHT RESPONSE COMES FROM OUR BRAIN. IMAGINE IT CAME BECAUSE THE BRAIN AND THE INTUITION FEELING WEREN'T SYNCHRONISED? THAT WOULD BE A SCIENCE AND SPIRITUAL RESPONSE THAT WOULD HAVE TO WORK IT OUT TOGETHER... ARE YOU SCIENCE OR SPIRITUAL, OR ARE YOU BOTH?

ANYWAY... I DIGRESS! WE CAN UNDERSTAND THE ENERGY IN THE THINGS WE ARE TOLD/TAUGHT AND NOT BELIEVE IT BECAUSE OUR FAMILY, FRIEND OR THE MAN/WOMAN ON THE TELEVISION SAID SO. SOMETIMES JUST LETTING IT SETTLE FOR A PERIOD OF TIME, BEFORE OVER-THINKING OR WRITING IT OFF. I WILL BE TALKING MORE ABOUT ENERGY IN THE MEDICINE CHAPTER, IT'S VERY IMPORTANT TO KNOW!

IF YOU RESEARCH ONLINE WHAT A CRISIS ACTOR IS, YOU'D BE SO SHOCKED. THE ACTING ROLES ARE ADVERTISED AS TV WORK, THEN EVERYONE IS GIVEN A NON-DISCLOSURE DOCUMENT TO SIGN, MEANING THAT THEY WILL BE PUNISHED BY THE SYSTEM IF THEY DISCLOSE ANY INFORMATION. BEFORE YOU DO RESEARCH, WHAT DO YOU THINK I MEAN BY CRISIS ACTOR? THERE ARE VIDEOS, PICTURES AND ARTICLES WAITING FOR YOU TO READ, WATCH AND LOOK AT, RIGHT AT YOUR FINGERTIPS! PUT A CUSHION ON THE FLOOR FOR YOUR JAW TO HIT, WHEN IT DROPS SO FAST! VIDEOS ALL OVER MEDIA SITES AND WILL LITERALLY SHOW YOU WHAT THE MEDIA DOES, WITHOUT ME HAVING TO EXPLAIN IN MY WORDS.

HOW WOULD YOU FEEL IF YOU BELIEVED LOTS OF HISTORY, BUT WHAT YOU ARE SHOWN THAT IT IS JUST MADE-UP FILMING TO MAKE YOU BELIEVE A NARRATIVE? DO YOU THINK THIS COULD BE POSSIBLE? INFORMATION FED TO THE MASSES THROUGH 6 MAJOR COMPANIES THAT OWN MOST OF THE MEDIA OUTLETS?

THERE HAVE BEEN NEWS REPORTERS STANDING IN FLOODS UP TO THEIR

WAIST AND PLACES BEING TOLD THAT THE WATER IS SO DEVASTATING, AFTER THE 'SCENE' IS FILMED, THEN YOU FIND OUT THAT THEY ARE ACTUALLY KNEELING DOWN AND ITS KNEE-DEEP WATER. THESE TYPES OF REPORTERS ARE CRISIS ACTORS! THIS IS THE DIFFERENCE BETWEEN TRUTH AND PROPAGANDA AND HOW PEOPLE ARE GIVEN THE SHOCK AND FEAR TO BE MUCH MORE EASILY CONTROLLED. IF THE QUESTIONS ARE NEVER ASKED, THE TRUTH WILL NEVER BECOME APPARENT. HOW CAN YOU PROVE WHAT YOU ARE WATCHING IS TRUTH? WHERE CAN YOU QUESTION IT? WHY, WHEN PEOPLE QUESTION IT, THEY ARE SHOT DOWN? REMEMBER THE TERM 'COGNITIVE DISSONANCE'

WHAT IS THE BEST APPROACH, BELIEVE EVERYTHING? IGNORE EVERYTHING? OR ASK QUESTIONS TO UNDERSTAND YOUR FEELINGS?

REMEMBER A SHORT WHILE AGO I MENTIONED ENERGY AND FEELINGS? PLEASE THINK ABOUT ALL MEDIA, NEWS, MOVIES, MUSIC, MAGAZINES ETC... JUST FOR A SECOND. WHEN YOU READ SOMETHING EXCITING, YOU BECOME EXCITED, WHEN YOU WATCH SOMETHING SCARY, YOU BECOME SCARED, WHAT IF YOU WATCH SOMETHING YOU 'THINK' IS REAL AND IT PUTS FEAR IN TO YOU? THIS CAUSES AN UNCONSCIOUS TRIGGER THAT CAN LAST A LIFETIME! THIS MEANS THAT YOU WILL NEED TO REHEARSE IT AWAY AND DEAL WITH IT, BECAUSE IT'S BEEN PROGRAMMED SUBLIMINALLY! HOW YOU DO THIS IS: CLOSE YOUR EYES, TAKE A DEEP BREATH AND RELAX. YOU THEN RUN THE SCENARIO IN YOUR HEAD AND MAKE UP YOUR OWN HAPPY OUTCOME, REPEAT MORE THAN 3 TIMES FOR MAXIMUM EFFECT. THIS ALSO WORKS FOR TRAUMATIC EXPERIENCES WE GO THROUGH... THAT IS HOW EASY IT IS TO PROGRAM THE BRAIN!

EVEN THOUGH SOCIAL MEDIA LOOKS LIKE YOU GET TO BE FREE, LIKE WHAT YOU WANT AND VIEW WHAT YOU WANT, YOU ARE ACTUALLY CONTROLLED WITHIN AN INCH OF YOUR LIFE! DO YOU BELIEVE THAT YOU ARE ABLE TO SEE ANY POST THAT IS ON SOCIAL MEDIA? DO YOU BELIEVE THAT YOUR POSTS ARE ABLE TO BE SEEN BY EVERYONE? WHO HAS A RIGHT TO CENSOR YOU? WHO HAS THE RIGHT TO LIMIT YOUR ACCESS TO INFORMATION? WHEN YOU SIGN UP TO THESE PLATFORMS, YOU AGREE TO THEIR TERMS OF SERVICE, WHICH MEANS YOU ARE NOT IN

CONTROL OF WHAT YOU POST, SAY AND DO. IT'S NOT THE FAULT OF THE PLATFORM, IT'S YOUR FAULT TO AGREE WITH THEIR RULES (YOU CONSENTED) SHADOW BANS, DELETED PROFILES…. IT WASN'T THEM, IT WAS YOU BREAKING THEIR RULES. THE WAY AROUND THIS IS TO CREATE YOUR OWN APP, WEBSITE OR BLOG AND HAVE PEOPLE COME TO YOU.

DO YOU EVER FEEL YOUR DEVICE IS WATCHING OR LISTENING TO YOU?

THE TRUTH IS, IT IS! EVERY SWIPE, EVERY WORD YOU ENTER, EVERY ONLINE STORE YOU VISIT IS RECORDED "IN A CLOUD". THE CLOUD IS MASS STORAGE FOUND IN COUNTRIES ALL OVER THE WORLD AND NOTHING IS EVER DELETED! I HAVE A FRIEND WHO IS ALSO FROM SCOTLAND AND HE IS AN ELECTRICIAN. HE WORKS IN THESE STORAGE BASES. THE ONE HE'S WORKING ON AT PRESENT COST ALMOST $700,000,000 TO BUILD AND THEY WILL MAKE THAT BACK THE FIRST MONTH FROM SELLING THE DATA TO COMPANIES ALL OVER THE WORLD. YOU ARE THE PRODUCT, WHETHER YOU BELIEVE IT OR NOT. DO YOU FEEL GOOD KNOWING THAT YOU ARE THE PRODUCT? THAT YOU AS A CONSUMER ACTUALLY ALLOW THE POWERS THAT BE TO CONTROL AND CHANGE SOCIETY AND YOUR BUYING HABITS THROUGH ADVERTISING?

AI… (ARTIFICIAL INTELLIGENCE) HOW CAN THEY MAKE A COMPUTER OR A ROBOT MORE INTELLIGENT THAN A HUMAN BEING? THE TRUTH IS, THEY CANNOT!

IMAGINE BRAINS BEING PROGRAMMED CONSTANTLY THROUGH ALL MEDIA AND ELECTRICAL DEVICES. WHAT HAPPENS IS, THEY BECOME PREDICTABLE THROUGH PATTERNS. ALL OF THESE DATA STORAGE FACILITIES ARE SELLING YOUR INFORMATION AND PATTERNS SO THAT YOU CAN BE MANIPULATED AND SUPPRESSED. I'LL EXPLAIN LATER IN THE BOOK… HOW YOU CAN BE YOU, DO YOU AND LIVE ON PURPOSE! THE HUMAN BRAIN IS NOTHING SHORT OF A MIRACLE, THERE WILL NEVER BE A COMPUTER OR ROBOT THAT CAN ACTUALLY MIMIC A HEALTHY HUMAN BRAIN EVER! IF THE BRAINS ARE CONTROLLED BY MEDIA AND ELECTRICAL DEVICES, LEADING TO PREDETERMINED BEHAVIOUR, OF COURSE AI WILL BE MORE INTELLIGENT! HOWEVER, IT STILL CANNOT BEAT A HEALTHY

HUMAN BRAIN THOUGH.

HOW LONG DO YOU SPEND WITH TV, PHONES, TABLETS AND LAPTOPS? DO YOU FEEL THE IMPLICATIONS ARE TAKING ITS TOLL? DO YOU KNOW WHO YOU REALLY ARE AND HOW TO BECOME MORE MENTALLY HEALTHY?

CHAPTER 10: THE ARMED FORCES

WHAT IS THE NAME OF A GROUP OF PEOPLE THAT THE GOVERNMENT ARE IN COMPLETE CONTROL OF? THE ARMED FORCES! COULD WE LEARN WHAT OUR GOVERNMENT THINKS ABOUT US BY THE WAY THAT THEY HANDLE THAT GROUP OF PEOPLE?

WHY DO WE HAVE AN ARMED FORCES? WHO ARE THEY PROTECTING, IF THEY ARE FIGHTING IN OTHER COUNTRIES? SURELY IF A SECURITY GUARD IS STANDING AT THE DOOR OF THE BANK, THEY ARE PROTECTING THE BANK... IS THE SECURITY GUARD PROTECTING THE BANK IF THE BANK IS IN SCOTLAND AND THE SECURITY GUARD IS IN ANOTHER COUNTRY???

I WRITE THIS CHAPTER AS A VETERAN OF THE BRITISH ARMY, I DID LONG ENOUGH IN THE ARMY TO REALISE THAT WHAT I WAS TOLD WASN'T TRUE. I SAW HOW I AND OTHER PEOPLE WERE PROGRAMMED AND TREATED. THERE WILL BE SHORT STORIES SHARED IN THIS CHAPTER, LOTS OF QUESTIONS ASKED TO YOU AND SOME ABSOLUTELY HUGE REALISATIONS MADE! I WOULD NEVER GIVE OPERATIONAL OR SENSITIVE INFORMATION AWAY TO ANYONE, WHAT I'M SHARING IS MY EXPERIENCE OF THE ENTITY I CHOSE TO LITERALLY SIGN MY LIFE AWAY TO, AT A TIME WHERE I WAS DOWN ON MY LUCK AND WANTING TO BE PART OF SOMETHING.

THERE ARE MANY DIFFERENT OPINIONS ON THE ARMED FORCES, THE SERVICEMEN AND WOMEN WHO SERVE AND HAVE SERVED. I'D LIKE TO GO INTO THIS IN A DEEPER SENSE, AS IT COULD BE MADE APPARENT THAT ALL OF US (THE PEOPLE) HAVE BEEN DUPED INTO WHAT THE ARMED FORCES REALLY ARE AND WHAT OUR GOVERNMENT WOULD DO IF THEY WERE IN COMPLETE CONTROL OF OUR LIVES!

IF CONSCRIPTION/DRAFTING CAME BACK, WOULD THIS BE FAIR? WOULD YOU GO WILLINGLY OR HAVE TO BE FORCED?

THE REASON I ASK. IS... IF YOU WERE WILLING TO DO YOUR BIT FOR YOUR COUNTRY AND POSSIBLY DIE IN A WAR, DOES THIS MEAN THAT YOU DON'T VALUE YOUR LIFE OR COULD IT MEAN THAT YOU JUST LIKE TO HELP? WHAT OTHER WAY COULD YOU HELP, OTHER THAN SIGNING YOUR LIFE AWAY?

BEFORE JOINING, I WAS NOT LIVING MY IDEAL LIFE, SO THE ARMY LOOKED LIKE THE (ONLY) CHOICE FOR ME. LET'S HAVE A LOOK AS TO HOW THE ARMED FORCES RECRUIT, WHO JOINS AND WHAT IT LOOKS FOR FROM AN OUTSIDE PERSPECTIVE OF HOW IT IS PERCEIVED BY THE NARRATIVE IT IS GIVEN BY THE POWERS THAT BE!

IF YOU HAVE A DEGREE AND JOIN THE ARMED FORCES, YOU ARE GIVEN AN AUTOMATIC HIGHER STATUS AS IT IS IN LIFE... THIS MEANS YOU HAVE THE CHOICE TO JOIN AS AN OFFICER, IF YOU CHOOSE TO GO IN AS AN OFFICER AND NOT THE BOTTOM LEVEL SERVICEMAN/WOMAN THERE IS A DIFFERENT TYPE OF TRAINING. DOES THIS MEAN THE INDIVIDUAL WITH THE DEGREE IS MORE INTELLIGENT OR THEY ARE JUST BETTER AT HOLDING INFORMATION?

IT'S TRUE THAT IF PEOPLE FEEL THEY WILL GAIN STATUS, A HIGHER LEVEL OF PAY, OR RECOGNITION...   THAT THEY WILL DO AS THEY ARE TOLD! JUST LIKE THEY DO IN THE CLASSROOM! DOES THIS MEAN, THE ARMED FORCES HIERARCHY IS FULL OF YES MEN/WOMEN (PEOPLE WHO FOLLOW ORDERS TO GET AHEAD)? IS THIS WHY THE ARMED FORCES NEVER CHANGES? IS THE HIERARCHY FULL OF PEOPLE THAT LIKE TO BE

TOLD WHAT TO DO WITHOUT QUESTION? EVEN IF IT IS WRONG AND PEOPLE CAN BE HURT MENTALLY, PHYSICALLY OR EVEN KILLED? IF ANY OF YOU WERE TRIGGERED BY THESE QUESTIONS, ASK YOURSELF WHY, AS I DID NOT BLAME ANYONE OR PUT ANYONE DOWN.

IF YOU JOIN AT THE ENTRY LEVEL AND YOU BEGIN YOUR ARMED FORCES CAREER, AS THE LOWEST OF THE LOW... YOU'D DO AS YOU ARE TOLD SO YOU WERE TO GET PROMOTED WOULDN'T YOU? I FOUND THAT WHEN A SERVICEMAN/WOMAN WAS PROMOTED THROUGH THE RANKS, THERE WAS LESS SH*T TO DEAL WITH AND A HIGHER PAY BAND! WHAT REASON WOULD A SERVICEMAN/WOMAN HAVE TO REMAIN IN THE LOWER RANKS OR MISBEHAVE? NOW WE CAN SEE HOW THE CONTROL IS EASY AND WHY THE SYSTEM CONTINUES TO GO ON LIKE IT ALWAYS HAS FOR SO LONG!

CLEARLY THERE IS DIVISION BETWEEN THE HIERARCHY AND LOWER RANKS, THIS IS NORMALISED IN SOCIETY, SO PEOPLE JUST ACCEPT IT. I AM SURE WE CAN AGREE THAT WE'D LIKE TO LEARN FROM SOMEONE WHO IS WELL VERSED IN A SUBJECT OVER SOMEONE WHO HAS LITTLE KNOWLEDGE, YES? WHEN AN INDIVIDUAL KNOWS MORE THAN ANOTHER, DOES THIS MEAN THEY SHOULD HAVE POWER OVER THEM? IF YOU SAID YES, IS THIS BECAUSE YOU ARE FULL OF KNOWLEDGE AND FEEL YOU HAVE POWER OVER OTHER PEOPLE?

ARE THE SERVICEMEN AND WOMEN SERVING THEIR COUNTRY OR JUST SERVING THE RANKS ABOVE THEM? THE REASON I ASK, IS THAT THE GOVERNMENT, INCLUDING THE PRESIDENT OF A COUNTRY, IS MEANT TO BE OF SERVICE TO THE PEOPLE (THE COUNTRY). THE SYSTEM IN PLACE, ALWAYS HAS A BLAME TO SOMEONE HIGHER THAN THEM, THEN THE PEOPLE AT THE BOTTOM CANNOT QUESTION THE PEOPLE AT THE TOP, AS IT IS BELIEVED THAT THE PEOPLE AT THE TOP ARE ABOVE THEM, WHEN IN FACT, THEY ARE ONLY ANOTHER HUMAN BEING!!! IT'S ACTUALLY MIND BLOWING WHEN WE STAND BACK AND LOOK AT IT AS A WHOLE!

LET'S LOOK AT WHO JOINS THE ARMED FORCES IN THE LOWER RANKS, NO JUDGEMENT, ONLY TRUTH! AS I SAID AT THE BEGINNING OF THE CHAPTER, I SIGNED UP BECAUSE I WAS UNHAPPY WITH MY LIFE, I WAS

GOING THROUGH A DIVORCE, I HAD INSECURITIES THAT CAUSED NARCISSISTIC BEHAVIOUR AND I WAS NOT HAPPY WITH THE MAN I HAD BECOME. I THOUGHT IT WOULD BE BEST TO BE BROKEN DOWN AND BUILT AGAIN! SO I SIGNED OVER ALL OF MY POWER TO A BUNCH OF STRANGERS THAT DIDN'T CARE ABOUT ME. SMART MOVE!! DOES THIS SOUND LIKE THE REASON YOU/SOMEONE YOU KNOW JOINED THE ARMED FORCES?

I BELIEVE THE RECRUITMENT TEAMS STRUGGLE TO GET HIGH SELF ESTEEM PEOPLE TO JOIN THE ARMED FORCES, AS THESE HIGH SELF ESTEEM PEOPLE WILL NOT FOLLOW ORDERS LIKE LOW OR NO SELF ESTEEM PEOPLE WOULD, THEREFORE THEY WILL BE HARDER TO CONTROL. SLOGANS LIKE "WANT TO BE PART OF SOMETHING?" OR "FEEL LIKE YOU DON'T FIT IN, IN THE OUTSIDE WORLD?" ARE FOR A REASON! A HIGH SELF ESTEEM MAN/WOMAN WILL NEVER NEED TO FIT IN ANYWHERE! IS THIS EXPLOITATION THE WAY THE ARMED FORCES RECRUIT PEOPLE? IF NO, WHAT DO YOU BELIEVE THE REASON IS TO HIRE LOW SELF ESTEEM PEOPLE THAT ARE EASIER TO CONTROL?

LET'S LIST REASONS WHY PEOPLE JOIN THE ARMED FORCES ALL OVER THE WORLD AND SEE IF WE CAN FIND A PATTERN! I BELIEVE PEOPLE JOIN THE ARMED FORCES FOR THE FOLLOWING REASONS: LOW SELF ESTEEM, NO HIGHER EDUCATION, CAN'T AFFORD HIGHER EDUCATION, CAN'T GET A JOB, HAVE BEEN IN TROUBLE AND WANT TO START A FRESH, WANT TO FEEL SECURE AND BE PART OF SOMETHING BIGGER, WANT TO HELP THEIR COUNTRY (BUT DON'T REALISE, TRAINING TO KILL PEOPLE IS NOT GOING TO HELP THEIR COUNTRY), ESCAPING FROM A LIFE THAT WAS NOT FULFILLED, BECAUSE THEIR FAMILY SERVED (WE WILL DISCUSS THIS IN MORE DETAIL), BECAUSE THEIR FAMILY HAVE NEVER SHOWN THEM LOVE, MAYBE THEY ARE WARPED AND THE THOUGHT OF WEAPONS AND KILLING MAKES THEM FEEL GOOD! DO YOU BELIEVE ANY OF THESE REASONS ARE THE RIGHT REASON TO JOIN?

I MENTIONED IN THE LAST PARAGRAPH, THAT PEOPLE JOIN THE ARMED FORCES BECAUSE THEIR PARENTS DID AND THEIR PARENTS BEFORE THEM. DO YOU THINK THIS IS THE RIGHT REASON TO JOIN? IF YES, WHY? SHOULD WE LIVE OUR LIVES THE WAY OUR FAMILIES SAY OR SHOULD WE

BE LIVING OUR UNIQUENESS SO THAT WE GET TO HIGH SELF ESTEEM BY OURSELVES?

SINCE MY UNIQUENESS IS COMPASSION-SERVER (I'LL EXPLAIN MORE LATER), WHICH MEANS I DO WHATEVER IT TAKES TO MAKE SURE OTHERS HAVE THEIR PAIN BEARED, I CANNOT STAND THE THOUGHT OF HURTING SOMEONE. I JOINED THE ARMED FORCES AND THE THOUGHT OF KILLING SOMEONE WAS HORRIFIC AS I ASKED MYSELF "WOULD I LIKE IT IF SOMEONEWAS TRAINED TO KILL ME OR SOMEONE I KNOW?" THE ANSWER WAS A BIG FAT NO!!! SO THE REASON THAT I JOINED WAS BECAUSE OF A FEW OF THE REASONS LISTED ABOVE AND I ONLY REALISED IT WAS A WRONG CHOICE AND I WAS LOSING ENERGY EVERY DAY I WAS IN SERVICE BECAUSE IT WENT AGAINST MY UNIQUENESS. I WAS FAR FROM THE ONLY ONE TOO! I WATCHED MANY A GOOD MAN/WOMAN BE BROKEN DOWN TO BE A ROBOT AND NOT A FREE THINKING HUMAN BEING... IT WAS TERRIBLE! IMAGINE NOT EVEN HAVING THE POWER TO QUESTION!!! THAT IS TRAGIC IN ITSELF! DO YOU BELIEVE SOMETHING IS RIGHT AND JUST IF YOU ARE NOT ABLE TO QUESTION IT?

BASIC TRAINING TAKES A FREE THINKING CIVILIAN (HUMAN) AND TURNS THEM INTO A SMALL COG IN A BIG MACHINE (ROBOT) SO THAT THEY FOLLOW ORDERS, DON'T QUESTION ANYTHING OR FEEL STRONG ENOUGH TO STAND UP FOR WHAT'S RIGHT AND JUST IN A SITUATION. IS IT FAIR TO TAKE A LIFE? IF SOMEONE TAKES A LIFE, DO THEY DESERVE THEIR LIFE TAKEN? IF YOU WERE ONLY DOING YOUR JOB AND FOLLOWING ORDERS TO TAKE SOMEONES LIFE, DO YOU DESERVE TO DIE? NOBODY HAS THE RIGHT TO TAKE A LIFE OF ANOTHER, IN MY BELIEF. WHAT DO YOU BELIEVE?

THE MILITARY IS RUN BY THE CROWN/GOVERNMENT. DOES THIS MEAN THE MILITARY SERVES THE CROWN/GOVERNMENT? WE ARE LED TO BELIEVE THAT THE MILITARY ARE TO PROTECT OUR COUNTRY, SO TO DO THAT, THEY ARE SENT AWAY TO POSSIBLY LOSE THEIR LIVES IN OTHER COUNTRIES. DOES THAT SOUND A LITTLE BACKWARDS? WE ARE TOLD THAT THE ENEMY IS OUT THERE... WHO DECIDES WHO THE ENEMY IS? WHY DO WE BELIEVE THAT THESE OTHER MEN AND WOMEN ARE

ENEMIES? I FOR ONE DON'T TRUST THE GOVERNMENT OR THE MEDIA, AS THEY LIE CONSTANTLY! WHY WOULD WE BELIEVE THAT THESE PEOPLE IN OTHER COUNTRIES ARE ENEMIES??? AS I COVERED IN THE PREVIOUS CHAPTER ON MEDIA MANIPULATION, WE ARE FED ANYTHING THEY WANT TO TELL US, THE MILITARY GOES INTO ANOTHER COUNTRY TO FLEX THEIR MUSCLES AND SERVICE MEN AND WOMEN FROM OUR COUNTRY DIE. IF SOMEONE CAME INTO OUR COUNTRY AND WE DECIDED TO PROTECT OUR ASSETS 'FROM THE ENEMY' DOES THAT MAKE IT OK? IS IT OK THAT ANYONE GOES INTO ANOTHER COUNTRY WITH THE INTENT TO RAID, STEAL, KILL OR TAKE?

THIS ONE IS GREAT!!! I WAS ORDERED, WHEN I WAS IN MY REGIMENT, TO GET ON A 'SCALE A PARADE' THIS MEANS THE WHOLE REGIMENT, INCLUDING ANY ATTACHED CAP BADGES. THE HIERARCHY WANTED TO ADDRESS US. WE ARRIVE IN SQUARE FORMATION, WHERE WE BEGIN TO BE SPOKEN TO ABOUT BREXIT (BRITAIN'S EXIT FROM THE EU). WE WERE TOLD HOW BAD IT WAS THAT WE WERE RUN BY THE EU AND THAT THEY WERE SYPHONING MONEY FROM THE COUNTRY AND THAT BRITAIN WOULD BE BETTER ON IT'S OWN. WE WERE TOLD THAT WE WEREN'T GOING TO BE FORCED TO VOTE, THAT MEANT THAT WE'D DO AS WE WERE TOLD. IF WE DID, WE'D GET TO LEAVE EARLY AND ENJOY OUR WEEKEND.

THE PARADE WAS DISMISSED AND THEN IT WAS DOWN TO THE SERGEANT MAJORS TO GET THE SERVICEMEN/WOMEN SORTED AND THERE WERE QUEUES OF PEOPLE LINED UP AT THE COMPUTERS, MANNED BY STAFF SERGEANTS, MAKING SURE WE ALL VOTED!!! I SAID I DON'T VOTE AND I DIDN'T KNOW ENOUGH ABOUT IT. I WAS TOLD THAT THE RIGHT DECISION WAS TO GO WITH THE MAJORITY FOR THE SAKE OF MY COUNTRY AND THAT MY WEEKEND DEPENDED ON IT. I KNEW I HAD MY SON THAT WEEKEND SO I BIT MY TONGUE AND DID IT,   I HAD BEEN FIGHTING IN COURT FOR A FEW YEARS BY THIS POINT. I COULDN'T STOP THINKING TO MYSELF, THAT EVERY REGIMENT WAS DOING THIS... IF WE WERE BEING 'GUIDED' TO VOTE THIS WAY 'WITH NO QUESTIONS' THERE WAS MORE THAN LIKELY MORE TO IT! THEN THE WIVES/HUSBANDS AND FAMILY MEMBERS WOULD BE INFLUENCED INTO VOTING FROM THE SERVICE MEN/WOMEN... THEN POSTING ON SOCIAL MEDIA WOULD MAKE THE

WORD SPREAD MORE. I STARTED TO SEE HOW THE VOTES ARE DONE IN REAL LIFE. IMAGINE THE OTHER INSTITUTIONS AND WORK PLACES THAT COULD DO THIS! MADNESS! DO YOU THINK THIS SOUNDS FAIR? WHAT DOES IT LOOK LIKE TO YOU?

I WAS FRIENDLY WITH A GUY, I'LL CALL HIM JASON (FOR PRIVACY PURPOSES). HE WAS 25, MARRIED AND HAD 3 KIDS WHO BELONGED TO HIS WIFE AND HER PREVIOUS PARTNER. JASON WAS LOVELY, REALLY STAND UP GUY AND A GREAT STEP-DAD TO THE KIDS FROM WHAT I HAD SEEN. HIS MRS WAS PLEASANT ENOUGH TOO AND THEY SEEMED HAPPY. THERE WAS A LOT OF MOVEMENT THIS YEAR, BEING DEPLOYED, OR PUT ON TRAINING COURSES. JASON WAS AWAY FOR A WHILE AND CAME BACK ON THE MONDAY TO HIS NORMAL LIFE ON BASE, SPENT A FEW DAYS WITH HIS WIFE AND KIDS. FRIDAY HE DECIDED TO GO TO SEE ONE OF THE GUYS AND WENT OUT FOR A COUPLE OF HOURS. HE FELT A LITTLE SICK SO DECIDED TO HEAD HOME EARLY. HE TURNED UP EARLY TO FIND HIS WIFE BENT OVER THE DINING ROOM TABLE, BEING SEEN TO BY WHAT WE CALLED A PAD PANTHER. A PAD PANTHER IS SOMEONE, USUALLY A MALE IN THE ARMED FORCES WHO GOES ROUND THE PADS (MILITARY HOUSING) SEEKING OUT THE WIVES OF THE SOLDIERS WHO ARE AWAY.

WHEN JASON SAW THIS, HE WAS DEVASTATED AND TURNED AND WALKED OUT. JASON'S WIFE SAID IT WAS THE FIRST AND ONLY TIME, WHICH LATER WAS FOUND OUT TO BE A LIE. JASON WAS THROWN OUT OF HIS HOUSE WITH NO BELONGINGS AND TOLD THAT HE WAS NOT ALLOWED TO CONFRONT THE PAD PANTHER, WHO WAS HAVING SEX WITH HIS WIFE, OR HE'D BE CHARGED!!!

HOW DO YOU FEEL THIS WAS DEALT WITH BY THE MILITARY AND WHY? I'LL BE HONEST, I FOUND HIS RIGHT TO VENT WAS TAKEN AWAY, HIS RIGHT TO BE A MAN WAS TAKEN AWAY, HE WAS SUPPRESSED AND THREATENED FOR HAVING EMOTION ON A SITUATION, WHILE THE PAD PANTHER WAS GOING ROUND AND BRAGGING, WITH NO BACKLASH. I COULDN'T BELIEVE WHAT WAS HAPPENING TO THE POOR GUY. I AM NOT ONE FOR FIGHTING, I ALSO DO NOT LIKE TO BE SUPPRESSED FROM EXPRESSING MYSELF, I COULD ONLY IMAGINE HOW JASON WAS FEELING

INTERNALLY.

IF YOU WERE IN THE ARMED FORCES AND WERE IN THIS SITUATION, HOW WOULD YOU REACT? DOES IT SOUND LIKE THEY HAVE THEIR SERVICEMEN/WOMEN'S MENTAL HEALTH IN THEIR BEST INTERESTS? I FOUND OUT, THIS HAPPENED A LOT!

THE NEXT GUY, GRAHAM, I HEARD OF, WAS A RIGHT HARD MAN AND THERE WERE NOT MANY PEOPLE WHO WOULD STAND UP TO HIM. HIS WIFE WAS HAVING SEX WITH ANOTHER PAD PANTHER AND WHEN GRAHAM FOUND OUT, HE FLIPPED! THE PAD PANTHER WENT INTO HIDING FOR 24 HOURS, WHILE GRAHAM WAS SHIPPED 500 MILES AWAY TO ANOTHER CAMP TO PROTECT THE PERPETRATOR! AWAY FROM HIS KIDS AND THIS PLACEMENT WAS FOR 12 MONTHS! DISGUSTING!

THERE WAS SO MUCH HAPPENING IN THE PRIVATE LIVES OF THESE SERVICEMEN/ WOMEN THAT WAS TAKING ITS TOLL ON THEIR MENTAL HEALTH AND THEY WERE TREATED LIKE THE SH*T ON THE BOTTOM OF THE SHOES OF THOSE IN CHARGE. I WAS NO DIFFERENT... EVERYONE HAD SOMETHING AND THE ENVIRONMENT WAS ABYSMAL. WOULD YOU LIKE TO SIGN UP? WOULD YOU ENCOURAGE ANY OF YOUR FAMILY AND FRIENDS TO SIGN UP?

THERE IS NO OUTLET FOR THESE SERVICEMEN/WOMEN TO BE EMOTIONAL, SO THEY HOLD IT IN UNTIL THEY DRINK ALCOHOL AND THEN LET LOOSE, GET THEMSELVES INTO TROUBLE AND UNDER MORE CONTROL, ITS HORRIFIC. SOME ENJOY THE ARMED FORCES, MANY, FROM MY EXPERIENCE DIDN'T. AS A HUMAN, YOU ARE BROKEN DOWN TO FEEL LOWER THAN A SNAKE'S BELLY, WITH NO SOVEREIGNTY, TO SERVE SOMETHING THAT DOES NOT SERVE YOU BACK. IS THIS A DECENT WAY TO LIVE?

WHEN THEY LEAVE THE FORCES, THIS IS WHEN THE SUICIDES HAPPEN, THE PTSD, THE HOMELESSNESS AND THE TROUBLE REALLY STARTS! IF YOU HAVE TO BE STRIPPED OF ALL SELF SOVEREIGNTY AND PROGRAMMED TO BE A MEMBER OF SERVICE PERSONNEL, DO YOU BELIEVE THAT YOU

SHOULD BE GIVEN TRAINING ON HOW TO BE YOURSELF WHEN YOU LEAVE? OF COURSE YOU SHOULD!! THIS IS WHY EX-SERVICEMEN/WOMEN STRUGGLE SO MUCH, THEY ARE GIVEN MONEY AND QUALIFICATIONS AND SENT ON THEIR WAY TO FEND FOR THEMSELVES, AFTER BEING TOLD WHAT TO DO FOR HOWEVER LONG THEY WERE IN!

IF BASIC TRAINING IS ONLY 12 WEEKS TO GET A HUMAN TO START ACTING LIKE A ROBOT, WHAT WOULD YEARS DO? WHAT BEHAVIOURS HAVE THEY LEARNED? WHAT WOULD THEY DO IF THEY GET FREEDOM? GO OFF THE RAILS?

SINCE MOST DON'T KNOW WHO THEY ARE WHEN THEY GO IN (I DIDN'T AND I WAS 30 YEARS OLD!), THERE IS NO CHANCE OF FINDING OUT WHEN THEY COME OUT. SOME WILL MAKE IT TO BE RESILIENT AND SUSTAIN A LIFE OF UNEASINESS. SOME WILL COME OUT AND HAVE TO FOCUS HARD AND WHEN THEY LOSE FOCUS, THEY CRASH AND BURN. SOME COME OUT, GET SCARED AND REJOIN. SOME COME OUT AND FEEL WORTHLESS SO COMMIT SUICIDE OR END UP CONSTANTLY INTOXICATED TILL THEY CAN NO LONGER LIVE.

I APPROACHED SOMEONE AT THE TOP FOR MENTAL HEALTH AT THE TRI-SERVICE MENTAL HEALTH BASE, EXPLAINED WHAT I HAD SEEN AND EXPLAINED THAT THERE IS ONLY ONE PATENTED WAY FOR VETERANS TO REALLY BE HELPED WHEN THEY COME OUT. I WAS SHOUTED AT, JEERED AT AND PUT DOWN. I THEN WENT TO ALL THE UK MILITARY CHARITIES AND EXPLAINED THE SAME THING... THEY ARE HURTING PEOPLE FURTHER AND WAS IGNORED AND SHOUTED AT.

IS THIS HOW OUR GOVERNMENT TREATS PEOPLE WHEN THEY HAVE COMPLETE CONTROL OVER THEM?

I CAN PROMISE, THERE IS A WAY THAT THE ONLY MODEL FOR THE MIND AND BRAIN IN THE WORLD COULD STOP 99.9% OF MILITARY SUICIDES ANYWHERE IN THE WORLD! THESE ARE HUMAN BEINGS LIKE YOU. DO THEY DESERVE LESS THAN YOU? DO YOU THINK GIVING MONEY TO CHARITIES THAT ARE HURTING THEM AND TREATING THEM ALL THE

SAME IS FAIR? WHY WON'T PEOPLE LET ME SPEAK AND SAVE THOUSANDS OF MILITARY PERSONNEL EVERY YEAR??

I, ALONG WITH THE TEAM I'M WITH, CAN HELP ANY HUMAN BEING GET IN TO FLOW AND CHANGE THEIR LIFE, IF THEY ARE WILLING TO CHANGE IT! I HOPE YOU CAN TAKE WHAT I'VE WRITTEN HERE, NOT AS NEGATIVE, BUT MORE TO THE POINT OF WHY... EVEN THE FACT THAT THESE PEOPLE SIGN THEIR LIVES AWAY AND MOST DON'T GET IT BACK PHYSICALLY OR MENTALLY... EVER!!! WE CAN ALL CHANGE THIS, WHO IS WITH ME?

WHAT DO YOU THINK IS THE FIRST STEP?

CHAPTER 11: SOVEREIGNTY OF SELF

YOU CAN PROBABLY SEE WHERE THIS BOOK IS HEADED AND THE PURPOSE OF IT ALREADY. THROUGH TRUTH MY WISH IS FOR EVERYONE TO DISCOVER THEMSELVES. THERE IS NO RELIGION HIGHER THAN TRUTH AND IF EVERYONE LIVED THEIR TRUTH, THE WORLD WOULD BE KINDER, MORE LOVING, MORE ABUNDANT... BUT SHARED EQUALLY, NO DICTATING, MORE UNDERSTANDING, MORE FRIENDLY... YOU GET THE PICTURE!

SELF SOVEREIGNTY CAN NOT BE GRASPED, UNTIL A MAN OR WOMAN UNDERSTANDS WHO THEY ARE ON THE INSIDE, THIS LEADS THEM TO UNDERSTAND THEIR BEHAVIOURS AND HOW THEY ARE SEEN ON THE OUTSIDE. PERSONALITY IS FROM THE LATIN "PERSONA" WHICH MEANS MASK. PERSONALITY IS THE BEHAVIOUR WE SHOW TO HIDE WHEN WE ARE UNBALANCED. PERSONALITY IS NOT WHO YOU ARE IN YOUR SOUL.

THERE ARE FAR TOO MANY PEOPLE ON THIS EARTH WHO TRY TO SHOW HOW THEY WANT PEOPLE TO SEE THEM AND THIS IS IN FACT HARMING

THE INDIVIDUAL AND ANYONE WHO COMES INTO CLOSE PROXIMITY. WHEN OTHERS GET HURT, THEY ALSO HURT OTHER PEOPLE AND BELIEVE ME, THE RIPPLE EFFECT COULD BE DEVASTATING!! LET ME EXPLAIN IN A VERY SHORT STORY!

DAVID AND PAM ARE A COUPLE AND GENUINELY DECENT PEOPLE, WHEN UNDER PRESSURE, LIKE MOST, THEIR PERSONALITIES CHANGE. THIS ONE FRIDAY NIGHT, THEY HAD AN ALTERCATION WHILST BEING DRUNK. EVERY TIME THEY ARE DRUNK THIS HAPPENS. IS THE ANSWER TO STOP DRINKING? OR IS THE ANSWER TO UNDERSTAND EACH OTHER BETTER WHEN DRUNK? ALCOHOL CAN HAVE A HUGE IMPACT ON THE BRAIN AND PEOPLE'S INHIBITIONS, THE TRUTH CAN COME OUT HARSHLY, THIS IS ANOTHER REASON TO KNOW THY SELF AND THOSE WE ARE INTERACTING WITH ON ANY LEVEL!

THEY ARE BOTH HAVING A NICE EVENING, BUT SUDDENLY DAVID MENTIONS SOMETHING THAT TRIGGERS PAM. PAM REACTS FROM THE TRIGGER AND DAVID CANNOT ACCEPT IT SO HE SAYS SOMETHING ELSE TO KEEP THE TRIGGER GOING. PAM THEN TAKES AN ORNAMENT FROM THE TABLE AND HITS DAVID WITH IT. NOW, BETWEEN THE ALCOHOL AND THE TRIGGER, WE HAVE TO BEAR IN MIND THAT PAM IS NOT IN CONTROL HERE. ANYWAY...

PAM LEAVES IN A BLIND RAGE AND PISSED OUT OF HER SKULL. SHE STOPS TRIGGERING AND BECOMES MORE FOCUSED AFTER A GOOD 15-20 MINUTES LATER BUT DOES NOT HAVE THE MEMORY OF HITTING DAVID, ONLY WHAT HE SAID. DAVID IS LYING PASSED OUT ON THE FLOOR, IN THE SITTING ROOM WITH A NASTY CUT ON HIS HEAD, NONE THE WISER. PAM NEEDS REASSURANCE AND CALLS HER GOOD FRIEND MAX. MAX IS A BIT OF A LAD AND IS GOING WITH PAM'S BEST FRIEND JANICE. JANICE IS HOME AT HER PARENTS AS SHE HAS WORK EARLY IN THE MORNING. LONG STORY SHORT, MAX GIVES PAM THE COMFORT SHE NEEDED AND THEN SOME EXTRA COMFORT... MEANWHILE DAVID STILL HASN'T MOVED A MUSCLE FOR HOURS. (I KNOW WHAT YOU ARE THINKING.)

IN THE MORNING PAM WAKES UP IN MAX'S BED, UNDRESSED AND ALSO

MAX UNDRESSED. THEY BOTH PANIC AND REALISE THE INEVITABLE HAPPENED AND FEEL INSTANT REMORSE. AS THEY AWAKEN, JANICE TURNS UP UNANNOUNCED BEFORE WORK TO COLLECT HER PASS TO GET INTO HER SECURE SECTION OF THE BUILDING AT WORK, ONLY TO FIND THESE TWO! THE PROVERBIAL S*IT HIT THE FAN. WE ARE NOW DOWN 2 RELATIONSHIPS! PAM MAKES HER WAY HOME, HUNGOVER AND FEELING TERRIBLE. HOW IS SHE GOING TO TELL DAVID THIS?

AS SHE WALKS THROUGH THE DOOR, SHE KNOWS THE HEATING HAS BEEN LEFT ON ALL NIGHT. FEELING STUFFY AND A LITTLE DIZZY, SHE CAN'T BELIEVE HER EYES TO FIND HER LIFELESS PARTNER ON THE FLOOR WITH A CUT HEAD. SHE DOES EVERYTHING SHE CAN BUT HAS NO LUCK REVIVING HIM. PAM THEN CALLS THE AMBULANCE AND TRIES TO BACKTRACK OVER HER NIGHT. LATER SHE IS BEING QUESTIONED BY THE COPS, NOTHING ABOUT THE ORNAMENT IS COMING TO MIND. PAM HAS LOST TWO FRIENDS, HAS KILLED AND LOST HER PARTNER TO A HEAD INJURY, DAVID'S MUM HAS LOST A SON, HIS FATHER A SON, HIS SISTERS A BROTHER AND EVERYONE CONNECTED TO HIM HAS LOST A PART OF HIM. ARE YOU STARTING TO SEE THE EFFECTS?

PAM IS DETAINED, STILL CANNOT REMEMBER A THING AND WHEN HER TRIAL COMES UP, SHE IS FOUND GUILTY AS THERE WAS NO MORE EVIDENCE TO SAY ANYONE ELSE WAS IN THE PROPERTY AND IS SENT TO PRISON, HER FAMILY HAVE NOW LOST A DAUGHTER, A SISTER AND HER FRIENDS HAVE LOST A FRIEND. A TRUE TRAGEDY REALLY!

NOW BECAUSE DAVID AND PAM'S FAMILY AND FRIENDS HAVE LOST THEM, THEIR PERSONALITIES CHANGE, WHICH CAUSES THEM TO SAY AND DO THINGS THAT CAN CAUSE HURT, LOSS, MISUNDERSTANDINGS. THIS LEADS TO OTHER PEOPLE HAVING THE SAME AND IT REPLICATES THROUGHOUT THE WORLD.

THE THING THAT CAUSED THIS WAS NOT THE ORNAMENT OR THE ACT OF VIOLENCE. IT WAS IN FACT THE COMMUNICATION NOT BEING RIGHT FROM THE START OF PAM AND DAVID'S RELATIONSHIP. THEY SPOKE TO EACH OTHER THE WAY THAT THEY THEMSELVES WANTED SPOKEN TO

AND NOT THE WAY THAT THE OTHER WISHED TO BE SPOKEN TO. THEY REASON FOR THIS IS THAT NEITHER OF THEM KNEW HOW THEY ARE SEEN BY OTHERS AND THEY ARE JUST GUESSING HOW TO SPEAK TO ONE ANOTHER. IF THEY KNEW EACH OTHER ON A SOUL LEVEL, THEY WOULD BE ABLE TO UNDERSTAND AND ACCEPT EACH OTHER. THEY WOULD BE ABLE TO SPEAK PAST THE BEHAVIOUR AND PERSONALITY OF THE MOMENT TO REACH THE UNIQUE INTANGIBLE SOUL OF THE PERSON.

THE IMPORTANCE OF COMMUNICATION AND UNDERSTANDING OF SELF AND OTHERS IS ABSOLUTELY IMPERATIVE AND IS THE REASON WHY SELF SOVEREIGNTY AND COMMUNITY IS SO BROKEN. IMAGINE THEY KNEW EACH OTHER'S UNIQUENESS AND HOW THEY WANTED TO BE SPOKEN TO IN ORDER TO GAIN ENERGY THEN APPLIED WHAT THEY KNEW? CAN YOU SEE ANY OTHER WAY THIS SITUATION COULD HAVE BEEN DISSOLVED?

THIS WOULD BE A GOOD TIME TO REALISE WHY WE DRINK ALCOHOL WHILE WITH OUR PARTNERS OR FRIENDS. ARE WE DRINKING BECAUSE WE ARE UNHAPPY? BECAUSE WE HAD A TOUGH WEEK, BECAUSE WE WANT TO RELAX AND SWITCH OFF, BECAUSE WE WANT TO ESCAPE FROM OUR THOUGHTS OR LIVES FOR A WHILE... THERE ARE AN ARRAY OF REASONS, BUT IT CAN ACTUALLY REMOVE YOUR CONSCIOUS SELF CONTROL AFTER 1 OR 2 DRINKS AND CAN AMPLIFY EVERYTHING YOU ARE FEELING MORE AND THE EFFECTS ON OTHERS CAN BE DEVASTATING (AS YOU JUST READ) HOW OFTEN DO YOU QUESTION YOURSELF AS TO WHY YOU ARE DRINKING ALCOHOL? HOW OFTEN DO YOU TAKE IT TOO FAR? HOW MANY TIMES DO YOU NEED TO LEARN THAT IS SOLVES LITERALLY NOTHING TO DRINK WHEN YOU NOT IN BALANCE OR FLOW?

WHEN WAS THE LAST TIME YOU THOUGHT ABOUT CONSIDERING OTHERS WHEN YOU SPEAK? HOW OFTEN DO YOU THINK ABOUT THIS? IF YOU DON'T SPEAK THE WAY OTHERS WANT TO BE SPOKEN TO, DO YOU DESERVE THE SAME TREATMENT?

IF SELF SOVEREIGNTY IS THE ABILITY TO LIVE FREELY, BY YOUR OWN CHOICES AND DECISIONS, DO YOU NOT THINK THAT IT IS BETTER THAT YOU FULLY KNOW AND UNDERSTAND YOURSELF FIRST? BEFORE YOU

TRIGGER AND FREAK OUT, BEFORE YOU BLAME OTHERS FOR YOUR CURRENT SITUATION, BEFORE YOU ACT OUT OF ANGER AND CANNOT CONTROL YOURSELF? DO YOU THINK YOU HAVE HAD THE FACILITIES TO KNOW YOURSELF SINCE BEING A CHILD? WERE YOU EVER TAUGHT TO BE YOURSELF OR TO CONFORM TO THE SOUND OF OTHER PEOPLES WORDS AND RULES?

SINCE YOUR BIRTH, THE GOVERNMENT/CROWN OR OTHER HIERARCHY HAVE SNEAKILY DECIDED TO TAKE CONTROL OF YOUR LIFE. FROM HOW YOU THINK, TO HOW YOU ACT AND EXPRESS YOURSELF, TO WHAT YOU PUT INTO YOUR BODY. IF YOU (THE PEOPLE) ARE SOCIETY, WHO DECIDES WHAT YOU AND THE MASSES DO, IN ORDER TO CREATE THE SOCIETY? WHY DO THE PEOPLE ON EARTH SUFFER SO MUCH, IF THE HIERARCHY ARE HELPING THEM LIVE A RIGHT AND JUST LIFE, AS GOD INTENDED?

I'M GOING TO TAKE YOU ON THE JOURNEY OF A BASIC LIFE, THIS IS THE LIFE OF MILLIONS AND MILLIONS OF PEOPLE SO PLEASE DON'T LAUGH, JUDGE, OR FEEL BAD. INSTEAD... I'D LIKE YOU TO FEEL WHAT YOU READ AND PUT YOURSELF IN THE POSITION AND WRITE DOWN WHAT YOU FEEL AND WHY, IT IS IMPORTANT THAT YOU ARE DESCRIPTIVE AS THIS IS YOU TALKING TO YOUR TRUE SELF, SO WRITE FROM YOUR HEART.

BORN INTO THIS WORLD, BECAUSE OUR PARENTS DECIDED TO HAVE A CHILD OR THE PREGNANCY WAS A SURPRISE. (THIS WAS NOT OUR CHOICE) GIVEN A NAME AND REGISTERED AS A CORPORATION TO THE GOVERNMENT (GIVEN A SOCIAL SECURITY NUMBER OR EQUIVALENT.. ALSO NOT OUR CHOICE). THEN WE ARE NURTURED IN A WAY OUR PARENT DECIDES (EVEN WHEN MOST HAVE NO IDEA WHO THEY ARE THEMSELVES, SO WE ARE REALLY JUST KEPT ALIVE AND PROGRAMMED). WE THEN GO TO PRESCHOOL THAT USUALLY HAS SOME SORT OF CURRICULUM (CONTROL) AND NOW WE REALLY GET MOLDED LIKE PUTTY! WE DON'T KNOW THE WAYS OF THE WORLD SO WE ARE TAUGHT THROUGH SCHOOL, HIGH SCHOOL, COLLEGE AND UNIVERSITY, THE WAY THE SO CALLED WORLD LEADERS WANT US TAUGHT, THEIR VERSION OF HISTORY, THEIR VERSIONS OF HOW WE HAVE TO CONDUCT OURSELVES, THEIR WAY OF

HOW OUR BRAINS ARE PROGRAMMED! ARE YOU STARTING TO FEEL LIKE CELEBRATING THIS LIFE YET OR DO YOU SEE INSTITUTIONS BELIEVE THEY NEED TO TREAT US ALL THE SAME AND AGAINST OUR UNIQUENESS BECAUSE IT IS EASIER FOR THEM?

WE START WORKING FOR A LIVING, USUALLY WITH A BOSS OR COMPANY OWNER, WE WORK THE WAY THAT THEY WANT, TO EARN THEM A LIVING AND WE GET GIVEN A CRUST, WHILE WE DO THE DIRTY/HARD WORK, THAT THEY DON'T WANT TO/CAN'T DO AND WE HAVE TO ACT BY THE COMPANY VALUES AND GUIDELINES, WHICH IS NOT TO BE OUR UNIQUE SELF.

RELATIONSHIPS ARE NEVER BUILT ON FULLY UNDERSTANDING ANOTHER, AS THERE IS NOTHING ON EARTH THAT ALLOWS A MAN OR WOMAN TO KNOW WHO THEY ARE AT ESSENCE, IN A WAY THAT THEY CAN EXPLAIN OR DETERMINE QUICKLY, SO PEOPLE TEND TO ACT MOSTLY ON EXPECTATION OF SOMEONE ELSE OR WITH THE PERSONALITY.

WHEN AND WHERE DO YOU GET TO BE YOURSELF? I WANT EVERYONE TO UNDERSTAND, THAT IF YOU HAVE TO ACT IN A CERTAIN WAY, THAT IS NOT YOU, IN ORDER TO EARN MONEY OR LIVE YOUR LIFE... YOU ARE NOT SOVEREIGN IN THE SLIGHTEST! DO YOU THINK YOU ARE SOVEREIGN? WHEN WAS THE LAST TIME YOU DID SOMETHING FOR YOU, THE WAY THAT YOU WANTED TO DO IT? HOW OFTEN DO YOU DO IT? HOW OFTEN CAN YOU DO THIS WITHOUT CAUSING ANY HARM TO ANYONE ELSE?

THROUGH MANY A CENTURY, THERE HAS BEEN HIDDEN INFORMATION, WHY WOULD THE ONES IN POWER HIDE ANY INFORMATION? WE ARE ALL HISTORY IN THE MAKING, BUT LIVING OUR LIVES ACCORDING TO THE PAST AND IN CYCLES! WHAT HAVE YOU DONE THAT HAS NEVER BEEN DONE BEFORE? WHY IS THIS? I BELIEVE IT IS BECAUSE WE AREN'T ALLOWED, THEN WE WILL SEE WE HAVE THE POWER AND THAT WOULD BE DANGEROUS TO A PROGRAMMED SOCIETY!

WE ARE PROGRAMMED TO THINK MONEY IS POWER, STATUS IS POWER, ASSETS ARE POWER, OR BEING ON A STAGE IS POWER! THE TRUTH IS...

POWER IS IN SELF SOVEREIGNTY, IN THE KNOWING OF SELF AND NOT CREATING A FALSE SELF. IMAGINE A WORLD, WHERE EVERYONE KNEW THEMSELVES SO WELL, THAT THEY NEVER HAD TO BE INSECURE OR FEEL WEAK, AS THEY WERE JUST DOING WHAT THEY WERE MEANT TO DO, WHAT WOULD IT LOOK LIKE?

THE FIRST STEP IN THIS PROCESS IS TO UNDERSTAND YOUR UNIQUENESS, REALISE AND ACKNOWLEDGE HOW YOU GAIN AND LOSE ENERGY. ONCE YOU EMBRACE THIS UNIQUENESS AND STOP TRYING TO BE SOMEONE ELSE, YOU CAN COMMUNICATE YOUR UNIQUENESS TO OTHERS AND IT BECOMES EASIER TO BE YOURSELF.

THE NEXT STAGE IS UNDERSTANDING AND ACKNOWLEDGING THE UNIQUENESS OF OTHER PEOPLE, WHO THEY ARE, HOW TO READ THEM AND ACCEPT THEM FOR WHO THEY ARE, WHILE INTERACTING IN A WAY THAT IS RIGHT AND JUST, BUT ALSO FAIR TO ALL PARTIES INVOLVED. IF YOU DON'T DO THIS, YOUR UNCONSCIOUS WILL BEGIN TO DEPRESS YOUR ENERGY.

WE THEN SHOULD LOOK AT OUR INTERACTIONS FROM AN OUTER PERSPECTIVE... THE COMMUNICATION GUIDELINES (THAT WE CAN CONTROL AND CHANNEL WELL THROUGH OURSELVES) WE NEVER MAKE STATEMENTS ON OTHER PEOPLE... IE: YOU ARE, YOU DON'T, YOU WON'T, YOU CAN'T... HOW OFTEN DO YOU THINK YOU DO THIS? I BELIEVE VERY OFTEN... INSTEAD, YOU MAKE THE STATEMENTS ON YOURSELF, SO THAT THE CONVERSATION IS COMING FROM YOUR VIEW, THAT CAN BE QUESTIONED AND UNDERSTOOD AND NOT MET HOSTILITY OR TAKEN AS BLAME... IE: I THINK, I FEEL, I BELIEVE, MY UNDERSTANDING IS... THIS MEANS ALL THAT YOU ARE TRYING TO CONTROL AND CHANNEL IS YOURSELF, ENSURING THAT YOU ARE NOT OUT TO CAUSE HARM OR START A FIGHT.

WOULD YOU WANT TO GO OUT AND HARM PEOPLE WITH YOUR COMMUNICATION ON PURPOSE? IF THE ANSWER IS YES, HOW SECURE ARE YOU WITHIN YOURSELF? DO YOU HAVE SELF ESTEEM ISSUES THAT NEED ADDRESSED? ALWAYS ASKING QUESTIONS IS VERY IMPORTANT! IT SHOWS

THAT YOU CARE, THAT YOU ARE WILLING TO UNDERSTAND AND LEARN ABOUT THE THOUGHTS, BEHAVIOUR OR ACTIONS OF ANOTHER, BEFORE YOU CONSIDER YOUR REPLY OR RETALIATION. HOW WOULD YOU FEEL IF EVERYONE STOPPED CONSIDERING YOU, BEFORE THEY REPLIED OR RETALIATED TO WHAT YOU HAVE SAID OR DONE? WILL YOU CONSIDER YOUR POSITION MORE CAREFULLY MOVING FORWARD IN THE FUTURE?

THE LAST STAGE IS BEING ON THE RECEIVING END OF INFORMATION COMING IN, UNDERSTANDING YOUR TRIGGERS AND REHEARSING THEM INTO A PLACE OF SILENCE, SO THAT WE DON'T OVERREACT WHEN SOMEONE SAYS SOMETHING THAT IS OUR ISSUE AND NOT THEIRS. YOU CAN DO THIS BY REALISING YOUR TRIGGER, CLOSING YOUR EYES , THEN YOU RUN THE SCENARIO THAT CAUSED THE TRIGGER TO HAVE A DIFFERENT ENDING OF YOUR CHOICE, DO THIS THREE TIMES OR MORE UNTIL YOUR TRIGGER IS SILENCED. THEN THERE IS THE BACKWARDS STEP (YEP! MORE QUESTIONS!) ASKING SOMEONE'S INTENTIONS, AS TO WHAT THEY SAID/DID, IN ORDER TO PROCESS YOUR FEELINGS, BEFORE YOU ENGAGE IN ANY ACT, THIS MAKES SURE THAT THEY KNOW THAT WHAT'S BEEN SAID OR DONE, THAT YOU ARE NOT FULLY HAPPY, THAT IT HASN'T BEEN AN UNCONSCIOUS BEHAVIOUR ON THEIR PART AND THAT YOU ARE WILLING TO UNDERSTAND. PERHAPS YOU MISUNDERSTOOD WHAT THEY SAID OR THEIR INTENTIONS? CAN YOU SEE THE IMPORTANCE OF ASKING QUESTIONS? WHICH PIVOTAL STAGES IN YOUR LIFE, DO YOU FEEL YOU COULD HAVE MADE LIFE EASIER FOR YOURSELF AND OTHERS IF YOU HAD ASKED QUESTIONS AND USED THE COMMUNICATION GUIDELINES?

WHY DO FIGHTS BEGIN? IS IT ALWAYS YOU THAT IS THE VICTIM? COULD IT BE TRIGGERS THAT YOU NEED TO WORK ON? OR COMMUNICATION GUIDELINES THAT YOU COULD USE? OR EVEN THAT YOU NEED TO MOVE ON FROM THE RELATIONSHIP?

ARE YOU ALWAYS CAUSING FIGHTS? WHAT TRIGGERS YOU? HOW WOULD YOU RATHER THESE CONVERSATIONS LOOKED IN FUTURE?

NOW, YOU SHOULD PROBABLY SEE THAT ALL YOU CAN CONTROL IN THIS LIFE IS YOU, YOUR BEHAVIOURS, YOUR REACTIONS AND YOUR THOUGHTS. THIS IS SELF SOVEREIGNTY!!! NOBODY ELSE ON THIS EARTH SHOULD EVER, EVER HAVE CONTROL OVER THIS! IF THEY DO, ITS BECAUSE YOU HAVE GIVEN IT AWAY OR YOU HAVE BEEN COERCED INTO GIVING YOUR SOVEREIGNTY AWAY. DO YOU REALISE WHEN YOU DO THIS? HOW ARE YOU GOING TO START TAKING YOUR SOVEREIGNTY BACK TODAY? WHO DO YOU NEED TO FORGIVE? WHO DO YOU NEED TO APOLOGISE TO, TO BE FORGIVEN?

THE LAST CHAPTER IN THIS BOOK, WILL TIE ALL CHAPTERS TOGETHER AND GIVE YOU A QR CODE AND WEBSITE, THAT WILL TAKE YOU TO YOUR FIRST STEP OF KNOWING WHO YOU ARE, HOW YOU ARE SEEN, HOW YOU DEAL WITH OR ACTION TASKS AND CONVERSATIONS, BUT ALSO... HOW YOU CAN FIND OUT THE BASICS OF OTHERS AND HOW YOU CAN INTERACT WITH THEM! PLEASE DON'T SKIP TO THE END, AS THERE ARE PLENTY MORE REALISATIONS TO COME, BEFORE YOU BEGIN THIS NEW JOURNEY OF TAKING YOUR POWER BACK!

ALL THIS TALK ABOUT WHO YOU ARE IN YOUR SOUL LEADS TO ANOTHER HUGE AREA...

CHAPTER 12: SPIRITUALITY

THIS CHAPTER IS GOING TO TAKE A FEW TWISTS AND TURNS... MANY PEOPLE BELIEVE SPIRITUALITY TO BE BUYING A FEW CRYSTALS, MEDITATING AND PRETENDING TO LOVE OTHERS WHEN THEY DON'T EVEN LIKE THEMSELVES.

WHAT IS SPIRITUALITY? WHAT IS YOUR DEFINITION?

SPIRITUALITY TO ME IS ABOUT THE MEANING OF LIFE, LOOKING PAST MATERIAL THINGS, FEELING MORE AND MOST OF ALL LIVING A LIFE OF

LOVE. IT'S ABOUT MORE THAN SELF... LOOKING AT THE MUCH BIGGER ENERGY FIELD THAN WHAT IS INSIDE OUR BODY, WORKING WITH THE RIGHT AND JUST... WE ARE ALL ENERGY!!

THERE WILL BE SOME SCIENCE IN THERE TOO BUT NATURE IS MEASURED BY SCIENCE AND WHEN SOMETHING IS CREATED, IT CAN USUALLY BE TRACED BACK TO NATURE AT SOME POINT, IE: THE PERSON WHO CREATED IT WAS CREATED BY NATURE.

REMEMBER JOHN LENHART, THE MAN I MENTIONED PREVIOUSLY WHO HAS A NON-CONTRADICTORY MODEL FOR THE MIND AND BRAIN? WHEN HE DEVELOPED THE MODEL HE REALISED ALL THE EXPERTS HAVE THE WRONG MODEL FOR THE BRAIN! EVERYONE THINKS THAT WE DO EVERYTHING WITH OUR CONSCIOUS BRAIN BECAUSE THAT IS THE PART OF OUR BRAIN WE CONTROL. IT TURNS OUT, THIS IS ONLY 10% OF OUR BRAIN.

ACTUALLY, ALL OUR BEHAVIOUR AND ENERGY IS IN OUR UNCONSCIOUS BRAIN. THE REASON PEOPLE ARE SUFFERING MENTALLY AND EMOTIONALLY AT A HIGHER RATE TODAY IS THAT EXPERTS ARE ENCOURAGING PEOPLE TO DO EVERYTHING THROUGH THIS 10% AND THEIR UNCONSCIOUS BRAIN IS FIGHTING THEM BY MAKING THEM FEEL SICKER. PEOPLE MAY WIN IN THE SHORT TERM, HOWEVER, IT ONLY RESULTS IN A MASSIVE CRASH IN THE LONG TERM.

DON'T BELIEVE THAT THE UNCONSCIOUS IS MORE THAN NINE TIMES MORE POWERFUL THAN THE CONSCIOUS AT MAKING US SICK OR HEALTHY? HOW DO YOU EXPLAIN THE PLACEBO EFFECT? DO YOU REALISE THAT FOR US TO BELIEVE A MEDICATION WORKS WE HAVE TO TRICK HALF OF THE PEOPLE INTO THINKING THAT THEY ARE GETTING THE MEDICATION AND THEY HAVE TO REMAIN ILL? WHY? BECAUSE THE UNCONSCIOUS BRAIN WILL HEAL US IF IT IS CONVINCED THAT WE ARE DOING SOMETHING TO TRY TO BE HEALED, WE CREATE THE PROGRAM AND THE BODY IS SELF HEALING AS WELL AS BEING ABLE TO THINK OURSELVES UNWELL!

FURTHERMORE, OUR MIND THAT IS IN CONTROL OF OUR TANGIBLE BRAIN IS INTANGIBLE. YOU ARE NOT YOUR BRAIN. YOU ARE YOUR MIND/SOUL WHICH IS THE INTANGIBLE DRIVER OF YOUR BRAIN!

IF I WERE TO ASK YOU WHAT GIVES YOU THE ENERGY TO LIVE, WHAT WOULD YOU SAY? WE DON'T NEED BATTERIES, WE DON'T CHARGE OURSELVES UP AT AN ELECTRICAL SOCKET (NOT ADVISABLE) AND FOOD IS THE FUEL THAT THE MYSTICAL ENERGY IN OUR BODY BURNS, THEREFORE IS NOT WHAT KEEPS US ALIVE... THOUGHTS ARE ENERGY, THEY CAN BE MEASURED IN FREQUENCIES, WHAT WE SEE, HEAR OR TOUCH ARE ALL FREQUENCIES THAT ARE SENT TO OUR BRAIN!! IT'S CRAZY!! WE ARE NOT TAUGHT ANY OF THIS THROUGH EDUCATION WHILE WE ARE GROWING UP. WHY IS THIS? IN FACT, I JUST SHOWED YOU WE ARE TAUGHT THE OPPOSITE!

DO YOU BELIEVE, THAT IF WE WERE TAUGHT WHO WE ARE PROPERLY FROM OUR EARLY YEARS, WE COULD BE SO MUCH MORE AND LIVE A LIFE WITH MORE LOVE AND ABUNDANCE?

I'M GOING TO TOUCH ON A FEW SUBJECTS THAT I LINK TO SPIRITUALITY AND WHAT I BELIEVE OTHER PEOPLE LINK TO SPIRITUALITY, THROUGH MY PRACTICES AND READING.

CRYSTALS:

I KNOW PLENTY PEOPLE WHO BELIEVE HAVING CRYSTALS ON TOP OF THEIR DRESSER MAKES THEM SPIRITUAL AND THAT WEARING A BRACELET FROM A CHEAP ONLINE STORE THAT THEY ONLY PAID POSTAGE FOR, WILL PROTECT THEM FROM SPIRITUAL ATTACKS AND HARM. THIS, IN MY BELIEF IS A LOT OF NONSENSE, GOOD FOR GIVING PEOPLE THE PLACEBO EFFECT, LIKE BELIEVING SOMETHING THAT ISN'T THERE AND GOOD TO FOLLOW TRENDS. THE AMOUNT OF PEOPLE WHO SAY "I'M REALLY SPIRITUAL" AND EXPLAIN THAT THEY GOT ALL OF THESE COOL STONES, THAT THEY KNOW NOTHING ABOUT, APART FROM THE FACT THEY ARE PRETTY!

CRYSTAL HEALING ON THE OTHER HAND, IS A THING... THERE IS NO SCIENTIFIC EVIDENCE TO SAY THAT IT ACTUALLY WORKS, BUT A LOT OF WHAT WE DO IN LIFE IS A PLACEBO... LIKE, BELIEVING WE CAN THINK OF SOMETHING THAT ISN'T THERE AND BECOME FEARFUL OF IT. WE CAN TAKE A TABLET, WITH LOTS OF CHEMICAL INGREDIENTS TO MAKE US 'FEEL BETTER' AND ALL THE INGREDIENTS CAN CANCEL EACH OTHER OUT SO THAT WE FEEL HEALED... PLACEBO!

OUR BODIES CAN HEAL THEMSELVES WITH SIGNALS FROM OUR BRAIN, SO IF PEOPLE BELIEVE CRYSTALS WORK FOR THEM, WHO ARE WE TO QUESTION CRYSTAL HEALING? CRYSTAL HEALING DOES NOT MAKE YOU SPIRITUAL, IF YOU LIVE THE WRONG LIFE. IT IS A HOLISTIC PRACTICE AND WHO KNOWS, THE CRYSTALS MIGHT EVEN HAVE SOME MAGICAL POWERS... HAVE YOU GOT AN OPEN ENOUGH MIND TO TRY?

MEDITATION:

"I'M SPIRITUAL BECAUSE I LIKE TO MEDITATE". THIS IS ANOTHER CRACKER I HAVE HEARD THROUGH MY JOURNEY OF LIFE! MEDITATION IS GREAT AND I GENUINELY PRACTICE IT BUT I DON'T BELIEVE IT MAKES ME SPIRITUAL.

VARIOUS TESTS OF FREQUENCY AND OTHER METHODS SHOW THAT THERE CANNOT BE NO ACTIVITY IN THE BRAIN, UNLESS YOU ARE DEAD!

SO WHY MEDITATE? WHY SIT IN PEACE? WHY TRY TO SWITCH OFF?

BEING PRESENT ALLOWS ANY OF US TO FEEL MORE GROUNDED, NOT OVERTHINKING THE PAST (DEPRESSION) OR WORRYING ABOUT THE FUTURE (ANXIETY). EVERY TIME WE MEDITATE, WE CLEAR OUR BRAIN AND SWITCH OFF FROM EXTERNAL INFLUENCES, WHICH ARE DISTRACTIONS. ANOTHER GREAT FACT TO UNDERSTAND IS: WHEN WE ARE DOING SOMETHING, WE ARE ALWAYS IN THE PRESENT, EVEN IF OUR THOUGHTS ARE NOT. YOU CANNOT PRACTICE BEING PRESENT BECAUSE

YOU ALWAYS ARE.

WHAT ARE WE REALLY DOING WHEN WE MEDITATE?

WE ARE BECOMING ONE WITH OUR BREATH BY FOCUSING OUR CONSCIOUS BRAIN FROM THE MADNESS OF EVERYDAY LIFE TO ONE INTANGIBLE THOUGHT; WE ARE HAVING 'ME TIME' WITH NO DISTRACTIONS. IT REALLY IS AN AMAZING PROCESS; THE BRAIN IS ESSENTIALLY A MUSCLE AND TRAINING IT TO FOCUS ON CUE IS A TALENT BUT TAKES PRACTICE, THE SAME AS ALSO TEACHING OURSELVES TO FOCUS ON ANYTHING OTHER THAN A SPECIFIC THOUGHT ON CUE.

DO WE NEED TO BE SPIRITUAL TO MEDITATE AND WE NEED TO MEDITATE TO BE SPIRITUAL? THE ANSWER IS WHAT YOU WISH IT TO BE. I BELIEVE THAT IT IS A GOOD, HEALTHY PRACTICE FOR ANY HUMAN TO SWITCH OFF FROM TANGIBLE DISTRACTIONS AND SWITCH FOCUS TO THE INTANGIBLE ENERGY/SOURCE. WE CAN'T TURN OUR BRAIN OFF BUT WE CAN QUIET OUR THOUGHTS AND WHEN PRACTICED REGULARLY, ALLOWS YOU TO BE PRESENT MORE OFTEN AND ABLE TO SWITCH OFF FROM DISTRACTIONS MORE EASILY.

ENERGY HEALING:

MOST PEOPLE WHO UNDERSTAND THE ENERGY OF THE HUMAN BODY, BEING AN EMPATH OR ARE TRAINED IN HOLISTIC PRACTICES, WILL KNOW THAT THE BODY HAS ITS OWN MAGNETIC FIELD. WE ARE NOT TAUGHT THIS GROWING UP EITHER AND THIS CAUSES MUCH CONFUSION TO PHYSICAL, MENTAL AND SPIRITUAL HEALTH AS WE TRANSITION FROM CHILD TO ADULT. WE CAN REALLY TRANSFER ENERGY ON TO OTHERS, AS WE LIVE ON A FREQUENCY/VIBRATION.

RECENTLY, RESEARCH IS SHOWING THAT HUMANS SYNC THEIR THOUGHT PROCESSES (ENERGY) TO OTHER HUMANS WHO ARE PHYSICALLY PRESENT. ARE YOU ABLE TO BRING PEOPLE UP TO YOUR THOUGHT

PROCESS OR DO YOU FIND YOURSELF SINKING DOWN TO THE THOUGHT PROCESSES OF OTHERS?

IMAGINE HOW MANY PEOPLE WHO FEEL SAD AND LOW, ARE ACTUALLY BEING DRAINED AND BROUGHT DOWN WITH SOMEONE ELSE'S ENERGY AND THERE IS NOTHING WRONG WITH THEM PERSONALLY... SPIRITUALITY CALLS IT VIBES, SCIENCE CALLS IT TRANSFERENCE. IMAGINE, LIVING ON A LOW FREQUENCY/VIBRATION CAUSED OUR IMMUNE SYSTEM TO BECOME WEAK AND OUR BODIES TO BE SUSCEPTIBLE TO PAIN AND DISCOMFORT... DIS-EASE CAUSES DISEASE!

I PRACTICE ENERGY HEALING; ANYONE WHO CAN BRING OTHERS UP TO THEIR LEVEL CAN DO IT! HOWEVER... IF A PERSON WAS NOT IN BALANCE WITH THEIR ENERGY, WOULD THIS BE BENEFICIAL TO A CLIENT? IF AN ENERGY HEALER DIDN'T KNOW THAT THEY TAKE ON THE CLIENT'S ENERGY, IT WOULD CAUSE THEM DISRUPTION TO THEIR LIVES TOO.. OR THE OPPOSITE, A SO-CALLED 'HEALER' CAN TRANSFER THEIR BAD SH*T TO CLIENTS WHEN OFF BALANCE. ITS SO SO IMPORTANT TO VIBE A CLIENT OR A PRACTITIONER.   I PERSONALLY DO NOT TRUST MANY PEOPLE WITH MY ENERGY AND PRACTICE HEALING MYSELF WITH INTENTION.

SOME PEOPLE ARE NATURALLY ON A HIGHER VIBRATION AND HAVE MORE HEALING QUALITIES THAT HAVE BEEN PASSED DOWN THROUGH GENERATIONS OR BY THEM HAVING A MORE BALANCED LIFE. EVEN JUST BEING IN THEIR SPACE CAN ALLEVIATE ANY LOW MOOD! HAVE YOU EVER CONSIDERED ENERGY HEALING FOR YOURSELF? HOW WOULD YOU KNOW THE RIGHT PRACTITIONER TO GO TO? AN APPLE CAN LOOK SHINY ON THE OUTSIDE AND BE ROTTEN AT THE CORE, BE CAREFUL!

I WILL ASK THE SAME QUESTION AGAIN... DOES ENERGY HEALING MAKE YOU SPIRITUAL? IS THIS A SOMETHING WE CAN ALL DO FOR EACH OTHER WITH INTENTION? ENSURING WE ARE ALL CONNECTED AND NOT DIVIDED? WE CAN ACTUALLY DO IT JUST BY TALKING IN CLOSE PROXIMITY OF ANOTHER, SO BE CAREFUL WHAT YOU ARE TALKING ABOUT!

I BELIEVE, LIKE I DO WITH MEDITATION, THAT ENERGY HEALING IS A

HOLISTIC PRACTICE, IT IS HEALTHY FOR PEOPLE'S INTERACTIONS TO DO IT BUT IT DOES NOT MAKE US SPIRITUAL PER SE. MORE STUDY INTO THE ENERGY OF THE HUMAN BODY IS NECESSARY FOR ALL PEOPLE. ENERGY HEALING IS USUALLY DONE WITH THE HEALING MUSIC FREQUENCY I MENTIONED IN THE CHAPTER ON MOVIES AND MUSIC. NOTHING STOPPING YOU GETTING INVOLVED IN COMING TOGETHER WITH OTHERS AND LEARNING A HOLISTIC PRACTICE. IT MEANS YOU CAN ONE DAY, HELP OTHERS IN YOUR OWN WAY THAT YOU HAVE LEARNED AND DEVELOPED AND THAT IS PURPOSE. WHAT WOULD STOP YOU? WHY WOULDN'T YOU WANT TO HELP OTHERS?

SPIRITUAL WARFARE:

THERE HAS BEEN A SPIRITUAL WAR GOING ON FOR A LONG, LONG TIME AND I BELIEVE IT IS NOW AT IT'S PEAK! REGARDLESS OF RELIGIOUS BELIEF, DARK VS LIGHT IS A REAL THING. I BELIEVE SPIRITUAL WARFARE IS NOT ABOUT CASTING SPELLS ON ONE ANOTHER AGAINST OUR WILL, BUT BREAKING DOWN THE HUMAN SPIRIT, TO THE POINT THAT PEOPLE ARE LOST, WEAK AND EASILY CONTROLLED BECAUSE THEY ARE DIVIDED. SPIRITS CAN'T DO ANYTHING TO YOU OTHER THAN INFLUENCE THE WAY YOU THINK WHICH LOWERS YOUR ENERGY. THAT IS SPIRITUAL WARFARE. HOW IS THIS DIFFERENT FROM WHAT PEOPLE CAN DO TO YOU? I HOPE YOU HAVE SEEN FROM THE PREVIOUS CHAPTERS, IT ISN'T ANY DIFFERENT.

CAN YOU IMAGINE A WORLD WHERE MOST PEOPLE LOVE OTHERS AND EVERYTHING IS SHARED? BEAUTIFUL ISN'T IT? COMPARE THAT THOUGHT TO WHAT YOU SEE AROUND ABOUT YOU DAILY… WHAT LOOKS BETTER? WHAT CAN YOU DO TO ADD SOMETHING TO CHANGING THIS?

WE WERE BROUGHT INTO THIS WORLD AS A TINY BABY THAT HAS TO LEARN EVERYTHING FROM SCRATCH. THE ONLY THING WE DON'T HAVE TO LEARN, IS HOW TO LOVE AND HOW TO GROW AS THOSE ARE THE TWO MOST NATURAL EXPERIENCES TO US AS HUMAN BEINGS NEXT TO

BREATHING AND FEEDING. THIS IS GREATLY AFFECTED AND, IN SOME CASES, DESTROYED DURING THE GROWING-UP PROCESS. LIFE IS MEANT TO BE SIMPLE, YET THERE ARE MANY UNNECESSARY OBSTACLES PUT IN OUR WAY, DUE TO HOW THE WORLD IS RUN. WHY WOULD WE NOT CREATE OUR OWN WORLD? IF WE CAUSE NO HARM TO ANY MAN, WOMAN OR CHILD... OR THEIR PROPERTY, WE ARE FREE TO LIVE. THE PROGRAMMING OF FEAR HOLDS US BACK BY LOWERING OUR ENERGY, THIS STEMS FROM CHILDHOOD. WHAT SCARES YOU? WHAT WOULD YOU PUT A STOP TO WITH THE CURRENT GOVERNMENT AND OTHER CORPORATIONS IF YOU COULD? WHAT WOULD YOU IMPLEMENT? WHAT IS LIGHT? WHAT IS DARK?

LOVE, GROWTH, HAPPINESS, JOY AND TOGETHERNESS ARE LIGHT. HATE, ABUSE, CHEATING AND ADDICTION ARE DARK. THERE ARE MANY MORE, I AM SURE YOU GET THE PICTURE. FOR THE PURPOSE OF THIS CHAPTER, I'D JUST LIKE TO ASK, WHAT DO YOU SEE AND HEAR MOST OF, DARK OR LIGHT? WHERE DO YOU SEE AND HEAR IT? TV, ONLINE, RADIO?

WHATEVER WE SEE, HEAR AND SPEAK, ACTUALLY PROGRAMS OUR UNCONSCIOUS BRAIN AND BECOMES THE WAY WE LIVE OUR LIVES. WHO CONTROLS THE TV, THE INTERNET AND THE RADIO? REMEMBER THE PREVIOUS CHAPTERS AND REALLY ASK YOURSELF, ARE WE PLAYING INTO THE HANDS OF THE DARK? EVEN THOUGH THE TEMPTATION, FORGETTING ABOUT THE LIGHT, IS DIVIDING HUMANITY TO AN ALMOST IRREPARABLE STATE, THERE IS STILL TIME TO CHANGE IT!!!

SPIRITUALITY... WHAT DO YOU THINK IT IS NOW?

I DON'T THINK IT IS RELIGION. YOUR RELIGION IS YOUR ANSWER TO THE THREE QUESTIONS EVERYONE'S UNCONSCIOUS WANTS ANSWERS TO:

1. WHY AM I HERE?

2. WHAT AM I GOING TO DO WHILE I'M HERE?

3. WHAT HAPPENS AFTER I LEAVE HERE?

RELIGION IS SOMEONE ELSE'S PLAN. I BELIEVE SPIRITUALITY IS TRUTH (THE GREATEST PLAN) WHICH IS A WAY OF LIFE AND A NEVER ENDING JOURNEY, NO MATTER YOUR RELIGION OR BELIEFS. A LIFE OF LOVE, KINDNESS AND MOST IMPORTANTLY, BEING AT ONE WITH OURSELVES THROUGH UNDERSTANDING. WHEN WE ARE BALANCED AND AT ONE WITH OURSELVES, ONLY THEN CAN WE REALLY LOVE OTHERS THE WAY THAT THEY NEED AND DESERVE! WE CAN ONLY GIVE WHEN WE ARE FULL AND THE POWERS THAT BE IN THIS WORLD UNDERSTAND THIS; THIS IS WHY SO MANY PEOPLE ARE RUNNING ON EMPTY, TRYING TO GIVE THEIR LAST, JUST FOR SOMEONE TO LOVE THEM. HOWEVER, YOU CAN'T GIVE SOMETHING THAT YOU DON'T FIRST HAVE!

CAN YOU BE HAPPY WITH NOTHING? DO YOU ACCEPT YOURSELF ENOUGH TO APPRECIATE HOW AMAZING YOU ARE? ARE YOU KIND AND HELP AS MANY PEOPLE AS YOU CAN ON YOUR JOURNEY? IF YOU ANSWERED YES TO ALL OF THESE QUESTIONS, IT'S A GOOD START!

YOU CAN LITERALLY BE HAPPY IF YOU CHOOSE TO BE, IF YOU REALISE YOU ARE THE ONLY ONE THAT CAN MAKE YOU HAPPY. YOU DON'T NEED TO SUCCUMB TO THIS SPIRITUAL WAR, YOU CAN FORGET WHAT THE SO-CALLED WORLD LEADERS AND NEWS IS SAYING AND LIVE A LIFE SO FREE, THAT ONLY WHAT YOU CHOOSE WILL BE IN YOUR LIFE. HOW DOES THAT SOUND? WHEN WILL YOU BEGIN TO LIVE YOUR TRUTH?

TRUTH IS SPIRITUALITY, TRUTH IS THE LIGHT.

CHAPTER 13: DRUGS

WHAT IS A DRUG? I BELIEVE IT TO BE A SUBSTANCE THAT WE USE TO ALTER OUR WAY OF FEELING, THINKING, LIVING AND WHAT WE SEE, NOT

NECESSARILY WHAT'S CLASSED AS LEGAL OR ILLEGAL.

PEOPLE USE DRUGS FOR ALL TYPES OF REASONS. THE MOST COMMON REASON, IN MY BELIEF, IS HABIT, WHICH MEANS PEOPLE DON'T EVEN KNOW WHY THEY ARE TAKING THE DRUG! THEY MAY HAVE BEGUN USING BECAUSE DRUGS CAN TAKE PEOPLE AWAY FROM THEIR LIVES FOR A MINUTE TO A FEW HOURS, BUT IT SEEMS TO END UP TAKING THEM AWAY FROM A FEW DAYS BINGE TO A LIFETIME OF LIVING A PERMANENT SUBSTANCE FILLED EXISTENCE.

THE LAWS MADE BY THE ESTABLISHMENT OF OUR COUNTRIES AND STATES, DEEMS MOST DRUGS ILLEGAL, THERE ARE EXCEPTIONS MADE FOR SOME SUBSTANCES IN CERTAIN COUNTRIES AND STATES AROUND THE WORLD AND THERE ARE SCIENTISTS AND ACTIVIST GROUPS CRYING OUT FOR THE OTHERS TO BE LEGALISED.

THE LIKES OF AYAHUASCA AND DMT HAVE HAD MAJOR RESULTS IN HELPING DEPRESSION, ANXIETY, ADDICTION AND RAISING LONG TERM HAPPINESS (SEROTONIN LEVELS) AND SCIENTISTS ARE LOOKING INTO MICRODOSING PSILOCYBIN MUSHROOMS AND OTHER SUBSTANCES TO ALLEVIATE TRAUMA AND OTHER SYMPTOMS OF LIFE FROM PEOPLE'S THOUGHTS AND BODY. AYAHUASCA AND DMT ARE NOT FOR THE FAINT HEARTED, I CAN SPEAK FROM EXPERIENCE THAT THESE GIVE US THE ANSWERS WE SEEK. I WILL TALK MORE ABOUT THIS IN THE MEDICINE CHAPTER AS I DON'T BELIEVE THESE ARE DRUGS WHEN USED IN CEREMONIAL OR MEDICINAL INSTANCES, WHICH ARE NOT PARTY OR CASUAL SETTINGS.

MY DEFINITION OF A DRUG FEELS TRUE TO ME AND I AM SURE THERE ARE PEOPLE WITH OTHER DEFINITIONS AND THAT IS GREAT! ON A PERSONAL LEVEL, TAKING SUBSTANCES ARE USUALLY FOR THE REASONS MENTIONED ABOVE. WHAT COULD THE OTHER REASONS BE FOR GROUPS/COLLECTIVES?

UNFORTUNATELY, DRUGS/SUBSTANCES ARE USED FOR CONTROL PURPOSES... THEY MAKE THE ESTABLISHMENT TRILLIONS! THERE ARE

DIFFERENT TYPES OF HUMAN BEHAVIOURS, FOR THIS TOPIC, I'M GOING TO SPLIT THEM IN TO CONFORMISTS AND NONCONFORMISTS, I'LL EXPLAIN IN SHORT.

CONFORMISTS: MOST DO NOT TAKE SUBSTANCES THAT ARE DEEMED ILLEGAL, LOOK DOWN ON OTHER PEOPLE WHO DO, THESE PEOPLE MIGHT WORK FOR THE ESTABLISHMENT/SYSTEM OR ARE SCARED OF BEING INCARCERATED AND RUN-INS WITH THE LAW.

NON-CONCORMISTS: WILL TAKE SUBSTANCES IF THEY WISH, LOOK AT PEOPLE TAKING SUBSTANCES AS 'JUST A THING', IF THEY WORK FOR THE ESTABLISHMENT/SYSTEM... THEY WILL BE DOING SO TO SERVE THEMSELVES AND NOT THE RULES, CAN BE FEARFUL OF RUN-INS WITH THE LAW OR BEING INCARCERATED BUT WILL TAKE THE CHANCE! THERE IS THAT CHANCE, THEY HAVE ABSOLUTELY NO REGARD FOR THE SYSTEM.

I IMAGINE, WE WILL ALL KNOW PEOPLE WHO DO, OR HAVE DONE DRUGS AT SOME POINT AT DIFFERENT STAGES OF THEIR LIVES. IT MIGHT HAVE BEEN A HARD TIME OR JUST BEING EXPERIMENTAL.

HOW CAN DRUGS/SUBSTANCES CONTROL MASSES?

PEOPLE WHO TAKE SUBSTANCES HABITUALLY ARE CALLED ADDICTS AND ARE DEEMED TO BE SICK. THEY WILL BELIEVE THEY ARE SICK BECAUSE THEY WERE TOLD BY 'A PROFESSIONAL' SO THAT THEY WILL NEED MEDICAL HELP (FUNDING BIG PHARMA). MY TRUTH IN THE MATTER IS THAT THE HUMAN BRAIN IS SO POWERFUL AND HABITUAL BEHAVIOURS CAN BE CHANGED BY SELF, THROUGH A WEANING PROCESS IN MY HUMBLE BELIEF. WHAT DO YOU BELIEVE? IF PEOPLE UNDERSTOOD HOW POWERFUL THEIR MIND IS, THEY COULD LITERALLY CHANGE THEIR LIFE, FREQUENCY AND HABITS TO LIVE A MORE FRUITFUL LIFE. INSTEAD, THEY ARE MADE TO FEEL LIKE THEY ARE WORTHLESS AND THAT WHAT THEY ARE DOING IS BAD, WRONG, WASTEFUL OR DEGRADING TO SELF OR SOCIETY. WHY WOULD THEY THINK THEY COULD STOP?

IMAGINE FOR A SECOND... PEOPLE WERE ENCOURAGED TO FEEL

POWERFUL AND NOT RELIANT ON THE SUBSTANCES OR THE SYSTEM, DO YOU BELIEVE THEIR HABITS WOULD CHANGE? DO YOU BELIEVE SOMEONE WHO IS DOWN ON THEIR LUCK AND TURN TO USING SUBSTANCES ARE REALLY THAT BAD TO BE LABELLED AN ADDICT OR CRIMINAL? PEOPLE ARE ADDICTED TO THE RELEASING OF BRAIN CHEMICALS THAT THE SUBSTANCES ALLOW THEM TO DO, NOT THE SUBSTANCES THEY ARE USING. THEY ARE THE GATEWAY TO FEEL GOOD!

WITHOUT USING NAMES OF GOVT/SYSTEM ENTITIES, SOME KNOW THAT SUBSTANCES/DRUGS ARE USED TO CONTROL THE PEOPLE. THIS CAN BE: LETTING THEM DEAL OR USE THEM IN ORDER TO SET THEM UP AND FINING THEM... THEN MAKING THE STATE MONEY. IT COULD BE THE FACT THAT MANY PEOPLE BECOME SICK BECAUSE OF USAGE AND END UP ON MEDICATION THAT MAKES BIG PHARMA MONEY. DO YOU BELIEVE A PILL CAN FIX SOMEONE'S SELF ESTEEM OR HEAL THEM FROM MENTAL AND EMOTIONAL TRAUMA?

HOW WOULD YOU FEEL ABOUT DRUGS, IF IT WEREN'T DRUMMED INTO YOU THAT THEY ARE ILLEGAL AND BAD? WOULD YOU FEEL DIFFERENTLY? MANY DRUGS/SUBSTANCES COME FROM PLANTS THAT ARE NATURALLY GROWN ON THIS PLANET. DO YOU BELIEVE ANY HUMAN, NO MORE HUMAN THAN YOU OR I, HAS THE RIGHT TO BAN THESE? COULD THERE BE ANOTHER USE FOR THEM, OTHER THAN RECREATIONAL? THERE IS A DEBATE ON THE CONSEQUENCES AND POSSIBILITIES OF LEGALISING CERTAIN DRUGS ALL OVER THE WORLD, MANY BELIEVE CRIME WOULD GO DOWN! MAYBE BECAUSE PEOPLE WON'T BE LOCKED UP FOR DOING THEM? MAYBE I'M JUST BEING SILLY, WHAT DO YOU THINK? DRUGS DON'T CAUSE CRIME... PEOPLE DO! ALCOHOL IS ONE OF THE WORST AND IS LEGAL!!

GOING BACK TO THE ESCAPISM THING... I KNEW A GUY, WE'LL CALL HIM ANDY, FOR THE SAKE OF HIS IDENTITY. ANDY HAD A STEADY JOB, A RELATIVELY HIGH INCOME AND A BEAUTIFUL FAMILY. ANDY WORKED HARD AND HIS WIFE AND KIDS WANTED FOR NOTHING! HE CAME HOME ONE DAY, EARLY FROM WORK TO FIND HIS WIFE DOING THE 'BARE BUM BOOGIE' WITH ANOTHER MAN. NATURALLY THE RELATIONSHIP BROKE DOWN AND THEN THE SYSTEM GOT INVOLVED AND GAVE HIS HOUSE TO

HIS WIFE, TOOK HIS KIDS AWAY BECAUSE SHE MADE UP LIES AND SLOWLY BUT SURELY ANDY'S MENTAL HEALTH DETERIORATED VERY QUICKLY.

AS TIME WENT ON, ANDY TURNED TO ALCOHOL TO COPE, HIS WIFE MOVED HER FANCY MAN INTO THE HOUSE WITH HIS KIDS AND HE RECEIVED CONSTANT HASSLE FROM HER. STILL NOT SEEING HIS BEAUTIFUL CHILDREN BECAUSE OF THE SPITE FROM HIS WIFE, HE WENT OFF THE RAILS. HE TRIED COCAINE FOR THE FIRST TIME. FOR THE FIRST TIME IN A LONG TIME, ANDY FELT FREE. HE BEGAN TO CHASE THIS FEELING... THIS IS WHERE THINGS GOT WORSE! STARTED DOING COCAINE AT WORK AND LOST HIS JOB, GOT INTO DEBT, LOST HIS HOUSE AND ENDED UP ON THE STREETS.

ANDY WAS A MAN THAT WAS RESPECTED BY HIS FAMILY, HIS PEERS AND THE MAJORITY OF PEOPLE HE MET AND NOW HE HAD NOTHING! GRANTED IT WAS A CHOICE TO BEGIN WITH, WHERE DID THE DESPERATION COME FROM? WAS IT THE SITUATION OF HIS WIFE OR WAS IT THE UNFAIR DECISION BY THE SYSTEM/ESTABLISHMENT THAT MADE HIM FEEL POWERLESS?

I, ALONG WITH HUNDREDS OF OTHERS CAN VOUCH FOR ANDY AND SAY HE WAS A STAND-UP HUMAN BEING THAT WAS TREATED UNFAIRLY AND DID NOT HAVE THE COPING MECHANISMS TO DEAL WITH THE SITUATION. DO YOU BELIEVE, FROM WHAT YOU HAVE JUST READ, THAT HE IS A BAD PERSON OR CRIMINAL?

PROGRAMMING FROM GROWING UP AND WATCHING TV, NEWS OR LISTENING TO OTHERS, TELLS US THAT ALCOHOL AND/OR DRUGS IS THE FIRST THING TO DO DURING OR AFTER A CRISIS... IS IT REALLY? LOSING SENSE OF SELF, LOSING VISION OR LOSING STRUCTURE CAN MAKE EVERY SITUATION MUCH WORSE. IT'S NOT THE DRUG, IT'S THE ADDICTION, OR BETTER YET, IT IS THE LACK OF BEING ABLE TO FIX THEMSELVES ONCE THEY BEGIN USING THE SUBSTANCE.

ANDY, AFTER A YEAR, MANAGED TO GET HIMSELF BACK ON THE STRAIGHT AND NARROW AND EVERYTHING WAS SORTED. HE HIT THE BOTTOM AND

THERE WAS NO OTHER WAY BUT UP. ANDY'S KIDS WERE OLD ENOUGH TO MAKE THEIR OWN DECISION AND THEY ENDED UP STAYING WITH HIM REGULARLY.

HOW DO YOU FEEL ABOUT DRUGS/SUBSTANCES AFTER READING THIS CHAPTER? WILL YOU GIVE COMPASSION FOR A SECOND TO PEOPLE YOU SEE AND CONSIDER WHAT THEY ARE TRYING TO ESCAPE FROM? MAYBE EVEN ASK THEM FROM A PLACE OF COMPASSION? WOULD YOU BE ABLE TO HELP THEM UNDERSTAND HOW POWERFUL THEY REALLY ARE BY RAISING THE ENERGY OF THEIR THOUGHT PROCESS?

CHAPTER 14: MEDICINE

THIS CHAPTER IS GOING TO GO IN VERY DIFFERENT DIRECTIONS, MAKE SURE YOU ARE COMFORTABLE! FROM HOLISTIC TO MANUFACTURED MEDICINE... EVEN DROPPING SOME BOMBSHELLS THAT MIGHT TRIGGER OR MAKE YOU FEEL UNCOMFORTABLE. THE INTENTION IS FOR YOU TO DO YOUR OWN RESEARCH, NOT TAKE WHAT I SAY AS GOSPEL AND KNOW HALF THE STORY! I ALSO DO NOT WANT ANYONE TO FEEL BAD.

WHAT IS YOUR DEFINITION OF MEDICINE?

IS IT SOMETHING THAT MAKES YOU FEEL BETTER? SOMETHING TO HEAL YOU? SOMETHING TO TAKE THE PAIN AWAY? SOMETHING TO HELP YOU DISCOVER YOURSELF? AN AID TO LATCH ON TO?

LET'S START WITH PHARMACEUTICALS!

THESE COME IN TABLETS, CREAMS, LIQUIDS, INOCULATIONS AND SPRAYS. WHO REALLY KNOWS WHAT'S IN THEM AND WHAT THESE DO/HOW THEY

WORK? THE EXPLANATION FOR HOW THESE WORK SEEMS TO CHANGE EVERY FIVE OR SO YEARS. WHO KNOWS HOW YOU ARE GOING TO REACT WHEN YOU TAKE OR ADMINISTER THEM? ONE SYSTEM CONTROLS THE MAKING OF THEM AND CONTROLS THE TEACHING OF A SELECT FEW AS TO HOW TO USE THEM, BASED ON EFFECTS THAT COME IN THE FORM OF AILMENTS, RASHES, PAIN, MENTAL CONDITIONS, NEUROLOGICAL CONDITIONS... SO BASICALLY WE ARE GUINEA PIGS IN A SENSE, NO?

THE COMPANIES MAKING THESE ARE AMONG THE FINANCIALLY RICHEST IN THE WORLD. IF THEY WERE REALLY HELPING, SURELY EVERYONE WOULD BE IN GOOD HEALTH RIGHT? AT THE VERY LEAST, SHOULDN'T THERE BE LESS PEOPLE WHO NEED MEDICATION OVER TIME? THAT MEANS THERE MUST BE SOMETHING CAUSING ALL OF THESE AILMENTS THAT HAVE US BUYING AND TAKING CHEMICALS TO 'GET BETTER'.

SO TO HEAL THE BODY WE NEED MEDICINE RIGHT? HOW ABOUT THE BODY HEALS ITSELF BECAUSE IT'S AN ABSOLUTE MARVELOUS CREATION? IS IT POSSIBLE THAT THE MEDICINE IS PREVENTING THE BODY FROM HEALING ITSELF? SOME PEOPLE DON'T TAKE ANYTHING AND ARE RARELY SICK, FUNNY THAT! THERE ARE PEOPLE WHO ARE LOADED WITH PHARMACEUTICALS AND ARE NEVER FULLY WELL... ALSO FUNNY EH?

THERE ARE A VERY SELECT FEW THAT ACTUALLY KNOW WHAT ALL OF THE SUBSTANCES ACTUALLY DO! DO YOU KNOW OR DO YOU JUST CONSUME, BASED ON THE WORD OF SOMEONE WHO IS BEING PAID TO HAND THEM TO YOU WITHOUT QUESTION, OR DO YOU NOT CARE ENOUGH TO LOOK?

I AM NOT GOING TO GO INTO EVERY MEDICINE OR EFFECTS, HOWEVER, I WILL TOUCH ON A FEW POINTS SO THAT YOU HAVE FOOD FOR THOUGHT AND CAN GO AND RESEARCH. LEARNING IS FUN RIGHT?

MENTAL HEALTH MEDICINE:

SOME OF THESE ARE PLACEBO AND IT'S THE PATIENT'S BELIEFS AND BEHAVIOUR THAT ACTUALLY CAUSES THEM TO FEEL BAD, BECAUSE THEY

DON'T KNOW THEMSELVES AT ESSENCE. SOME BLOCK YOUR SEROTONIN RECEPTORS SO THAT YOU WILL NEVER BE TRULY HAPPY, OTHERS GIVE YOU FAKE HAPPY CHEMICALS SO THAT YOU ARE NUMB OR RELIANT ON THE PHARMACEUTICALS... IT WOULDN'T BE SUCH A BIG BUSINESS IF YOU GOT BETTER WOULD IT? SO IF EVERYONE WAS TO END UP ON A TYPE OF MEDICATION, THEN SOMEONE IS MAKING BILLIONS, ALL THE WHILE THE PEOPLE OF THE WORLD ARE SUPPRESSED.

WHAT ABOUT THE MAN OR WOMAN DIAGNOSING ANOTHER INDIVIDUAL WITH MENTAL ILLNESS... DO THEY KNOW THEMSELVES OR ARE THEY FOLLOWING PROTOCOL WITHOUT QUESTION? DOES THE MAN OR WOMAN DIAGNOSING THE PATIENT/CLIENT KNOW WHO THE PATIENT/CLIENT IS AND HOW THE PROCESS OR SEE SITUATIONS TO DETERMINE IF THEY JUST DON'T KNOW THEMSELVES PROPERLY? IF A PROGRAMMED BRAIN IS NOT SETTLING WITH THE WAY THAT THE BRAIN WAS INTENDED TO BE, THEN THERE WILL BE NO HAPPINESS, AND STRESS, SUICIDE OR EVEN BAD BEHAVIOUR NO? DO YOU REALISE THAT THERE IS A PROCESS FOR HOW TO BEGIN TAKING ANTIDEPRESSANTS BUT THERE IS NO PROCESS FOR HOW TO STOP TAKING THEM?

LET'S BEGIN WITH YOUR DEFINITION FOR 'MENTAL HEALTH'? WHAT IS IT?

THE NON-CONTRADICTORY DEFINITION FOR MENTAL HEALTH IS; UNDERSTANDING HOW TO REPAIR THE THOUGHT PROCESS. IT CAN'T BE TO FIX THE THOUGHT PROCESS AS THAT WOULD ONLY MAKE IT THE SAME AS IT WAS BEFORE IT WAS DAMAGED, MEANING FIXING IS ONLY TEMPORARY. TO REPAIR SOMETHING, MAKES IT STRONGER. HOW CAN WE MAKE THE THOUGHT PROCESS STRONGER??? BY US UNDERSTANDING OUR OWN AND BEING ABLE TO EXPLAIN IT IN WORDS.

THE 'EXPERTS' DEFINE MENTAL HEALTH AS ABSENCE OF NEGATIVE THOUGHTS AND FEELINGS. IS IT POSSIBLE TO NEVER HAVE ANOTHER NEGATIVE THOUGHT OR NEGATIVE FEELING FOR THE REST OF YOUR LIFE? NO! THIS DEFINITION MEANS NO ONE HAS MENTAL HEALTH. THIS IS WHY WE DON'T SEE PROGRESS IN 'MENTAL HEALTH'. IT'S IMPOSSIBLE!

NOTICE, A HEALTHY BODY IS NOT ONE THAT NEVER GETS INJURED; IT IS ONE THAT IS ABLE TO REPAIR ITSELF FROM INJURY. LIKEWISE, 'MENTAL HEALTH' IS WHEN A PERSON IS ABLE TO REPAIR THEIR OWN THOUGHT PROCESS. HOW DOES MEDICATION HELP YOU REPAIR YOUR OWN THOUGHT PROCESS? WILL MEDICATION EVER PROVIDE MENTAL HEALTH?

IMAGINE THERE WERE TEN STAGES TO MENTAL HEALTH, STAGE ONE BEING THE CAUSE THROUGH TO STAGE 10 BEING THE EFFECTS. PSYCHIATRISTS AND PSYCHOLOGISTS ARE GIVEN STAGES THREE TO TEN. THIS MEANS THAT THEIR DIAGNOSIS IS BASED ON A GENERIC WAY OF WORKING, WHEN IN REALITY EVERYONE IS UNIQUE AND DIFFERENT. VERY DIFFICULT TO COMPREHEND, WOULDN'T YOU AGREE? THIS IS ONE OF THE BIGGEST REVELATIONS OF THIS BOOK!

STAGE ONE WOULD BE KNOWING YOUR INTANGIBLE UNIQUENESS (MIND/SOUL) AND STAGE TWO WOULD BE KNOWING HOW YOUR TANGIBLE BRAIN WORKS AND PROCESSES. THE STAGES THREE TO TEN WOULD WORK IF THEY WERE DONE BASED ON THE INFORMATION FROM THESE FIRST TWO STAGES AND APPLIED IN YOUR EVERYDAY LIFE, WORK, INTERACTIONS AND RELATIONSHIPS. SURELY IF THESE WERE ALL FLOWING, THERE WOULD BE NO MENTAL HEALTH ISSUES, UNLESS THERE WAS SOMETHING FROM BIRTH THAT CAN'T BE CHANGED, A MEDICAL SIDE EFFECT/INJURY OR PHYSICAL INJURY.

IN ESSENCE, WE HAVE NOT BEEN PRIVY TO THE INFORMATION AS TO WHO WE ARE, SO WHAT TYPE OR PERCENTAGE OF PEOPLE WOULD BE LIVING THE LIFE THAT IS MEANT FOR THEM? I'VE BEEN LEAD TO BELIEVE ITS AROUND FOUR PERCENT! THAT LEAVES 96% OF PEOPLE EITHER STRUGGLING, ON MEDICATION OR MESSING UP THEIR LIVES WITH TRIAL AND ERROR! IS THAT NOT A TERRIFYING NUMBER? THIS IS WHERE THE ONLY MODEL FOR THE MIND AND BRAIN IN THE WORLD COMES IN HANDY... YOU CAN DO LIFE ON PURPOSE AND FLOW DAILY! IT DOESN'T MEAN LIFE ISN'T HARD SOMETIMES OR YOU DON'T RUN INTO UNWANTED SITUATIONS, IT MAKES YOU REALISE YOU ARE NOT THE SITUATIONS AND YOU CAN STILL GAIN ENERGY BY TAKING ON THE ISSUE IN A WAY UNIQUE TO HOW YOU WERE DESIGNED!

ADJUVANTS

ALL OVER THE WORLD THERE ARE PEOPLE WHO ARE DIVIDED INTO GROUPS OF PEOPLE WHO ARE QUITE HAPPY BEING INOCULATED AND THOSE WHO HAVE RESEARCHED. I AM NOT A PROFESSIONAL IN THE MEDICAL FIELD, I AM A MAN FOR THE PEOPLE OF THIS WORLD AND I WISH EVERYONE TO BE HEALTHY, HAPPY AND IN THE KNOW.

IN 1983 CHILDREN USED TO GET AROUND 8 INOCULATIONS IN THEIR CHILDHOOD, NOW SOME CHILDREN ARE GIVEN 70 PLUS INNOCULATIONS... WHO PROFITS FROM THE SALES? NOT THE PEOPLE, NOT THE DOCTORS, NOT THE SCIENTISTS! AS USUAL, IT'S THE CORPORATIONS! SO AGAIN, WHY WOULD SOMEONE GET INOCULATIONS IF THEY WERE MEANT TO KEEP THEM HEALTHY BUT THEY STILL BECAME ILL OFTEN? IS IT SOME OF THE INGREDIENTS THAT ARE NO LONGER PRESENT AT A LOW LEVEL DUE TO THE NUMBER OF INOCULATIONS? DO THEY DO WHAT THEY SAY ON THE PACKAGING BUT ALSO CAUSE HARM?

THE HUMAN BRAIN AND BODY EACH HAS A CONSCIOUSNESS, HOWEVER THE BRAIN IS THE PART OF THE BODY THAT WORKS WITH BOTH CONSCIOUSNESS AND THOUGHTS, WAVES OF FREQUENCY PASSING THROUGH ALL THE TIME. WHAT IF THE BRAIN WAS BECOMING DAMAGED WITH THE ADJUVANTS, RATHER THAN THE ACTIVE INGREDIENTS? FOR TALKING SAKE, ALUMINIUM AND FORMALDEHYDE ARE BOTH HIGHLY TOXIC AND WOULD KILL IF THESE WERE INGESTED. DO YOU KNOW WHAT THESE ARE? WILL YOU READ ON WITHOUT LOOKING THESE UP AND WHAT THEY DO TO THE BODY? WILL YOU CHOOSE TO SEE HOW TOXIC THESE ARE?

ALUMINIUM IS A NEUROTOXIN AND IS CLASSED AS 'SAFE' (SAFE MEANING NOT INSTANT NOTICABLE HARM) AS AN ADJUVANT AS IT'S IN LEVELS THAT USUALLY DON'T KILL, HOWEVER, THESE LEVELS CAN CAUSE SOME SORT OF BRAIN DAMAGE, NOT NECESSARILY NOTICEABLE BUT WILL STOP THE BRAIN FUNCTIONING 100%. DOES THAT SOUND LIKE SOMETHING YOU'D WANT OR WANT YOU, YOUR FAMILY MEMBERS AND FRIENDS TO HAVE? IT IS ALWAYS A CHOICE AND AS HUMAN BEINGS, WE SHOULD ALWAYS HAVE

THAT CHOICE AND THE REAL TRUTH AS TO WHY A PROVEN POISON IS USED AT ALL. CHECK INGREDIENTS IN EVERYTHING! WHY WOULD YOU ONLY TRUST AND BLINDLY DO?

THE NEXT TWO INGREDIENTS I WISH TO BRING UP WILL SPARK HUGE CONTROVERSY AND INFORMATION SHOULD BE LOOKED INTO, RATHER THAN TAKE AS GOSPEL... THE SAME AS ANY INFORMATION WE ARE GIVEN IN LIFE.

MRC5 IS USED IN VACCINATIONS. IT IS A DIPLOID CELL THAT COMES FROM AN ABORTED 14-WEEK-OLD MALE CAUCASIAN FOETUS. IF YOU KNOW ABOUT CHROMOSOMES, YOU WILL KNOW THAT MALES ARE (XY) AND FEMALES ARE (XX).

HEK293 HAS 12 VARIANTS AND COMES FROM THE KIDNEY OF A FEMALE FOETUS ABOUT THE SAME AGE. YOU CAN CHECK THIS FOR YOURSELF.

FROM WHAT I HAVE RESEARCHED... HUMAN DIPLOID CELLS CAN ALTER A MAN OR WOMAN'S DNA AT A CELLULAR LEVEL. THE CHROMOSOMES FROM A FEMALE FOETUS WILL BE (XX) AND A MALE (XY). IMAGINE AT A CELLULAR LEVEL, THIS WAS BEING INJECTED INTO CHILDREN AND ADULTS. IMAGINE MIXING (XX+XY) OR (XY+XX). HOW DO YOU FEEL IT WOULD AFFECT THE BODY AND BRAIN? REMEMBER HORMONES AND DIPLOID CELLS ARE VERY DIFFERENT, WOULD YOU LIKE TO LOOK IN TO THIS? WHY GO WITH THE FLOW AND NEVER ASK QUESTIONS OR RESEARCH? LAZINESS?

CAN YOU THINK HOW DISASTROUS IT WOULD BE FOR MALES TO BE INJECTED WITH FEMALE AND FEMALE TO BE INJECTED WITH MALE. WHAT DO YOU THINK COULD HAPPEN? CONFUSION OF GENDER MAYBE? HAVING DIFFERENT FEELINGS, POSSIBLE THOUGHTS OF CHANGE IN SEX? IF YOU FEEL THIS IS TOTALLY OUTRAGEOUS, I FEEL THE SAME AND I'D PICK REAL SCIENCE OVER CONSPIRACY ANY DAY, HENCE I AM BRINGING THIS SUBJECT UP AND ASKING YOU TO LOOK DEEP INTO THE SCIENCE BEFORE BLOCKING OUT THE INTERNAL CONFLICT OR SHUNNING THE SUBJECT.

WRITE DOWN WHAT YOU FIND IN YOUR OWN WORDS AND YOU'LL NOT NEED TO BE A SCIENTIST OR A PROFESSOR TO WORK OUT THE POSSIBILITIES. THEN LOOK AT SOCIETY, THE WAY THAT THE NARRATIVE IS, THE PEOPLE WHO ARE SEGREGATED UNDER THE PRETENCE OF PROTECTION.

WE ARE ALL HUMAN, DOES IT MATTER ABOUT THE PERSONAL CHOICES PEOPLE MAKE OR FEEL WITHOUT CHOICE, IF THEY ARE NOT HURTING ANYONE? WOULD IT BE HUMANE IF THERE WERE LARGER POWERS AT BE THAT WERE MESSING ABOUT WITH EXPERIMENTAL DRUGS AND CHROMOSOMES, ESPECIALLY WITHOUT FULL DISCLOSURE AND CONSENT, BECAUSE THEY ARE NEVER QUESTIONED? ARE PEOPLE REALLY SO LAZY THAT THEY BLINDLY EAT, DRINK AND INGEST THINGS THAT THEY KNOW NOTHING OF?

IMAGINE IT HAD THE EFFECTS OF UNKNOWING CHANGE AND SO MANY JUST WENT ALONG WITH IT... COULD IT BE ENOUGH FOR A MALE OR FEMALE TO FEEL LIKE THEY ARE IN THE WRONG BODY, BECAUSE IT'S NOT BEEN CHANGED ON A HORMONAL BASIS, BUT A CELLULAR LEVEL? COULD IT MEAN THAT THE INTERNAL CONFLICT IS INVISIBLE? IF A CELL OR CHROMOSOME NATURALLY CHANGES CURRENT DNA, SHOULD MORE QUESTIONS NOT BE ASKED? AGAIN, CAN YOU REALLY DEMONISE PEOPLE FOR ASKING QUESTIONS?

AS FAR AS I'M LEAD TO UNDERSTAND, CELLS MULTIPLY... A LITTLE LIKE GERMS. I COULD BE WRONG, WOULD YOU LIKE TO DO A LITTLE DIGGING ON THIS? WRITE DOWN WHAT YOU FIND!

DO YOU STILL BELIEVE ALL MEDICINE IS HERE TO ONLY MAKE US BETTER?

NATURAL MEDICINE

IN THE PHYSICAL WAYS THAT WE ARE ALL PRETTY MUCH THE SAME, WE

CAN UNDERSTAND THAT WE ARE ALL PART OF THE SAME CONSCIOUSNESS, WE ALL BREATHE THE SAME AIR AND ALL NEED FOOD AND WATER TO SURVIVE. THERE ARE NATURAL MEDICINES THAT BEEN USED FOR THOUSANDS OF YEARS CALLED HOMEOPATHIC THERAPIES/REMEDIES, THESE HAVE BEEN MADE ILLEGAL, HARD TO GET HOLD OF OR AT LEAST WRITTEN OFF WITHOUT PROOF. FOR THE MAJORITY OF DISEASE OR INFECTION, THERE WILL BE SOMETHING ON EARTH THAT CAN BE GROWN OR BE USED TO HEAL THE HUMAN BODY. HAVE YOU LOOKED INTO HOMEOPATHY OR HOMOEOPATHIC MEDICINES BEFORE? WOULD YOU LIKE TO HEAL THE CAUSE, RATHER THAN MASK THE EFFECTS?

PLANT MEDICINE

BECAUSE MENTAL HEALTH SEEMS TO BE THE BIGGEST PANDEMIC OF THE 2020'S SO FAR (IN MY BELIEF) AND THE WAR ON CONSCIOUSNESS IS RAGING ON, I'D LIKE TO SHOW EXAMPLES OF HOW PLANT MEDICINE CAN WORK TO IMPROVE QUALITY OF LIFE AND THE PROOF I HAVE WITNESSED WHERE 157 PEOPLE IN UNDER 24 MONTHS CEASED TO USE MENTAL HEALTH MEDICATION, PRESCRIBED BY MEDICAL REGURGITATING PEOPLE FOR MONEY, ALL BY THE ONE MAN, WHO WORKED WITH GOD/THE UNIVERSE GUIDING HIM, GIVING THEM BELIEF, UNDERSTANDING AND HAPPY CHEMICALS FROM THE EARTH.

AYAHUASCA

AYAHUASCA HAS BEEN USED IN THE AMAZON JUNGLE FOR THOUSANDS OF YEARS AND IS AN EXTREMELY PSYCHEDELIC NATURAL MEDICINE (TERM USED BY INDIGENOUS PEOPLE AND NOT GOVERNMENT OR OTHER CORPORATIONS) WITH HEALING CAPABILITIES LIKE NOTHING ELSE DUE TO THE INSIGHT THAT IS GIVEN FROM SELF, WHICH OCCURS DURING THIS EXPERIENCE AND IT IS INCREDIBLE!! THROUGH STUDY AND SELF ADMINISTERING, I FOUND THAT THIS WAS THE MOST PROFOUND AND LIFE-CHANGING EXPERIENCE EVER. I WILL EXPLAIN THE REASON WHY I BELIEVE THAT THE HEALING IS DIFFERENT FROM WHAT I LEARNED FROM YOUTUBE, HEALERS, SHAMEN AND OTHERS WHO HAVE BEEN ON A

JOURNEY WITH THIS MARVELOUS MEDICINE.

THE MAIN ACTIVE INGREDIENT IS DIMETHYLTRYPTAMINE (DMT) AND THE PROCESS CAN LAST FROM 3-6 HOURS OF INTENSE PSYCHEDELIC VISIONS AND INSIGHTS. WE ARE TAUGHT THAT DRUGS ARE BAD. WHAT ABOUT NATURAL HEALING SUBSTANCES, THAT HAVE BEEN DEMONISED AND CATEGORISED WRONGLY BY THE GOVERNMENT AND CORPORATIONS THAT CAN ALLOW PEOPLE TO UNDERSTAND MORE ABOUT THEMSELVES? SHOULD NATURAL SUBSTANCES BE BANNED IF THEY HELP PEOPLE? WHO GIVES PEOPLE THE RIGHT TO THINK THAT THEY CAN PLAY GOD WITH OTHER HUMAN BEINGS?

IN THE SWINGING 60S MANY PEOPLE TOOK PSYCHEDELICS AND IT WAS ALL PEACE, LOVE, SEX AND HAPPINESS! THE POWERS AT BE THEN BANNED THE USE OF THESE. CONTROL AND PROGRAM THE PEOPLE AND THEN YOU HAVE IT: A DULLED DOWN, CONTROLLED SOCIETY. THIS MEDICINE, IN MY BELIEF, OR IN THE PURE FORM OF DMT, IS THE MOST FREEING EXPERIENCE TO COME FROM ANY SUBSTANCE I HAVE EXPERIENCED, BUT NOT IN AN ADDICTIVE MANNER, IN MY BELIEF.

WE SAW THAT SEROTONIN IS A SUBSTANCE THAT WE PRODUCE TO FEEL HAPPINESS (LONG TERM), SO THAT WE FEEL CONTENT AND ARE CONTENT BY 'JUST BEING'. THROUGH ALCOHOL, NARCOTICS, PROCESSED FOODS AND POOR THOUGHT PROCESSES, WE DO NOT PRODUCE THIS CHEMICAL (SEROTONIN) ANYWHERE NEAR AS MUCH AS WHAT WE SHOULD, IF AT ALL! MOST MENTAL HEALTH MEDICATION (ANTIDEPRESSANTS AND ANTIPSYCHOTICS) PRODUCE OTHER CHEMICALS AND TRICK THE BRAIN INTO THINKING IT IS HAPPY! THE CHEMICAL MOLECULAR STRUCTURE OF DIMETHYLTRYPTAMINE (DMT) IS ALMOST IDENTICAL TO THAT OF SEROTONIN!! THIS IS WHERE IT BECOMES INTERESTING.

THERE IS ONLY ONE MOLECULE BETWEEN THE TWO, WHICH MEANS WHEN INGESTED IN AYAHUASCA FORM, IT'S PUMPED AROUND THE BODY AND IGNITES THE SEROTONIN RECEPTORS IN THE BRAIN, THE EFFECTS ARE 3-6 HOURS. WHEN VAPORISED IN PURE DMT FORM, IT LASTS 7-12 MINUTES, NO COME DOWN, VERY INTENSE AND AS I'M LEAD TO BELIEVE,

CANNOT BE TESTED IN A COMMON DRUG TEST FOR EMPLOYMENT OR SPORTS, AS OUR BODY NATURALLY PRODUCES IT ANYWAY, ABSOLUTELY MIND BLOWING!

THE MAN I MENTIONED, WHO HAS HELPED 157 PEOPLE TO STOP USING MENTAL HEALTH MEDICATION AND WHO WAS SLOWLY AND SAFELY SETTING THEM FREE   USED THIS 75% OF THE TIME WITH PEOPLE AND HAS HAD A FULL SUCCESS RATE! THESE 157 WHO CAME OFF REALISED THEY DON'T NEED ANYTHING BECAUSE THEY RECEIVED INTANGIBLE, DARE I SAY 'SPIRITUAL', INSIGHT! THE PROCESS WAS JUST A KICK IN THE ASS AND PROMPTED THE TRANSITION! THE SUBSTANCES SHOULD ALWAYS BE USED UNDER SUPERVISION AND WITH SOMEONE EXPERIENCED AND I AM NOT SUGGESTING PEOPLE GO AND DO ANY OF THIS, I'M JUST GIVING INFORMATION AND ASKING QUESTIONS!

WHAT PEOPLE NEED TO REMEMBER IS... WE HAVE BEEN PROGRAMMED FOR DECADES TO FEEL WE FIND HAPPINESS FROM THE OUTSIDE VIA OTHER PEOPLE, TANGIBLE THINGS, PHYSICAL BEHAVIOUR, AMONG OTHER THINGS. THIS MEANS THAT WE LITERALLY GET A SHORT-TERM BUZZ, IN ORDER TO DISTRACT US. WE PRODUCE ENDORPHINS AND DOPAMINE, WHICH MAKES US THINK THAT WE ARE HAPPY AND DISTRACTED AT THE TIME AND FORGET THE LONG-TERM BALANCE, CONTENTMENT AND HAPPINESS. THIS LEADS TO GREEDY AND SHALLOW WAYS OF LIVING THAT WILL LEAD US TO CRASHING AND BURNING EVENTUALLY, WITH NO WARNING!!! TRY GETTING OUT OF THAT WHEN YOU DON'T KNOW WHO YOU ARE OR YOUR PURPOSE!

I WAS NOT CURED BY A DRUG. I WAS PROMPTED BY THE AYAHUASCA/DMT EXPERIENCE THAT RESET MY PERSPECTIVE AND ALSO GAVE ME SPIRITUAL INSIGHT. I DID NOT CONSUME ALCOHOL OR HAVE INTERCOURSE FOR SOME TIME AFTER AYAHUASCA, THEY WERE BOTH MY GO TO FOR HAPPINESS. THE AYAHUASCA EXPERIENCE HAS BEEN KNOWN TO STOP ALMOST ALL ADDICTIVE BEHAVIOURS AND THE EFFECTS ARE HAPPINESS. ANY UNDERLYING MEDICAL CONDITIONS OR PRESCRIPTION DRUGS SHOULD BE CAREFULLY CONSIDERED BEFORE CONSIDERING DOING THE CEREMONY WITH SOMEONE WHO SPECIALISES IN THESE PRACTICES.

ALWAYS ASK A SHAMAN OR SOMEONE VERY KNOWLEDGEABLE IN THE PRACTICE. IF USED WITH MEDICATION THAT BLOCKS SEROTONIN, IT CAN CAUSE SEROTONIN SYNDROME, AS WELL AS OTHER SYMPTOMS THAT DON'T SOUND VERY PLEASANT. RESEARCH BEFORE ANYTHING IS KEY!

IS IT SOMETHING YOU'D CONSIDER RESEARCHING? IT'S GOOD TO LEARN NEW INFORMATION, WE WERE FORCED TO DO IT AS KIDS, BUT WE DONT DO IT AS MUCH AS ADULTS.

KAMBO

KAMBO IS ANOTHER INDIGENOUS MEDICINE, NON PSYCHEDELIC AND IMPACTS THE BODY IN A POSITIVE MANNER. IT HAS 120 PEPTIDES. PEPTIDES ARE STRINGS OF 2 OR MORE AMINO ACIDS AND THESE ARE LIKE BUILDING BLOCKS AT A CELLULAR LEVEL. KAMBO HAS BEEN KNOWN TO HAVE AN ALL-OVER EFFECT TO THE PHYSICAL AND MENTAL WELLNESS OF A HUMAN BEING. I HAVE ALSO EXPERIENCED THIS ON SEVERAL OCCASIONS AND HAVE WORKED WITH PRACTITIONERS WITHIN THIS PROCESS. THE MAN I TOLD YOU ABOUT WITH HIS 157 PEOPLE NOW THRIVING FROM NOT USING MENTAL HEALTH MEDICATION, USES THIS PROCESS AS PART OF THEIR PURGE ALSO, IF THEY CHOOSE TO DO SO.

KAMBO IS THE SECRETION OF THE AMAZONIAN MONKEY FROG, IT HAS BEEN USED BY HEALERS AND SHAMAN FOR AT LEAST TWO THOUSAND YEARS, NO FROGS ARE HARMED IN THE EXTRACTION OF THE MILKY SECRETION FROM THEIR SKIN EITHER.

THE PROCESS IS SIMPLE, YET EFFECTIVE. THE PEOPLE WHO ARE ON THE RECEIVING END, FAST FOR AROUND 12 HOURS PRIOR, SO THAT THEY HAVE AN EMPTY STOMACH. WHEN THEY TURN UP TO THE PRACTITIONER'S PLACE OF RESIDENCE OR CEREMONY, THEY ARE GIVEN A CHAT AS TO WHERE KAMBO WAS FIRST FOUNDED. THEY WILL USUALLY HEAR THE STORY OF KAMPU, THE SHAMAN FROM THE AMAZON JUNGLE WHO HAD CONSUMED AYAHUASCA AND WENT ON A SEARCH THROUGH THE JUNGLE

TO FIND A CURE TO HELP THE SICK VILLAGERS. HE WAS MET BY THE FROG AND SHOWN THE PROCESS TO HEAL THEM. THIS IS FOLLOWED BY EXPLAINING THE PROCESS.

THE NEXT STAGE IS CLEANING THE SKIN. ONCE CLEAN, THERE WILL USUALLY BE THREE TO FIVE TINY BURNS (GATES) MADE BY A BURNING PIECE OF WOOD, SIMILAR TO AN INCENSE STICK. ANOTHER WIPE TO REMOVE THE BURNED SKIN TO EXPOSE THE LYMPHATIC FLUID, THIS IS THE BODY READY FOR THE SMALL AMOUNTS OF KAMBO TO BE PLACED ONTO THE EXPOSED GATES. THIS IS NOT PAINFUL.

WITHIN 5-10 MINUTES OF THE KAMBO BEING PLACED ON, THE EFFECTS ARE HEAT AND NAUSEA, SOMETIMES A FEELING OF BEING LIGHTHEADED. WATER IS THEN CONSUMED TO ENCOURAGE THE PURGE OF THE BILE IN THE STOMACH, THIS CAN BE ALMOST CLEAR TO BEING ALMOST BLACK, DEPENDING ON HOW TOXIC THE CLIENT'S BODY IS. THERE WILL BE A PURGE FOR TEN TO FIFTEEN MINUTES, SOMETIMES MORE AND THIS ALLOWS THE STOMACH TO RESET.

THE HUMAN BODY HAS THE LYMPHATIC SYSTEM, IN SHORT; THIS WORKS IN A WAY WHERE THE LYMPH NODES ACTUALLY TAKE IN ANY TOXINS OR INFECTIONS, PASS THEM THROUGH THE SYSTEM AND ALLOWS THE BODY TO EXPEL THE TOXINS SAFELY. THE HUMAN BODY IS SO SUPER INTELLIGENT, THAT IT HAS A CODE FOR JUST ABOUT ANYTHING ON THIS EARTH THAT IS UNDESIRABLE OR HARMFUL TO THE BODY. THE INFECTION, VIRUS OR POISON COMES INTO THE BODY, THE INTELLIGENT LYMPHATIC SYSTEM KICKS IN AND REMOVES AS MUCH AS IT POSSIBLY CAN!

THE HUMAN BODY DOES NOT HAVE A 'CODE' FOR KAMBO, YOU CAN LITERALLY FEEL THE HEAT RUNNING UP AND DOWN YOUR BODY, SCANNING FOR WHAT TO DO WITH THIS SUBSTANCE. IN RESPONSE TO THIS, IT RELEASES OLD TOXINS AND WASTE FROM THE LYMPHATIC SYSTEM, THESE ARE PUMPED INTO THE STOMACH OF THE CLIENT AND THEN THE PURGE HAPPENS.

WITHIN 20-30 MINUTES AFTER THE CEREMONY, THERE IS A FEELING OF PEACE, THE DARK CLOUD (PANEMA) HAS GONE, THE BODY HAS RESET (DEPENDING ON HOW MUCH PURGING WAS DONE, YOU MAY NEED TO GO BACK), A YUMMY BOWL OF SOUP AND THEN YOU ARE ON YOUR WAY HOME. THE EFFECTS OF REMOVING THE TOXINS CAN LAST MONTHS!

THIS HAS BEEN TRIED AND TESTED FOR OVER TWO THOUSAND YEARS. IF IT SOUNDS RIDICULOUS BUT THE FACT 90% OF FOODS IN SUPERMARKETS ARE FULL OF PROCESSED INGREDIENTS AND CHEMICALS SOUNDS NORMAL, MAYBE IT'S THE PROGRAM YOU HAVE BEEN LIVING BY? OPENING OUR MIND AND BODIES TO NATURAL WAYS, CAN NOT ONLY HAVE HEALING BENEFITS, BUT THEY ALSO ALLOW US TO REALLY FEEL AND BECOME MORE IN TUNE WITH OURSELVES AND OUR SURROUNDING ENERGY.

MUSHROOMS

MUSHROOMS ARE A FUNGI AND AROUND THE WORLD ARE USED FOR COOKING, TAKING PEOPLE ON PSYCHEDELIC JOURNEYS, BUT ALSO USED FOR HEALING. IN SOME COUNTRIES, THE MUSHROOMS WITH PSILOCYBIN ARE DEEMED ILLEGAL TO CONSUME, SELL OR POSSESS. DO YOU THINK THIS SOUNDS FAIR, CONSIDERING WE CAN FORAGE FOR THEM AND USE THEM TO EXPAND OUR CONSCIOUSNESS? WE ARE TOLD IN THE UK (SCOTLAND), WHERE I'M FROM, THAT THESE ARE DRUGS AND BAD... BUT WE ARE AGAIN, ENCOURAGED TO TAKE CHEMICALS PRESCRIBED BY A SYSTEM THAT WISHES US TO BE CONTROLLED AND NOT FREE. I'M STILL TRYING TO GET MY HEAD AROUND THAT ONE, I HAVE BEEN TRYING TO WORK IT OUT A WHILE! WHAT IS YOUR THOUGHTS?

THERE ARE MANY (NON-MAINSTREAM) SCIENTIFIC STUDIES, THAT SAY THE PSILOCYBIN ACTUALLY HEALS NEURAL PATHWAYS IN THE BRAIN, BY EXPANDING THE THOUGHT PROCESS AND IS BEING USED (LOW KEY) TO TREAT DEPRESSION IN PEOPLE. MUSHROOMS SHOULD NOT BE USED WHILE ON MEDICATION FOR MENTAL HEALTH OR IF THERE ARE ANY

UNDERLYING ISSUES WITH MENTAL HEALTH OR THE BRAIN, WITHOUT PROPER UNDERSTANDING AND A KNOWLEDGEABLE DOCTOR/SHAMAN PRESENT.

MICRODOSING HAS BECOME SERIOUSLY POPULAR WITHIN THE WESTERN WORLD OVER THE LAST FEW YEARS. MANY PEOPLE ARE LOOKING FOR THE NEXT THING TO WAKE THEM UP, TO DISTRACT THEM FROM LIFE, TO LOOK COOL AND SOME TO HEAL. EVERYTHING IS INTENTION. THE EXPERIENCES I HAVE HAD INVOLVE VERY LOW DOSES 0.1 - 0.25G FOR A MICRODOSE AND 1.85-2G FOR A CEREMONY. IT'S NOT FOR RECREATIONAL PURPOSES AND I FEEL, AS A HUMAN BEINGS, WE HAVE FULL SOVEREIGNTY OVER OUR CHOICE OF FOOD, MEDICINE, AND INFORMATION WE WISH TO CONSUME. WE ARE INDIVIDUAL SYSTEMS THAT CREATE ONE BIG ENERGETICAL SYSTEM AND WHEN THE BIG SYSTEM IS MADE UP OF LOTS AND LOTS OF BROKEN PIECES... IT DOESN'T WORK!

MY EXPERIENCES WITH MUSHROOMS HAVE BEEN NOTHING SHORT OF MIND BLOWING! ALL LOVE, BEING ABLE TO UNDERSTAND MY HIGHER SELF THROUGH A KNOWING AND IT'S LIKE A DEEP MEDITATION THAT I DON'T GET DISTRACTED FROM.

AS MUCH AS I HAVE LOVED WRITING THIS CHAPTER AND DISCUSSING MY RESEARCH AND VIEWS, I'M IN NO WAY CONDONING THE USE OR PURCHASE OF SUBSTANCES. I AM IN NO WAY COERCING OR PERSUADING ANYONE TO DO ANYTHING OF THE SORT. REMEMBER, IT IS THE INTANGIBLE EXPERIENCE THAT PROVIDES SPIRITUAL INSIGHT AND NOT THE MEDICINE ITSELF THAT BRINGS THE HEALING. I AM MERELY JUST EXPLAINING MY EXPERIENCES AND THOSE OF OTHER PEOPLE AND SHOWING SOMETIMES OTHER METHODS CAN BE USED, BUT CONSULT AN EXPERT IN THE FIELD (WHICH I AM NOT).

THE PEOPLE OF THE WORLD DO NOT NEED ANYTHING TO KEEP THEM ALIVE APART FROM CLEAN AIR, WATER, FOOD, AND ALSO IMPORTANTLY TO KNOW WHO THEY ARE AND THAT THEY DON'T HAVE TO COPE, WHEN THEY CAN LIVE THEIR LIVES AS THEMSELVES. THIS ONLY HAPPENS WHEN THEY BREAK THE HABITS OF A LIFETIME AND REALLY BEGIN TO DO LIFE

ON PURPOSE, WITHOUT THE MANIPULATION OF ANY OTHER LIVING BEING OR SYSTEM. I WILL EXPLAIN MORE IN THE LAST CHAPTER TO BRING EVERYTHING TOGETHER AND INSTRUCTIONS AS TO HOW YOU CAN DO IT!

CHAPTER 15: FOOD

RESEARCH IS BEGINNING TO FOCUS IN ON THE MAIN CAUSE FOR THE PEOPLE NEEDING MORE MEDICATION. DO YOU KNOW WHAT IT IS? THE FOOD WE EAT AND DRUGS WE TAKE (LEGAL OR NOT)

DO WE EAT BECAUSE WE ARE HUNGRY AND TO SURVIVE, OR DO WE EAT TO ENSURE OUR BODY IS HEALTHY AND FUELED TO LIVE A FULL AND HEALTHY LIFE? DO WE EAT BECAUSE IT PROVIDES A DISTRACTION THAT COMFORTS US OR ARE WE COMPLETELY UNAWARE OF WHY WE EAT WHAT WE EAT?

I'M SURE THERE WILL BE MIXED ANSWERS TO THE ABOVE QUESTIONS, AS WE ARE TAUGHT TO EAT WHEN WE ARE HUNGRY AND NOT ABOUT HOW OUR BODY WORKS PROPERLY FROM WHEN WE ARE YOUNG, THEREFORE WE CAN BE MANIPULATED THROUGH LIFE AND BECOME CUSTOMERS TO THE PHARMACEUTICAL COMPANIES AND CORPORATIONS OF TOXIC FOOD, ALL BECAUSE OUR BODIES ARE UNHEALTHY. AFTER WE BECOME UNHEALTHY, WE ARE PRONE TO INFECTIONS, FATIGUE AND DISEASE. DO YOU EAT WELL?

MANY PEOPLE SAY MONEY RUNS THE WORLD, IN SOME INSTANCES I'D HAVE TO AGREE, THIS IS MOSTLY BECAUSE OF CONSUMERISM AND LIFESTYLES. IT'S NOW A TREND TO EAT HEALTHILY, RATHER THAN HEALTH BEING MADE MANDATORY, AS THERE IS MORE MONEY TO BE MADE WHEN THE SICK ARE TREATED WITH WHAT WE BELIEVE TO BE MEDICINE. WHEN DO YOU FEEL WE SHOULD BE TAUGHT ABOUT OUR BODIES AND HOW TO EAT PROPERLY? IF REAL FOOD IS THE MEDICINE AND THE FUEL, DO YOU BELIEVE WE'D BE SICK ANYWHERE NEAR AS OFTEN AS WE ARE?

I'M NOT A DIETITIAN OR WELL VERSED IN FOOD SCIENCE, THIS CHAPTER IS NOT GOING TO HELP YOU WITH WEIGHT LOSS OR GIVE YOU THE ULTIMATE DIET TO FOLLOW. I AM MORE INTERESTED IN YOU ASKING YOUR QUESTIONS WHEN IT COMES TO YOUR BODY AND UNDERSTANDING WHAT YOU ARE PUTTING INTO IT AND WHY: CARCINOGENS, ACIDITY LEVELS, CHEMICALS, PROCESSED GARBAGE AND ANYTHING IN BETWEEN.

IF YOU COULD LIVE LONGER AND HEALTHIER, WOULD YOU DO WHAT IT TAKES TO MAKE IT HAPPEN? DO YOU FEEL THAT EATING AND DRINKING WELL IS BORING AND LESS FUN? WOULD YOU CHOOSE WHAT YOU BELIEVE TO BE FUN OVER HEALTH? DO YOU THINK YOU CAN CHOOSE TO EAT HEALTHY OR DO YOU HAVE AN ADDICTION TO OVEREATING UNHEALTHY FOOD?

E-NUMBERS

THESE ARE PUT IN FOODS IN THE UK, I'M NOT SURE ABOUT THE REST OF THE WORLD, OR IF OTHER COUNTRIES HAVE OTHER NAMES FOR THESE SO CALLED INGREDIENTS. THE TRUTH IS, BY LAW THE PROCESSED FOOD COMPANIES HAVE TO DISCLOSE THE E-NUMBERS ON THE BACK OF FOOD PACKETS SUCH AS E951- ASPARTAME.

HAVE YOU HEARD OF THIS BEFORE? ASPARTAME WAS BANNED IN 1980 IN THE UNITED STATES, AS IT CAUSED BRAIN LESIONS, CANCER AND BRAIN TUMOURS. ASPARTAME- E951 IS USED WIDELY AS A SWEETENER IN DRINKS, SNACKS, ALCOHOL, DESERTS AND 'DIET FOODS'. E951 IS USED, AS IT IS AROUND 200 TIMES SWEETER THAN SUGAR, WITHOUT BEING SUGAR!

WHEN YOUR BODY CONSUMES SUGAR, YOU PRODUCE INSULIN TO EFFECTIVELY BURN OFF THE SUGAR IN YOUR SYSTEM. IMAGINE YOUR BODY THINKS IT HAS 200 TIMES THE AMOUNT OF SUGAR COMING IN, WOULD YOU PRODUCE MORE OR LESS INSULIN? I BELIEVE WE'D PRODUCE MORE INSULIN, THAT MEANS IT WOULD HAVE NO SUGAR TO BURN, AS IT WAS A SWEETENER, YES? NOW IMAGINE THE EXCESS INFLAMMATION TO YOUR ORGANS AND BLOOD VESSELS, DOES THIS SOUND HEALTHY? WHAT

HAPPENS WHEN YOUR BODY HAS INFLAMMATION? YES... INFLAMMATION ALLOWS THE BODY TO BE OPEN TO DISEASE, SUCH AS CANCER!

NOW BEFORE WE BLAME THE COMPANIES THAT PUT THIS IN THE FOOD, WE MUST UNDERSTAND THAT WE CHOOSE TO EAT THESE FOODS. SUGAR AND SWEETENERS ARE PROBABLY THE MOST ADDICTIVE OF SUBSTANCES IN THE WORLD AND THE MOST DANGEROUS. DO YOU THINK IT IS RIGHT TO GIVE A CHILD A SUGARY SWEET AS A TREAT, EVEN IF IT WAS TOXIC TO THE BODY? DOES IT SIT WELL WHEN YOU KNOW YOU COULD BE GIVING A CHILD SOMETHING THAT CAN CAUSE CANCER AS A TREAT?

WHEN WE CONSUME ASPARTAME, IT ACTUALLY METABOLISES INTO FORMALDEHYDE WITHIN THE BODY, WHICH IS IN FACT, HIGHLY TOXIC! THIS MEANS THAT YOU ARE POISONING YOURSELF THROUGH METABOLISING THE ASPARTAME, THEREFORE... THESE COMPANIES CAN NOT BE HELD LIABLE AND PEOPLE ARE KILLING THEMSELVES AND MAKING THEMSELVES ILL WITH WHAT THEY CHOOSE TO EAT AND DRINK. FORMALDEHYDE ON ITS OWN, CAUSES IRRITATION TO THE SKIN, NOSE AND EYES... IMAGINE WHAT IT'S DOING INSIDE A HUMAN BODY!

IF SOMEONE WAS ASKED TO DRINK FORMALDEHYDE, THEY'D PROBABLY SAY NO, BUT THEY'D EAT ASPARTAME AS ITS SWEET AND NOT A POISON (AS SUCH) UNTIL IT METABOLISES. THESE COMPANIES ARE CLEVER, THEY BELONG TO THE SAME SYSTEM THAT TEACHES US THROUGH SCHOOL. CONVENIENT WE DON'T LEARN ABOUT THESE PRODUCTS, BUT WE LEARN MEDICINE IS GOOD, RATHER THAN THE CAUSE OF WHAT MAKES US SICK! YOU CAN LOOK INTO WHY HITLER USED ASPARTAME TO WEAKEN THE BRAINS OF HUMANS, SO THAT THEY BECAME YES MEN AND WOMEN IN WW2... THAT'S DEFINITELY AN INTERESTING BIT OF FACT FINDING, ESPECIALLY WHEN YOU LOOK AT SOCIETY TODAY AND HOW PEOPLE JUST ACCEPT ANYTHING!

NOT ALL E-NUMBERS ARE BAD. THERE ARE SOME HARMLESS ONES, SUCH AS E164-SAFFRON, E160-PAPRIKA, E300-VITAMIN C AND E500-SODIUM BICARBONATE.

THERE ARE ONES TO BE ESPECIALLY WARY OF: E102, E104, E110, E122, E124 AND E129. WILL YOU GIVE YOURSELF A LITTLE WHILE TO RESEARCH? WOULD YOU LIKE TO HELP THE PEOPLE YOU KNOW, ESPECIALLY CHILDREN TO BE HEALTHIER? DO YOU KNOW IT'S ACTUALLY ABUSE TO GIVE THESE PRODUCTS TO ANY ADULTS OR CHILDREN? ESPECIALLY NOW YOU HAVE READ THIS.... IT IS NOW A CHOICE!

MONOSODIUM GLUTAMATE (MSG) E621- IS A FLAVOUR ENHANCER AND IS USED IN PROCESSED FOODS AND AFFECTS THE REPRODUCTIVE SYSTEM AND THE BRAIN IN A NEGATIVE MANNER. PLEASE DO YOUR RESEARCH. THERE IS ALSO A CHEMICAL WE PRODUCE CALLED LEPTIN, THAT TELLS US WHEN WE HAVE HAD ENOUGH TO EAT. MSG WHICH INTERRUPTS THE SIGNALLING SO THAT WE EAT MORE THAN WE SHOULD, ALSO HAS BEEN LINKED TO EATING DISORDERS!

MEAT AND VEGANISM

A HUGE FIGHT JUST NOW TO SAVE THE PLANET AND THE ANIMALS, IT'S ALL GOING A BIT MAD, STAUNCH BELIEFS BEING PUSHED AND FORCED. PEOPLE JUDGING OTHERS AND THE GOVERNMENT TURNING PEOPLE AGAINST THE OLD NARRATIVE, BASED ON 'NEW-SCIENCE' (ALSO KNOWN AS AGENDA). THE TRUTH IS BOTH SIDES ARE BEING PLAYED! THE MEAT EATERS ARE EATING MEAT FROM ANIMALS THAT HAVE BEEN RAISED ON ANTIBIOTICS AND STEROIDS, IN POOR AND UNSANITARY CONDITIONS. THE VEGANS ARE NOT EATING OR KILLING ANIMALS, BUT ARE EATING GENETICALLY MODIFIED VEGETABLES THAT HAVE BEEN SPRAYED WITH ALL SORTS OF CHEMICALS, THAT DO KILL MILLIONS OF INSECTS AND ANIMALS. WHO IS ACTUALLY BENEFITING HERE?

OUR SKIES ARE SPRAYED WITH ALUMINIUM AND BARIUM TOO AND THESE ARE CALLED CHEMTRAILS AND THEY NOW ADMIT THIS BY TALKING ABOUT CLOUD SEEDING, WHICH WILL ALSO BE ON THE VEGETABLES, CONSUMED BY THE ANIMALS THAT ARE EATEN AND THEN BY THE CONSUMER! A GOOD HEAVY METAL DETOX AND BEING CONSCIOUS OF WHAT GOES INTO YOUR FOOD AND INEVITABLY YOUR BODY IS IMPORTANT. YOU CAN ALSO RESEARCH THE COMPANIES THAT SPRAY THE

VEGETABLES WITH PESTICIDES, YOU'LL FIND THAT THEY ARE OWNED BY... YES! YOU GUESSED IT! PHARMACEUTICAL COMPANIES NOW POISONING ALL YOUR FOOD SO YOU BECOME A CUSTOMER FOR THEIR DRUGS! GO ONTO A FREE SEARCH INTERNET SOURCE LIKE DUCKDUCKGO... ALL THE INFORMATION IS THERE.

ARE YOU TOO LAZY TO RESEARCH? WHY DOES SOMEONE'S DIET CHOICES HAVE ANYTHING TO DO WITH ANOTHER HUMAN BEING, UNLESS THEY ARE BEING CARED FOR? I WAS TOLD A JOKE, "HOW DO YOU KNOW WHEN SOMEONE IS A VEGAN?" "THEY'LL LET YOU KNOW" I DIDN'T LAUGH, BUT IT DID MAKE ME THINK. MAYBE IT'S BECAUSE VEGAN PEOPLE WANT TO LOOK LIKE THEY ARE GOOD AND WANT TO DO THE RIGHT THING, BUT ARE TRYING TO INFLUENCE OTHERS IN A WAY WHERE IT IS DAMAGING. MAYBE IT'S BECAUSE SOME HAVE SUCH BELIEFS AND HAVE INSECURITIES THAT THEY NEED CONTROL.

THE MEAT EATERS ARE JUST AS HARDCORE IN THEIR BELIEFS, THEY PUT THE VEGANS DOWN, BELIEVETHAT THEY ARE MEANT TO EAT MEAT, AS IT'S ALWAYS BEEN DONE. DO YOU THINK IT'S RIGHT THAT PEOPLE JUDGE EACH OTHER ON WHAT THEY EAT? WHAT WOULD WORK BETTER THAN MINDING YOUR OWN BUSINESS WHEN IT COMES TO OTHER PEOPLE'S EATING HABITS?

IF YOU DON'T LIKE IT, DON'T LOOK. AGENDA 2030 AND THE TIME BEYOND IS AIMING TO BAN MEAT FOREVER! ALL THANKS TO THE UNELECTED WORLD ECONOMIC FORUM AND OTHER SO CALLED WORLD LEADERS. WILL YOU GIVE IT UP EASILY?

WHILE WE ARE ON THE SUBJECT OF FOOD, I'D LIKE TO TALK A LITTLE ABOUT FAT CELLS. THESE ARE ACTUALLY VERY CLEVER INDEED! A LOT OF PEOPLE BELIEVE IF YOU EAT FATTY FOODS, YOU BECOME OVERWEIGHT AND IT'S THAT SIMPLE, WHEN REALLY THERE IS MORE TO IT.

OUR SKIN IS THE BIGGEST LIVING ORGAN ON OUR BODY AS A HUMAN BEING, IT'S THERE TO PROTECT OUR INTERNAL ORGANS FROM ANY OUTSIDE THREATS. OUR SKIN DOES A PRETTY GOOD JOB. WHAT ABOUT IF

THERE WAS AN INTERNAL THREAT? WHAT IF 90% OF FOOD AND DRINK STUFFS WERE PROCESSED OR HAD CHEMICALS IN THEM?

OUR SKIN LOOKS ONE WAY ON THE OUTSIDE, HOWEVER, ON THE INSIDE WE HAVE A FAT LAYER, SOME THICKER THAN OTHERS. IF THERE IS A THREAT TO OUR INTERNAL ORGANS, THESE CELLS WILL HOLD ONTO THE THREAT, TO ENSURE IT DOES NOT GO INTO OUR INTERNAL ORGANS. IF IT WAS JUST THE CASE THAT WE HOLD FAT, BECAUSE WE EAT FAT, IT WOULD BE SIMPLE TO LOSE WEIGHT WOULDN'T IT? I HAVE HEARD "ALL I DRINK IS DIET DRINKS AND FOOD" THIS USUALLY MEANS ITS PROCESSED AND PEOPLE STILL PUT ON WEIGHT BECAUSE THE SKIN IS SOAKING UP AND STORING TOXINS.

TO MAKE MORE OF AN INTERESTING POINT, THAT OF COURSE YOU CAN RESEARCH EASILY, FOOD ISN'T WHAT WE ARE TOLD. WHAT WE PUT IN OUR MOUTHS METABOLISES AND THE CHEMICAL MAKEUP CHANGES. THIS MEANS THESE CAN BE A THREAT TO OUR INTERNAL ORGANS. I SPOKE ABOUT ASPARTAME METABOLISING AS FORMALDEHYDE ALREADY. YOUR SKIN WILL HOLD ONTO THAT POISON. IMAGINE HOW MANY OTHER SUBSTANCES THERE ARE! SO IF YOU DRINK DIET DRINKS, WITH ASPARTAME AND ARE NOT LOSING WEIGHT, YOU NOW HAVE A BETTER IDEA AS TO WHY! ALSO, THE OILS YOU COOK YOUR FOOD IN CHANGE WHEN HEATED UP TOO, INFORMATION IS FREELY AVAILABLE, WHEN YOU CHOOSE TO LOOK FOR IT AND READ.

DO YOU FEEL DIFFERENT AFTER READING THIS CHAPTER? WILL YOU TAKE BETTER CARE, WHEN FEEDING YOU AND YOUR FAMILY, ESPECIALLY CHILDREN? (IF YOU HAVE OR KNOW ANY)

FOOD COMPANIES AND PHARMACEUTICAL COMPANIES ARE IN CAHOOTS, THEY ARE NOT HERE TO FEED YOU FULL OF GOODNESS. HOPEFULLY, YOUR CHOICE FROM TODAY ONWARDS IS TO MAKE MORE OF AN EFFORT. FOOD IS YOUR MEDICINE, REAL FOOD!

ARE YOU GOING TO MAKE A CHANGE? ARE YOU GOING TO STAY AS YOU ARE?

CHAPTER 16: PARENT/CHILD RELATIONSHIPS

PARENTAL ISSUES ARE MASSIVE NOW AND HAVE BEEN FOR A LONG TIME. ALTHOUGH IT'S A FACTOR AS TO WHY PEOPLE ACT AND BEHAVE A CERTAIN WAY, IN MOST PEOPLE'S LIVES, IT'S NOT WHAT THE CAUSE IS. IN FACT, IT'S THE PROGRAMMING FROM THE INDIVIDUAL'S REPETITIVE BEHAVIOUR, BASED-ON THEIR REACTIONS TO WHAT WAS DONE OR NOT DONE TO THEM BY THEIR PARENTS. THIS MEANS PEOPLE'S BEHAVIOUR IS HOW THEY WERE RAISED AND HOW THEY RESPONDED TO IT. THIS, MIXED WITH THE NOT KNOWING OF ONE'S SELF, IS SET UP FOR DISASTER AND WE ARE NEVER TAUGHT DIFFERENT!

ARE WE NOT TAUGHT DIFFERENT BECAUSE NOBODY KNOWS HOW TO TEACH IT? IS THE BIGGER SYSTEM HOLDING BACK INFORMATION SO THAT WE ARE EASIER TO CONTROL/MANIPULATE IF WE HAVE NO IDENTITY OF SELF?

IF YOU HAVE ANYTHING RELATED TO CHILDHOOD THAT YOU HOLD ON TO, IS IT BECAUSE YOU MAYBE HAD AN EXPECTATION THAT WASN'T MET? DID YOUR PARENT KNOW WHO THEY WERE AT SOURCE AND WHO YOU WERE AT SOURCE SO THAT YOU COULD HAVE BEEN GIVEN WHAT YOU NEEDED, RATHER THAN WHAT THEY WANTED TO GIVE?

WE ARE TOLD TO ACT A CERTAIN WAY AND FULFILL OUR PARENTS' EXPECTATIONS FROM BIRTH REALLY. WE ARE FED AT CERTAIN TIMES TO SUIT THEIR AGENDA AND LIFESTYLE. THINGS LIKE: "IF I FEED THE BABY AT 6PM THEY WILL GO TO SLEEP FOR THE NIGHT" OR "I'M CREATING THEIR ROUTINE BECAUSE ITS BEST FOR THEM". WHO SAYS IT'S BEST FOR THEM? ISN'T IT TO BETTER SUIT THE PARENT?

PARENTING NOWADAYS, IN MY EYES, IS TRIAL AND ERROR BASED ON THE UPBRINGING THAT THE PARENT HAD FROM THEIR PARENT/GUARDIAN. THEY CHOOSE WHAT THEY LIKED FROM THEIR CHILDHOOD, PROJECT THAT ONTO THEIR CHILD/CHILDREN AND ADAPT IT TO WHAT THEY'D HAVE LIKED. WOULD YOU AGREE? DO YOU SEE THIS IN YOU OR OTHERS YOU KNOW? I KNOW I'VE DONE THIS.

DOES THAT MEAN THAT IS HOW SOCIETY CHANGES: THROUGH PROGRAMMING THE PARENTS, SO THAT THEY PUT IT ONTO THEIR KIDS? RULES CHANGING AND TRANSFERENCE OF POWER?

AS KIDS, WE LEARN FROM THE BEHAVIOUR WE SEE AND THE WORDS WE HEAR WHICH WILL MOSTLY BE DETERMINED FROM HOW OUR PARENTS WERE WITH US. SOME PARENTS DON'T MIND THEIR KID SAYING CUSS WORDS, OTHERS JUST THINK IT'S A WORD. SOME LIKE THEIR KIDS TO EAT HEALTHY AND MAKE THEM DO IT, OTHERS ARE JUST GRATEFUL THAT THEY ARE EATING AND LET THE KID CHOOSE, REGARDLESS OF HOW NUTRITIONAL THE FOOD IS.

WHAT I HAVE JUST INTRODUCED THIS CHAPTER WITH IS ALL PRETTY MUCH SURFACE LEVEL, THESE ARE THE THINGS THAT PEOPLE HANG ON TO, REBEL AGAINST AND ALLOW TO TAKE UP SPACE IN THEIR BRAIN, WHILE USING THE SAME BRAIN TO STEER THEM THROUGH LIFE AND USUALLY INTO THE WRONG PLACE, WHILE LOSING ENERGY!

IF A PARENT WAS TO SPEAK TO A CHILD THE WAY THAT THE CHILD 'NEEDS' TO BE SPOKEN TO, ACCORDING TO THEIR UNIQUENESS, DO YOU EVER THINK THERE WOULD BE HALF THE PROBLEMS IN THE WORLD? WOULD IT MAKE EVERYONE'S LIFE EASIER? IF KIDS WERE UNDERSTOOD FROM CHILDHOOD AND, MOST IMPORTANTLY, KNEW THEMSELVES?

WHERE DOES CRIME COME FROM? A CRIMINAL, RIGHT? THE CRIMINAL ADULT WAS ONCE A CHILD, EVEN STILL IS A CHILD, BUT LEARNED THE WRONG BEHAVIOUR BY STEERING THROUGH LIFE, NOT KNOWING WHO THEY ARE. WHAT IF I WERE TO TELL YOU THAT MOST OF THE CRIMINALS LOCKED UP IN JAIL WERE MISUNDERSTOOD KIDS IN ADULT BODIES THAT

MADE A SERIES OF WRONG CHOICES? AS MUCH AS IT WAS A CONSCIOUS DECISION TO MAKE THE WRONG CHOICE, HOW COULD THIS HAVE BEEN PREVENTED? THE PARENTS COULD HAVE UNDERSTOOD THEM BETTER AND THIS COULD HAVE CHANGED THE FUTURE OF THE HUMAN BEING WHOM THEY CREATED!

BET YOU THINK THAT SOUNDS DRAMATIC? HOW WOULD YOU EXPLAIN IT?

A YOUNG MALE, CALLED JACK, COMES FROM A WEALTHY FAMILY, HAS PARENTS THAT LOVE HIM, HAS WENT TO THE BEST SCHOOLS, WANTS FOR NOTHING AND IS STILL NOT HAPPY. HE ENDS UP GETTING INVOLVED IN FRAUD AND DRUGS TO GIVE HIMSELF PURPOSE. THIS IS BECAUSE HE DIDN'T KNOW WHO HE WAS INSIDE, HE HAD TO START DOING THINGS ON THE OUTSIDE TO BECOME ENERGISED AND DISTRACTED FROM HOW HE FEELS DAILY. HE GETS INVOLVED WITH THE LAW, ENDS UP COMMITTING SUICIDE. THE PARENTS SAY, "WE GAVE HIM EVERYTHING, HE HAD MANY CHANCES TO CHANGE AND DIDN'T, WHAT ELSE COULD WE HAVE DONE?"

IF YOU ASKED HIS PARENTS WHO THEIR CHILD WAS UNIQUELY, HOW HE GAINED AND LOST ENERGY, HOW HE SHOULD HAVE LIVED ACCORDING TO HIS UNIQUENESS, DO YOU THINK THEY COULD ANSWER? ME NEITHER!

MOST PEOPLE DON'T KNOW WHO THEY ARE, SO THE CHANCES OF UNDERSTANDING OTHERS AT SOURCE IS LITERALLY IMPOSSIBLE. WE HAVE SEEN THE BEHAVIOUR IS THEIR PERSONALITY; THE PERSONA/MASK THAT HAS BEEN CREATED BY THE CHILD WHEN THEY ARE UNBALANCED, BASED ON HOW THEY HAVE BEEN ALLOWED TO ACT/BEHAVE ACCORDING TO THEIR PARENT/GUARDIAN.

DO YOU NOW SEE THE IMPORTANCE OF UNLEARNING FROM THE PAST AND LEARNING BETTER FOR THE FUTURE?

CODEPENDENT PARENTING IS BECOMING AN ISSUE NOWADAYS AND I DON'T FEEL IT'S AS BAD IN SOME COUNTRIES AS IT IS IN OTHERS. LET ME EXPLAIN WHAT IT IS.

HOW MANY PARENTS/GUARDIANS SAY "MY KID IS MY BEST FRIEND" OR "CAN'T LIVE WITHOUT MY BESTIE"? IT'S BECOMING A LOT MORE ISN'T IT?

THIS IS AN EXTREMELY IMPORTANT SUBJECT AS IT'S SEEN TO BE CARING, WHEN IN FACT IT IS SMOTHERING AND REALLY TAKES THE CHILD'S CHILDHOOD SELF DEVELOPMENT AWAY. I CAN HEAR YOU THINKING "BUT WHY IS IT BAD?" LET ME BREAK IT DOWN IN STAGES, SO THAT THERE ARE NO MISINTERPRETATIONS AND I CAN PUT MY INTERPRETATION INTO PERSPECTIVE.

FIRST STAGE OF CODEPENDENT PARENTING: THE REASON FOR HAVING A BABY WOULD BE FOR THE COUPLE/INDIVIDUAL FEELING EMPTY, BORED, UNHAPPY AND USE THE BABY FOR HAPPINESS, THUS GIVING PURPOSE OR FULFILLMENT. THIS IS DAMAGING FROM THE GET GO AS FULFILLMENT SHOULD BE ATTAINED FROM WITHIN BEFORE THE BABY IS BORN, IF POSSIBLE, TO BE SURE YOU ARE GIVING BABY FULL CARE. THE KNOWING OF SELF AND GAINING ENERGY DAILY, ALL BY OURSELVES IS THE KEY TO NOT HAVING ATTACHMENT.

NOW I HAVE SPOKEN ABOUT 'CODEPENDENT PARENTING' WOULD THIS TRIGGER YOU? IF SO, WAS IT FROM EXPERIENCING THE EFFECTS FROM YOUR PARENT OR GUARDIAN? OR IS THE TRIGGER BECAUSE THIS IS YOU DOING IT TO YOUR KIDS?

SO MANY PEOPLE ARE LOOKING FOR THE UNCONDITIONAL LOVE. THEY ARE LOOKING FOR THE ONE THAT THEY CAN LOVE, NO MATTER WHAT. WHERE DOES THIS NEED COME FROM? NOT BEING LOVED AS A CHILD OR BY A PARENT? A SERIES OF BAD RELATIONSHIPS? LACK OF SELF ACCEPTANCE BASED ON THE PREVIOUS?

THE SECOND STAGE IS WHEN BABY ARRIVES AND ALL THE LOVE (OR ATTACHMENT) IS GIVEN TO THE CHILD AND NONE TO SELF. THIS IS WHERE THE DOWNWARDS SPIRAL BEGINS. YOU CAN'T GIVE TOO MUCH LOVE, BUT YOU CAN GIVE TOO MUCH ATTACHMENT; CUDDLES WHEN THE PARENT/GUARDIAN IS DOWN IN THE DUMPS AND NOT FEELING GOOD. THIS IS NOT FOR THE CHILD, IT'S FOR THE PARENT. SHOWERING WITH

CONSTANT GIFTS AND ATTENTION AS TO SHOW MORE LOVE WHEN IT ISN'T NECESSARY. DISCIPLINING THE CHILD WHEN THE PARENT IS UPSET OR WORSE, NOT DISCIPLINING THE CHILD BECAUSE THE PARENT IS HAPPY. DOES THIS SOUND FAMILIAR FROM YOUR LIFE OR THE LIFE OF SOMEONE YOU KNOW? IT DOESN'T SOUND VERY UNCONDITIONAL DOES IT?

THE THIRD STAGE IS WHEN THE CHILD BEGINS TO GROW UP IN THE IMAGE THE PARENT/GUARDIAN WISHES TO CREATE... THE WAY THAT THEY DRESS, THE ACTIVITIES THAT THEY ARE INVOLVED IN, EVEN HOW THEY SPEAK SO THAT THEY ARE THE MOST POLITE OR 'THE COOLEST KID', SO THAT THE PARENT GETS THE PRAISE! ARE YOU STARTING TO SEE THE PICTURE?

THE FOURTH STAGE IS WHEN THE PARENT NOW HAS A CHILD THAT THEY CAN TALK TO ABOUT PERSONAL THINGS LIKE RELATIONSHIPS, WORK, FAMILY AND PROBLEMS. THIS IS WHERE THEY BECOME 'THEIR BEST FRIEND'. THEY TALK TO THEM IN A WAY THAT THEY ARE USING THE CHILD TO VENT THEIR EMOTIONS AND THIS THEN BEGINS TO POISON THE MIND OF THE CHILD AND THEY BEGIN TO TAKE THE DEPENDENT PARENT'S VISION AS THEIR OWN AND WILL BEGIN TO SEE THE WORLD THROUGH THEIR PARENT'S EYES. CHILDREN ARE NOT EMOTIONALLY READY TO COPE WITH ANY OF THIS AS THEY HAVE LITTLE LIFE EXPERIENCE AND ARE NOT EMOTIONALLY MATURE. DO YOU OR ANYONE YOU KNOW LET YOUR CHILD IN TO YOUR PERSONAL ADULT CONVERSATIONS?

THE FIFTH STAGE IS WHEN THE CHILD IS NOW A TEEN AND HAD NOT BEEN TREATED AS THEY SHOULD WHEN BEING BROUGHT UP, THAT IS, ACCORDING TO THEIR UNIQUENESS. THEY HAVE BEEN TREATED ACCORDING TO THE PARENT'S UNIQUENESS BECAUSE THE PARENT HAD BEEN TREATED ACCORDING TO THEIR PARENT'S UNIQUENESS. DID YOU EVER WONDER WHY PROBLEMS WITH THE LAW AND ADDICTION BEGIN AROUND 14 YEARS OLD?

THE REASON IS; AROUND 13 YEARS OLD EVERYONE GOES THROUGH THE

BIGGEST BRAIN EVENT IN THEIR LIFE CALLED "SYNAPTIC PRUNING". PRIOR TO 13 YEARS OLD, EVERY CHILD HAS ACCESS TO ALL THEIR BRAIN, WHICH IS WHY THEY ARE SO SMART. THEIR BRAIN CAN BE SEEN AS A FOREST AND HOW THEY WERE TRAINED TO USE THEIR BRAIN WORE SPECIFIC PATHS IN THEIR FOREST.

AROUND 13 YEARS OLD, THEY LOSE ACCESS TO THOSE TREES THAT AREN'T ON THE PATHS THAT THEY HAVE CREATED. FURTHERMORE, PUBERTY TURNS THESE PATHS INTO SUPERHIGHWAYS THAT THEY WILL WANT TO DRIVE DOWN AS FAST AS POSSIBLE. IF THESE SUPERHIGHWAYS AREN'T IN LINE WITH THEIR UNIQUENESS, THEN THE INTANGIBLE DRIVER OF THEIR MIND/SOUL IS GOING TO CRASH AND THE TEENAGER IS GOING TO GET SUPER FRUSTRATED BY THEIR INABILITY TO DRIVE PATHS THEY USED TO BE ABLE TO DRIVE OR NOW WANT TO DRIVE ACCORDING TO THEIR UNIQUENESS.

THE CHILD'S NEURAL PATHWAYS REDUCE TO THE ONES THEY USE THE MOST (THE PROGRAMMED ONES), MEANING THE CHILD'S BRAIN DOESN'T MATCH WHO THEY WERE BORN TO BE AND THEN THE TROUBLE STARTS FOR THE PARENT! CLASHES IN PERSONALITY, BEHAVIOUR PROBLEMS, POSSIBLY THE CHILD EVEN BECOMING ALMOST RECLUSIVE AS THEY DON'T UNDERSTAND THEMSELVES! IT'S NOT SOUNDING NICE IS IT?

WHEN THE CONFLICTS COME ABOUT, THE PARENT WILL BE FIGHTING THEMSELVES (WHAT THEY CREATED). THE PARENT STILL HAS NO IDEA WHO THEIR CHILD REALLY IS AND IT'S SCARY! THIS CAN BE MAKE OR BREAK IN THE RELATIONSHIP TOO AS MOST CODEPENDENT PARENTS/GUARDIANS WILL PUNISH THE CHILD FOR THE BEHAVIOUR TAUGHT, OR PUNISH THE CHILD FOR TRYING TO FIND THEIR OWN WAY IN THEIR MUCH CONFUSED BODY AND BRAIN.

I KNOW YOU ARE PROBABLY THINKING THIS SOUNDS A LITTLE DRAMATIC, LOOK AROUND AND WATCH IT HAPPEN EVERYWHERE!

THE SIXTH STAGE CAN GO A COUPLE OF WAYS, IT CAN LEAD TO THE PARENT CREATING EXACTLY WHAT THEY WANTED (THE PRIZE CHILD

THAT WILL NEVER KNOW TRUE FULFILMENT) OR CREATING THE PROBLEM CHILD THAT IS NEVER HAPPY, NEVER SETTLED AND HAS TO TRY AND GAIN ENERGY BY REBELLING AND TRYING DIFFERENT WAYS TO FEEL THEMSELVES... NARCOTICS, CRIME, NO FOCUS OR PURPOSE, SOMETIMES EVEN SUICIDE!

THERE ARE GOOD PARENTS OUT THERE AND I FEEL THAT THEY WILL NOT BE TRIGGERED BY WHAT THEY JUST READ AND MAY EVEN APPRECIATE GETTING AN EXPLANATION FOR WHAT THEY HAVE SEEN. THERE COULD BE SOME CRINGING OR FEELING LOTS OF GUILT AT THIS POINT IN THIS CHAPTER, THIS IS NOT JUDGEMENT, THIS IS BEING PRESENTED WITH CHOICE. WHICH ONE ARE YOU IF YOU HAVE KIDS?

IN THE FINAL CHAPTER, WE WILL TALK ABOUT HOW TO DISSOLVE PROBLEMS, WHICH IS MORE THAN JUST SOLVING THEM. CODEPENDENT PARENTING IS THE PARENT TRYING TO SOLVE THE ISSUE OF RAISING A "GOOD KID" AND WE HAVE SEEN THAT IT RESULTS IN THE CREATION OF EVEN MORE PROBLEMS.

WHAT IS THE DISSOLVE TO CODEPENDENT PARENTING? IS IT NOT HAVING CHILDREN UNTIL THE PARENT KNOWS, UNDERSTANDS AND ACCEPTS THEMSELVES, WITHOUT ATTACHMENTS? IS IT GIVING THE CHILD WHAT THE CHILD NEEDS, BASED ON WHO THEY ARE AT SOUL LEVEL?

NOW YOU HAVE READ THIS, WHAT WOULD YOU CLASS AS A GOOD PARENT? HOW DO YOU THINK A CHILD CAN BE UNDERSTOOD FROM A YOUNG AGE AND NURTURED AND NOT PROGRAMMED?

EVERY HUMAN BEING BORN INTO THIS WORLD HAS A PURPOSE, A JOB TO DO AND THINGS TO LEARN TO COMPLETE THEIR SOUL'S JOURNEY THAT SHOULD NOT BE MANIPULATED. CHILDREN SHOULD NOT BE WHAT A PARENT WANTS THEM TO BE SO THAT THEY CAN BE PROUD.

MY FRIEND AND COLLEAGUE JOHN LENHART (FLOWCESS.COM), THAT I'VE MENTIONED IN PREVIOUS CHAPTERS, HAS THE ONLY NON CONTRADICTORY MODEL FOR THE MIND AND BRAIN AND SO HE IS ABLE

TO HELP PARENTS RAISE THEIR CHILD ON PURPOSE BY UNDERSTANDING THE CHILD'S UNIQUENESS, WHICH INCLUDES THEIR INTANGIBLE DRIVER, PICTURE PERSPECTIVE, AND PROCESSING STYLE OF THE BRAIN. IS THAT NOT UNBELIEVABLE?

WITH THE HEALTHY COMMUNICATION GUIDELINES I MENTIONED EARLIER, THIS WOULD ENSURE THAT THE CHILD IS SPOKEN TO AND UNDERSTOOD PROPERLY AND WILL HAVE A HEALTHY BRAIN THAT WILL LEAD TO HEALTHY BEHAVIOR. WOULD YOU DO IT ON PURPOSE IF YOU THOUGHT YOU COULD? WILL YOU DO THIS NOW THAT YOU KNOW YOU CAN? WE SAY CHILDREN FROM AROUND 8-9 CAN DO THE QUIZ, DESIGNED TO UNDERSTAND THEM AND OLDER AS THEY ARE DEVELOPING TOO QUICKLY UP UNTIL AGE 7.

MOST PEOPLE IN JAIL ARE JUST KIDS THAT WEREN'T UNDERSTOOD AS CHILDREN AND, AS MUCH AS THE PRISONS ARE BIG BUSINESS, WE AS PEOPLE CAN ENSURE THAT EVERYONE IS UNDERSTOOD AND THAT WOULD SEVERELY LOWER CRIME AND SUICIDE! HAVE YOU EVER HEARD OF THE SYSTEM OFFERING A DISSOLVE? THEY USE REWARD AND PUNISHMENT ON PEOPLE WHO DON'T KNOW THEMSELVES WHICH IS KNOWN AS RESOLVE AND TREATS PEOPLE LIKE ANIMALS! TEACH PEOPLE AND TREAT THEM THE WAY THAT THEY WANT TO BE TREATED! IF THAT IS HOW A DOG IS TREATED, HOW WILL IT WORK ON HUMANS? WE WILL TALK MORE ABOUT THIS IN THE LAST CHAPTER.

I MET JOHN WHEN HE ASKED MY DEFINITIONS FOR 'LEADER' AND 'PARENT'. WHAT ARE YOUR DEFINITIONS FOR LEADER AND PARENT? DO YOU THINK THAT THEY ARE THE SAME?

JOHN SAID A LEADER FACILITATES THE PURPOSE AND PROGRESS OF ANOTHER, SO PARENTS CAN BE LEADERS, HOWEVER, THEY ARE SOMETHING MORE. A BIRD TEACHES THEIR YOUNG TO FLY. WHAT OUGHT HUMANS TEACH THEIR YOUNG?

THE WORD "MAN" COMES FROM THE SANSKRIT WORD "MANU" WHICH MEANS "TO THINK". THIS MEANS PARENTS OUGHT TO TEACH THEIR

CHILDREN HOW TO THINK. NOTICE, THIS IS NOT WHAT TO THINK, THAT IS PROGRAMMING. THIS IS NOT WHY TO THINK, THAT OUGHT TO BE OBVIOUS: SO YOU AREN'T PROGRAMMED.

I HAVE BEEN ENCOURAGING YOU TO LEARN HOW TO THINK SINCE THE BEGINNING OF THIS BOOK! DO YOU KNOW HOW TO THINK?

IF PARENTS DON'T KNOW HOW TO THINK, WHO DO THEY LOOK TO IN ORDER TO TEACH THEIR KIDS HOW TO THINK?

CHAPTER 17: EDUCATION

I USED TO FEEL I WAS WELL EDUCATED IN WAYS OF LIFE. AS MUCH AS I WASN'T HIGHLY EDUCATED IN CERTAIN SUBJECTS, I COULD ALWAYS RESONATE WITH WHAT PEOPLE WERE SAYING IN TERMS OF ENERGY AND UNDERSTANDING THEM AS PEOPLE. TURNS OUT IT WAS A TALENT THAT WAS NATURAL TO ME BUT NOT EVERYONE.

PEOPLE OF ALL BACKGROUNDS, FROM STREET LIVING TO HIGH FLYING MILLIONAIRES, FELT THAT THEY COULD TALK TO ME ABOUT EVERYTHING AND I'D UNDERSTAND. THEN WHEN THEY ASKED ABOUT MY EDUCATION, THEY'D BE SHOCKED AS I DIDN'T HAVE MUCH. IT IS LIKE A WISDOM THAT HAS BEEN GIVEN OVER TIME AND A TRUTH THAT CANNOT BE ARGUED, UNLESS I'M TALKING TO SOMEONE WHO IS MORE ON THE CLOSED-MINDED SIDE. I WAS ABLE TO ACCEPT OPINIONS, VISIONS AND UNDERSTANDING OF OTHERS, WHILE SEEING THE BALANCED TRUTH.

THE DEFINITION OF EDUCATION TO ME IS: BEING TAUGHT ABOUT A SUBJECT WHILE BEING ABLE TO QUESTION AND RESEARCH, TO GROW A SUBJECT; LEARNING HOW TO THINK. WHAT WOULD YOUR DEFINITION OF

EDUCATION BE?

THE DEFINITION OF INDOCTRINATION TO ME IS: BEING PROGRAMMED INTO A ONE-TRACK WAY OF THINKING, WHILE NOT BEING ABLE TO QUESTION THE NARRATIVE; LEARNING WHAT TO THINK. WHAT WOULD YOUR DEFINITION OF INDOCTRINATION BE?

LET'S START WITH PRE-SCHOOL AND KINDERGARTEN:

I TOUCHED ON PARENTING IN THE EARLIER CHAPTER AND SINCE WE KNOW THE PARENT IS THEIR FIRST TEACHER, MOST CHILDREN WILL THINK LIKE THEIR PARENTS IN MOST WAYS, AS THEY ARE NOT ABLE TO QUESTION THE ADULT. IS THIS EDUCATING A CHILD OR INDOCTRINATING THEM?

CHILDREN THEN GO TO A CHILD MINDER OR PRE-SCHOOL WHERE THEY ARE TAUGHT TO EXPLORE, BUT WITHIN THE REALMS OF CONTROL AND RULES OF SOCIETY. THEN THEY GO TO KINDERGARTEN. WHAT DO YOU THINK HAPPENS IN THE CLASS? HAS A KINDERGARTEN TEACHER EVER BEEN HONEST WITH YOU?

IT TURNS OUT, THE CHILDREN PLAY OUT THEIR HOME ISSUES DURING SCHOOL PLAYTIME AND THE TEACHER LEARNS EVERYTHING ABOUT THE FAMILY. "BRIAN, COME HERE AND BE THE DADDY. YOU CAME HOME DRUNK AND I'M MAD AT YOU." DO YOU KNOW WHERE THE CHILDREN REALLY LEARN THE RULES FOR SOCIETY? FROM OTHER CHILDREN!

THIS IS WHERE THE FIRST CONFLICTS OF LIFE COME INTO PLAY FOR THE POOR CHILDREN… INCLUDING YOU, WHEN YOU WERE YOUNG. THE RULES OF SOCIETY, DO NOT ALWAYS COINCIDE WITH WHAT HAPPENS IN THE HOME. HOW IS A TEACHER SUPPOSED TO DEAL WITH ALL THE CHILDREN? DO THEY TREAT EACH CHILD ACCORDING TO THEIR UNIQUENESS OR AT THE VERY LEAST HOW THEIR PARENTS WANT THE CHILD TO BE TREATED?

NO, AND THIS CAUSES CHILDREN TO BE TREATED LIKE A COLLECTIVE OF WILD ANIMALS, WHO NEED TO BE TAMED, JUST IN TIME FOR THEM TO

START PRIMARY SCHOOL, SO THAT IT ISN'T A FREE FOR ALL AND THEY CAN THEN BE TAUGHT WITHOUT ANY DISRUPTION TO OTHER STUDENTS. WHY WOULD THEY BE DISRUPTIVE?

WHAT WOULD THE BENEFITS BE FOR LETTING A CHILD TEACH THE ADULTS WHAT THEY WANT AND NEED, WHILE THE ADULT'S ONLY ROLE IS TO PROTECT THEM FROM HARM OR INJURY, NURTURING THEIR UNIQUENESS AND ENCOURAGING THEM TO EXPLORE SAFELY?

PRIMARY:

PRIMARY SCHOOL IS WHERE CHILDREN LEARN HOW TO READ, WRITE, INTERACT AND BE THE BEST (NOT THEIR UNIQUE BEST) WITHIN A SOCIETY DRIVEN MACHINE, ALL TAUGHT THE SAME THINGS IN A ONE SIZE FITS ALL MANNER. IF THEY DON'T MEET THE REQUIREMENTS, THEY ARE GIVEN EXTRA TUITION TO PUSH THEM FURTHER INTO THE ONE WAY OF WORKING.

THEY ARE SOFTLY PUSHED UNTIL THEY MANAGE OR BREAK AND BECOME A HINDRANCE TO THE SYSTEM AND ARE MADE TO FEEL INADEQUATE BY NOT BEING UNDERSTOOD, WHILE WATCHING OTHERS BE REWARDED FOR BEING SMART AND WELL BEHAVED AS THEY EASILY COMPLY AND ARE ABLE TO DO THE TASKS AND SOAK IN THE DOCTRINE MUCH EASIER. DO YOU THINK THIS SOUNDS FAIR?

YES, THIS WILL ALL BE TRIGGERING WHOEVER IS READING JUST NOW, BUT WHY? WERE YOU THE KID THAT EXCELLED? WERE YOU THE KID THAT WASN'T UNDERSTOOD? OR WERE YOU THE KID LIKE ME THAT WASN'T ON A SIDE, BUT KNEW SOMETHING WASN'T RIGHT ABOUT THE WHOLE SYSTEM?

CHILDREN ARE NOW DIAGNOSED AT A YOUNG AGE.... ADD, ADHD, ASPERGERS, DYSLEXIA AND A WHOLE RIDICULOUS AMOUNT OF OTHER NEGATIVE LABELS AT A YOUNG AGE. DO YOU FEEL THIS WILL SET THEM UP FEELING POWERFUL IN LIFE? IF THEY CAN'T LEARN A CERTAIN WAY, SHOULD THEY BE LABELED AND FEEL NOT GOOD ENOUGH? WHEN ARE

YOU GOING TO STAND UP FOR THE CHILDREN?

WHAT IF THE WAY A CHILD (HUMAN BEING) LEARNS IS DIFFERENT, DUE TO THEIR UNIQUENESS, HOW THEIR BRAIN HAS HABITUATED, HOW THEY ARE OR AREN'T UNDERSTOOD? WOULD THAT NOT MEAN THE SYSTEM, TEACHERS AND PARENTS SHOULD BE WORKING FOR THE CHILD?

MY FRIEND JOHN LENHART HAS WORKED WITH SCHOOLS LONG ENOUGH TO REALISE SCHOOL IS MADE FOR THE CHILDREN THAT ACT MOST LIKE A COMPUTER. THE FURTHER AWAY A CHILD IS FROM ACTING LIKE A COMPUTER, THE MORE THE CHILD IS DIAGNOSED WITH A PROBLEM. HAVE YOU EVER HEARD OF A POSITIVE DIAGNOSIS?

FINDING OUT THE CHILD'S UNIQUENESS IS A POSITIVE DIAGNOSIS AND IT LEADS TO CHILDREN UNDERSTANDING HOW THEY LEARN. IT NOT ONLY HELPS THE TEACHER DEAL WITH THE CHILD'S BEHAVIOUR, BUT IT CAN CATCH STUDENTS UP THAT ARE TESTING MORE THAN A YEAR BEHIND IN COMPETENCY! ISN'T THIS BECOMING MORE IMPORTANT BECAUSE OF HOW FAR THE KIDS GOT BEHIND DURING COVID?

WHEN YOU UNDERSTAND HOW THE MIND AND BRAIN WORK, SEVERAL ISSUES IMMEDIATELY BECOME APPARENT WHEN THINKING ABOUT PRIMARY SCHOOL KIDS.

FIRST, NINE YEAR OLDS ARE INTERNALLY MOTIVATED TO ACHIEVE A REWARD. TEN YEAR OLDS ARE EXTERNALLY MOTIVATED TO AVOID A PUNISHMENT, WHICH IS WHEN MOST PEOPLE LOSE THEIR CREATIVITY. WHY? BULLYING! TEN YEARS OLD IS WHEN KIDS LEARN THE EASIEST WAY TO FEEL GOOD ABOUT YOURSELF IS NOT TO DO GOOD, BUT TO TEAR SOMEONE ELSE DOWN.

SECOND, WOULD YOU LET AN 11 YEAR OLD TEACH YOU HOW TO DATE? NO? WHY NOT? ACTUALLY, YOU ARE TOO LATE BECAUSE YOU ALREADY DID! ALL OF US LEARNED HOW TO DATE FROM OTHER KIDS WHEN WE WERE AROUND ELEVEN YEARS OLD. WONDER WHY RELATIONSHIPS AND MARRIAGES FAIL? IT'S BECAUSE WE ARE FOLLOWING A PLAN CREATED BY

AN ELEVEN YEAR OLD!

THIRD, WE DON'T LEARN BY FOCUSING ON A SUBJECT. WE LEARN BY DOING WHICH INVOLVES MORE THAN ONE SUBJECT AT A TIME. DO YOU THINK PEOPLE LEARN A SECOND LANGUAGE BETTER AT HOME OR SCHOOL? STUDIES SHOW IT'S AT HOME BECAUSE THE STUDENT ISN'T CONFINED TO JUST LEARNING THE LANGUAGE; THEY LEARN IT THROUGH APPLICATIONS. SCHOOL IS NOT ABOUT LEARNING, IF IT WAS, WE WOULD TEACH DIFFERENTLY. SCHOOL IS ABOUT FINDING OUT WHO THE SMARTEST KIDS ARE, SO THE KIDS ARE TAUGHT IN A WAY THAT MAKES LEARNING HARD.

FINALLY, WHAT DO YOU THINK HAPPENS TO A TEACHER'S THOUGHT PROCESS WHEN THEY SPEND THEIR DAY SURROUNDED BY DOZENS OF KIDS? THE TEACHER SYNCS INTO THE GROUP'S THOUGHT PROCESS RATHER THAN GETTING THE KIDS TO SYNC INTO THEIRS. THIS ISN'T THAT BAD WHEN THE GROUP IS 9 YEAR OLDS AND YOUNGER. HOWEVER, AS THE KIDS GET TO THE BULLYING AGE, THE TEACHER'S THOUGHT PROCESS BEGINS TO SUFFER. IS THIS THE PERSON YOU WANT TO TEACH YOUR CHILD HOW TO THINK? I HOPE NOT BECAUSE EVERY TEACHER WILL TELL YOU THAT, THAT IS NOT THE JOB THEY SIGNED UP FOR. THEY ARE THERE TO TEACH THE CHILD WHAT TO THINK.

WHY IS THERE NOT A METHOD IN PLACE TO DETERMINE THE UNIQUENESS OF A CHILD? WHAT DO YOU THINK ABOUT THE SYSTEM WHEN BROKEN DOWN LIKE THIS AND EXPLAINED? WE HAVE NOT EVEN REACHED PUBERTY IN THIS CHAPTER SO FAR FOR THE POOR KIDS, AND THE SYSTEM WE ARE PROGRAMMED TO LOVE AND ADHERE TO ISN'T LOOKING RIGHT AND JUST IS IT? CAN YOU EVEN SEE WHAT PROBLEMS EXIST? WHAT'S YOUR DISSOLVE ON THE SITUATION?

HIGH SCHOOL:

HIGH SCHOOL IS WHERE THE KIDS GET TO GO INTO THE BIGGER SCHOOL, FULL OF PRE-PUBESCENT AND HORMONAL MIXED TEENS TO EXPLORE THEMSELVES, WHILE NOW LOOKING TO WORK TOWARDS

COLLEGE/UNIVERSITY, TO HAVE THAT CAREER. THE GOOD ONES, THAT BEHAVE, THAT SOAK IN EXACTLY WHAT THEY ARE TAUGHT, WHILE STUDYING HARD ARE USUALLY PROMISED A JOB IN THE SYSTEM. THE SYSTEM BEING THE LARGE MACHINE THAT CONTROLS ALL OF HUMANITY... LAW, HEALTH CARE, MEDICINE, FINANCE, ALONG WITH OTHERS THAT I'M SURE YOU CAN ADD TO THE LIST.

WORKING FOR THE SYSTEM IS SOLD TO THE TEENS AS SUCCESS. THEY GET AROUND TWO YEARS TO PROVE THEIR ACADEMIC SKILLS (IN THE UK ANYWAY) TO THEN BE PUT IN CLASSES, BASED ON MERIT AND ACHIEVEMENT.

THERE WILL BE SOME OF YOU THINKING THIS IS NORMAL, BUT WHAT IF THE LOWER CLASSES WERE MORE CAPABLE, IF ONLY THEY WERE TAUGHT DIFFERENT? WHAT IF THEY WEREN'T BEING TAUGHT ACCORDING TO THEIR UNIQUENESS AND THE SYSTEM WAS FAILING THEM? WHAT IF THE CREAM OF THE CROP WAS ONLY INDIVIDUALS THAT FITTED INTO A CERTAIN BOX TO KEEP THE SYSTEM FROM BEING DISRUPTED AND THE SYSTEM LOSING CONTROL? I'LL TALK MORE ABOUT THIS LATER!

NOW, WE HAVE TEENS WHO HAVE BEEN CONTROLLED FROM BIRTH, ALL THE WAY TO HIGH SCHOOL AND GOING THROUGH PUBERTY. WE ARE TAUGHT THAT GOING THROUGH PUBERTY IS THE ROAD TO BECOMING AN ADULT, WHILE PART OF THIS IS TRUE, THERE IS ANOTHER HUUUGE PROCESS THAT HAPPENS AT THE AGE OF 13 AND WE SAW IT'S CALLED SYNAPTIC PRUNING, WHICH I SPOKE OF IN THE PREVIOUS CHAPTER. THIS IS WHAT DETERMINES IF A TEEN WILL GROW OLDER WITH A HEALTHY, EXPANSIVE BRAIN, OR THE CLOSED MINDSET WE SEE IN THE MAJORITY OF ADULTS TODAY, WHICH CAUSES SO MUCH DIVISION AND BREAKS DOWN THE COMMUNITY OF HUMANKIND.

I SUGGEST SOME STUDY ON SYNAPTIC PRUNING TO UNDERSTAND FULLY OR GO ON TO MY 'TRUTH IN THE 2020S' YOUTUBE CHANNEL TO FIND OUT MORE. THERE IS SO MUCH LIFE-CHANGING FREE INFORMATION ON THERE THAT YOU CAN APPLY TRUTH TO YOUR LIFE (ON PURPOSE) AND LIVE THE LIFE YOU WANT TO REALLY LIVE.

WHILE OUR SYNAPSES ARE PRUNED THROUGH THE SYNAPTIC PRUNING PROCESS, IT IS SUPERCHARGED BY PUBERTY AND THIS IS WHERE WE ALL GET LOST AND ATTACH OURSELVES TO OTHER PEOPLE'S WAYS OF WORKING, CHOOSE CAREERS BASED ON MONEY OR FAMILY EXPECTATION AND EVEN BECOME THE WORST VERSION OF OURSELVES AND NEVER UNDERSTAND HOW TO BREAK THE CYCLE, WHICH LEADS US TO LIVE AN UNFULFILLED LIFE. ADD IN THE PRESSURE TO SUCCEED AND YOU CAN SEE WHY BULLYING IS SO VICIOUS IN HIGH SCHOOL!

WE ALL HAVE A UNIQUE MIND AND BRAIN. THE BRAIN IS THE CAR AND THE MIND IS THE DRIVER. BEFORE SYNAPTIC PRUNING, IT'S AS IF WE ARE ABLE TO DRIVE ANY CAR. HOWEVER, AFTER SYNAPTIC PRUNING, WE END UP WITH ONLY ONE CAR AND THERE'S A 2% CHANCE IT MATCHES OUR UNIQUENESS. IF WE'VE BEEN BULLIED TO THE POINT THAT WE KEEP THAT PATHWAY AFTER SYNAPTIC PRUNING, OUR CHANCES OF GETTING THE RIGHT CAR IS CLOSE TO ZERO.

CHOOSING THE WRONG TYPE OF CAR TO TAKE US THROUGH LIFE AND AS MUCH AS IT SOUNDS TRIVIAL, IT'S IMPERATIVE TO BE IN THE RIGHT CAR. EXAMPLE: IF YOU HAVE A SLOW SUNDAY DRIVER MIND, BUT CHOOSE A RACE CAR TO GET THROUGH LIFE, YOU ARE NOT AT ONE WITH YOURSELF. IF YOUR BRAIN IS A 25 TONNE TRUCK BUT YOUR MIND IS A RACE CAR DRIVER, AGAIN IT'S NOT GOING TO WORK.

WITH THE INTANGIBLE DRIVER QUIZ AT FLOWCESS.COM/INTANGIBLEDRIVER, A CHILD BETWEEN 8 AND 12 (JUST BEFORE SYNAPTIC PRUNING) CAN BE UNDERSTOOD, SPOKEN TO AND BE TREATED THE WAY THAT THEY WANT TO BE TREATED SO THEY FLOW THROUGH LIFE AND DON'T HAVE TO STRUGGLE TO FIND OUT WHICH CAR THEY DRIVE THROUGH TRIAL AND ERROR! PUBERTY WOULD ACTUALLY TURN THEM INTO A GENIUS! MORE THAN 100 YEARS AGO, TEENAGERS REGULARLY MADE BENEFICIAL CONTRIBUTIONS THAT CHANGED THE WORLD!

HOW IMPORTANT DO YOU FEEL IT IS TO HAVE THIS INFORMATION? HOW DIFFERENT WOULD YOUR LIFE HAVE BEEN IF YOU WERE ABLE TO

MAINTAIN A HEALTHY BRAIN FROM AGE 13? I'VE WITNESSED IT, IT'S BEAUTIFUL!

COLLEGE/UNIVERSITY:

FOR SOME PEOPLE, GOING TO COLLEGE/UNIVERSITY IS A CHOICE, TO OTHERS IT'S PUSHED ON TO THEM BY FAMILY OR PEERS. CHOICES COME FROM THE FALSE DEFINITION OF SUCCESS WHICH CAN BE: TO BE FINANCIALLY RICH; TO BE THE BEST; TO HAVE THE MOST; TO HIDE BEHIND THE LABEL OF A TITLE TO HIDE INSECURITIES. I'M NOT SAYING ALL, JUST A MAJORITY AND A LOT OF THIS IS DONE WITHOUT PEOPLE THINKING ABOUT IT. WHAT IS YOUR DEFINITION OF SUCCESS? WHY DID YOU MAKE YOUR DECISION FOR THE CAREER/JOB YOU ARE IN? WAS IT MONEY? DESPERATION? EASE OF LIFE? LACK OF SELF BELIEF? IF NONE OF THESE, PLEASE WRITE YOUR OWN ANSWER DOWN AND WHAT YOU'D DO IF YOU COULD.

IF COLLEGE/UNIVERSITY IS YOUR TRADE TRAINING, THIS MEANS THERE IS A CLEAR DIRECTION AS TO WHERE YOU WANT TO GO, THERE ISN'T ALWAYS A JOB AT THE END, SO THIS MEANS MANY GO THROUGH THE PROCESS AND END UP DOING SOMETHING ELSE! THIS CAN BE TRAGIC IN SOME CASES, BUT A BLESSING IN OTHERS. AS PEOPLE GROW AND TIME PASSES, THEY CAN OPEN UP TO DIFFERENT AVENUES AND IT CAN HAVE A POSITIVE OR NEGATIVE EFFECT. IMAGINE KNOWING WHAT CAR TO DRIVE AND CHOOSING A CAREER THAT YOU DON'T HAVE TO WORK SO HARD AND IT'S SO NATURAL TO YOU THAT YOU ENJOY IT! WOULD YOU SIGN YOUR KIDS UP? WOULD YOU SIGN UP?

WHEN YOU LOOK AT THE PEOPLE WHO HAVE BENEFITED HUMANITY THE MOST, DO YOU THINK THEY WERE VERY SIMILAR TO A COMPUTER? STUDIES HAVE SHOWN THAT OVER 60% OF THE PEOPLE WHO HAD THE MOST IMPACT ON MODERN HUMANITY HAD SERIOUS ISSUES IN SCHOOL! A COMPUTER CAN ONLY DO WHAT IT HAS BEEN PROGRAMMED TO DO. INNOVATION COMES FROM THOSE STUDENTS WHO ARE DECLARED PROBLEM STUDENTS. ARE WE ELIMINATING MORE OF THESE PEOPLE FROM OUR FUTURE AS WE BECOME MORE EFFICIENT WITH OUR

DIAGNOSING OF CHILDREN?

THERE'S AN OLD SAYING ABOUT THE FUTURE OF COLLEGE STUDENTS. THE ONES WHO GET ALL A'S BECOME PROFESSORS AT THE UNIVERSITY. THE ONES WHO GET ALL B'S GET GOOD JOBS. THE ONES WHO GET C'S GET BAD JOBS. THE ONES WHO GET D'S OR FAIL OUT BECOME THE PEOPLE THAT THE COLLEGE NAMES THEIR BUILDINGS AFTER!

THE SYSTEM:

DO YOU KNOW WHAT WAS THE ORIGINAL GOAL OF THE CURRENT EDUCATION SYSTEM THAT WE HAVE HAD FOR OVER 100 YEARS?

THE SYSTEM THAT EDUCATES/INDOCTRINATES IS TAUGHT FROM EARLY YEARS TO CONDITION THE MINDS OF YOUNGSTERS TO BE ABLE TO WORK IN FACTORIES!

MANY WILL SAY THAT IT IS HEALTHY AND NEEDED, WHILE OTHERS WILL SAY THAT IT'S BAD TO TRY TO PROGRAM EVERY HUMAN BEING THAT GOES TO PRESCHOOL/KINDERGARTEN, PRIMARY, HIGH SCHOOL, AND COLLEGE/UNIVERSITY WITH THE SAME TEACHINGS, BECAUSE THE STUDENTS ARE NOT BEING TREATED LIKE A UNIQUE HUMAN BEING. INSTEAD, HUMANS ARE TREATED LIKE COMPUTERS AND ANIMALS, PROGRAMMED AND TAUGHT ON THE PUNISH AND REWARD METHOD WHICH IS IN FACT NOT RIGHT AND JUST. WHAT DO YOU THINK OF THE EDUCATION SYSTEM, FROM YOUR OWN PERSPECTIVE AND WHAT WOULD YOU DO TO IMPROVE/DISSOLVE IT?

LET'S LOOK AT WHAT INTELLIGENCE IS! IS IT BEING ABLE TO SOAK IN EVERYTHING YOU ARE TOLD LIKE A COMPUTER? OR IS IT THE ABILITY TO THINK FOR YOURSELF AND LOOK FOR TRUTH? WHY ARE PEOPLE WHO THINK FOR THEMSELVES DEMONISED IN ANY OF THE EDUCATION INSTITUTIONS?

I, MYSELF UNDERSTOOD MOST THINGS AT SCHOOL, BUT FOUND MYSELF EITHER SWITCHED ON WITH THE THINGS I LIKED OR SWITCHED OFF WITH

THE THINGS I DIDN'T LIKE. DO YOU THINK IT IS FAIR TO PUSH ANY HUMAN BEING THROUGH SOMETHING THEY DON'T LIKE AND CAN'T CONNECT WITH, IN ORDER TO ASSESS THEM ON IT AND COMPARE THEM TO THE PEOPLE WHO ARE SWITCHED ON TO IT?

WHAT IF I TOLD YOU THAT THE HUMAN BRAIN IS HALF INFORMATION AND HALF EMOTION. THINK ABOUT IT, IF I SAY "VANILLA ICE CREAM" AND I SAY "DOG CRAP", YOU HAVE TWO DIFFERENT EMOTIONS, HOPEFULLY! HUMANS RETAIN INFORMATION TO THE SAME DEGREE AS THE EMOTION. THE MORE POSITIVE THE EMOTION, THE MORE LIKELY THEY WILL RETAIN IT. COMPUTERS LEARN REGARDLESS OF THE EMOTION. WHICH ONE DOES EDUCATION THINK WE ARE?

PERSONALLY, WHEN I BECAME SWITCHED OFF, I WAS DISRUPTIVE, I WAS RESTLESS AND THIS WAS UNFAIR TO THE STUDENTS THAT WERE SWITCHED ON IN THAT CLASS BECAUSE I LESSENED THEIR GOOD EMOTION TO THE INFORMATION. WHOSE FAULT WAS THE DISRUPTION TO OTHERS, MINE OR THE WAY THE SYSTEM IS DESIGNED TO HAVE ME THERE? THERE IS NO ASSESSMENT DONE TO THE STUDENT TO FIND OUT IF THE DRIVER AND THEIR CAR IS SUITED TO THE ROAD OR CONDITIONS!!!

TO FINISH THIS CHAPTER, I WOULD LOVE YOU TO ASK YOURSELF: IS A HUMAN THAT HAS HIGHER EDUCATION/INDOCTRINATION A BETTER HUMAN THAN ANOTHER? WHY ARE THEY HELD IN HIGHER REGARD? WHY DOES THE UNQUALIFIED ROAD SWEEPER GET LESS RESPECT THAN THE LAWYER? IS IT FAIR THAT THEY GET LESS, WHEN BOTH ARE USING THE SAME AMOUNT OF TIME FROM THEIR LIVES TO WORK FOR A LIVING?

THE TRUTH IN MY EYES IS: MOST OF THE PEOPLE WHO SPEND THEIR TIME WITH THEIR HEAD IN THE BOOKS, BEING CAREER FOCUSED AND HAVE A GREAT DRIVE FOR OUTER SUCCESS, WILL DO ANYTHING TO GET THERE AND THERE IS LESS CHANCE THAT THEY WILL ASK THE 'WHY' QUESTIONS. THEY WILL JUST ACCEPT 'THIS IS' AND DO WHAT THEY HAVE TO. FOR THIS, THE SYSTEM PAYS THEM HANDSOMELY WITH LARGE PAY PACKETS.

THE SYSTEM KNOWS THAT MOST PEOPLE WILL NOT JEOPARDISE ANY PUBLIC SUCCESSES FOR THE SAKE OF QUESTIONING A NARRATIVE. THIS HAS BEEN CAREFULLY PROGRAMMED INTO THE BRAINS OF ANY CAPABLE HUMAN FROM A YOUNG AND EASILY IMPRESSIONABLE AGE FOR OVER 100 YEARS.

THE EGO THAT IS ATTACHED TO THIS PROCESS IS NOT ALWAYS HEALTHY AND LEADS TO MOST PEOPLE LIVING AS A LABEL AND NOT AS THEMSELVES. THIS IS A TRAGEDY, SO MANY SPECIAL SOULS ARE CONTROLLED IN THIS WAY, WHILE IT LOOKS LIKE FINANCIAL FREEDOM AND SUCCESS, MANY HAVE MINIMAL DEPTH OR QUESTIONING SKILLS, WHILE FEW OF THEM ARE TRULY FULFILLED BECAUSE THEY ARE TOO SCARED TO LOSE MONEY OR FACE, BY BEING THEMSELVES. HOW DO YOU FEEL ABOUT WHAT YOU HAVE JUST READ?

THE SO-CALLED FAILURES, THE NOMADS, THE REBELS, THE LESS EDUCATED/INDOCTRINATED... YOU FALL INTO THE SAME CATEGORY AS ME. YOU MAY HAVE BEEN TOLD THAT YOU ARE AN UNDERACHIEVER, YOU COULD HAVE DONE BETTER, SOCIETY DOESN'T ALWAYS ACCEPT YOU. YOU ARE THE REVOLUTION, BECAUSE YOU ASK QUESTIONS! YOU ARE THE ONES WHO UNCONSCIOUSLY KNOW IN YOUR BRAIN AND YOUR MIND, THAT THINGS AREN'T RIGHT AND YOU DON'T BELONG IN THE SYSTEM. YOU HAVE BEEN SEGREGATED LONG ENOUGH AND CAN JOIN FORCES IN LOVE AND UNDERSTANDING FOR ALL. WE CAN CREATE A NEW WORLD, OUTSIDE OF THE SYSTEM! WHERE YOU FIND OUT WHO YOU REALLY ARE, WHAT SWITCHES YOU ON AND WHAT TYPE OF DRIVER YOU ARE FOR YOUR CAR! IT'S NOT TOO LATE!

THE SYSTEM WILL NEVER BE TAKEN DOWN AS IT IS TOO BIG AND STRONG. ANOTHER SYSTEM IS THE ANSWER, RATHER THAN FEEL A FAILURE FOR TRYING TO MAKE THIS ONE BETTER. YOU ARE THE MASSES, YOU ARE THE POWER, YOU ARE THE LIGHT!

HOW WOULD YOU BEGIN THE REVOLUTION? HOW WOULD YOU START BRINGING EVERY TYPE OF HUMAN TOGETHER? NO MATTER THEIR PROGRAMMED BELIEFS, IT ALL STARTS WITH UNLEARNING, BREAKING

FREE OF THE SO CALLED 'MATRIX' AND REALLY LIVING ALL OF OUR PURPOSES!

CHAPTER 18: CONVENIENCE

WHAT IS CONVENIENCE? WHAT CONVENIENCES DO YOU LIKE? WHAT DO YOU FEEL IS A MUST HAVE?

THIS CHAPTER IS ONE OF THE MOST IMPORTANT IN THIS WHOLE BOOK AND WHEN YOU REALLY CHECK YOURSELF AND BECOME AWARE OF WHAT IS HAPPENING AROUND YOU, LIFE WILL CHANGE FOR THE BETTER... FOR EVERYONE!

I COULD HAVE CONVENIENTLY MADE THIS BOOK AN ON-LINE BOOK AND IT WOULD HAVE BEEN ESPECIALLY CONVENIENT FOR EVERYONE TO HAVE AND DOWNLOAD, BUT IT WOULD NOT HAVE HAD THE DESIRED EFFECT ON THOSE WHO WANTED TO CHANGE THEIR LIFE AND SEE THE WORLD FOR WHAT IT IS, AS YOU CANNOT WRITE IN THE BOOK IF IT'S AN ONLINE DOCUMENT. I CANNOT MAKE YOU SEE THROUGH MY EYES AND WOULDN'T WANT TO. ALL I WISH IS FOR YOU TO LOOK THROUGH YOUR OWN, THROUGH YOU ANSWERING QUESTIONS THAT YOU'D NOT USUALLY BE ASKED.

IF PEOPLE ARE EXPECTED TO DO LESS FOR THEMSELVES, IT WILL HAVE A KNOCK ON EFFECT WITH THEIR BEHAVIOR AND EVEN THEIR THOUGHTS. THEIR TRUST WILL BE PUT INTO OTHER PEOPLE TO DO THINGS FOR THEM... INCLUDING THINK!!! LET'S LOOK AT HOW SOCIETY AND THE WORLD HAS CHANGED OVER THE LAST DECADE, ESPECIALLY IN THE LAST FEW YEARS, WHILE THE 'WORLD EMERGENCY PANDEMIC' WAS AT ITS MOST FIERCE!

I CANNOT AND WILL NOT PUT DOWN OR TALK ILL OF ANY COMPANY OR CORPORATION, I WILL EXPLAIN WHAT COMPANIES AND CORPORATIONS ARE DOING. IF THE READER (YOU) WORKS OUT WHO IT IS AND WHAT'S GOING ON, THAT WILL BE THEIR OWN TAKE ON WHAT I HAVE SAID, HOWEVER... IT MAY NOT OR MAY BE TRUTH DEPENDING ON THE INDIVIDUAL AND THEIR APPROACH TO TRUTH, WHILE DETACHING FROM OPINION.

FIRSTLY... WHO MADE THE MOST MONEY DURING THE PANDEMIC? DO YOU THINK THAT THIS WAS COINCIDENTAL? IF THE POWERFUL GOT RICHER AND MORE POWERFUL BECAUSE OF A PANDEMIC, WHAT WOULD CAUSE THEM TO WANT TO HELP US AVOID THE NEXT ONE? IS THERE A CHANCE THAT THE WORLD IS RUN BY A SMALL GROUP OF EXTREMELY WEALTHY INDIVIDUAL OR POSSIBLE SOCIOPATHS/PSYCHOPATHS, WHO BOUGHT OTHER INDIVIDUALS TO DO THEIR WORK FOR THEM? IF ONE NARRATIVE WAS TO BE PUSHED GLOBALLY, WHY WOULD OR WOULDN'T YOU QUESTION IT? WHAT IS AN EXPERT? ARE THEY PAID TO BE AN EXPERT OR FOR YOU TO BE TOLD THEY ARE ONE?

I SPENT HALF OF THE 'GLOBAL PANDEMIC' CLASSED AS HOUSELESS. I LIVED IN A CONVERTED VAN, WITH MY DOG AND HAD NO REAL PLACE TO CALL HOME. IT WAS INSPIRING AND LIBERATING!

SINCE I HAD NO PLACE TO CALL HOME, I HAD THE PRIVILEGE TO TRAVEL THE UK AND SLEEP PRETTY MUCH ANYWHERE, WHICH LET ME SEE THE WORLD FROM A DIFFERENT PERSPECTIVE AND HOW DIFFERENT TOWNS AND CITIES DEALT WITH SUCH A CRISIS. WHAT I DID NOTICE WAS THE AMOUNT OF CONVENIENCES THAT HAD BEEN PUSHED AND ADVERTISED IN THE TIME LEADING UP TO THIS DARK TIME FOR THE WORLD AND ITS PEOPLE. THESE CORPORATIONS WERE COINING IT IN!

THERE WAS A LARGE CORPORATION THAT MADE FORTUNES INTRODUCING THEIR WAY OF WORKING TO TAXI COMPANIES. THIS WAS VERY CLEVER AS TO HOW IT WAS PUSHED AND MADE SO CONVENIENT TOO. THE MONSTER BECAME SO BIG, THAT JUST ABOUT EVERY COMPANY IN THE UK THAT I OBSERVED, AND THE REST OF THE WORLD (THAT I

HEARD), HAS TO SUCCUMB TO THIS WAY OF WORKING TO REMAIN IN BUSINESS.

IT WAS SOLD TO THE TAXI COMPANIES AS A CONVENIENCE AND TO THE CUSTOMER AS A CONVENIENCE, SO NO QUESTIONS WERE ASKED! EASY MONEY... KNOW WHEN OUR CAR ARRIVES... SAFETY FOR MEN AND WOMEN TRAVELLING... NO NON HIRES... WATCH YOUR DRIVER IN REAL TIME... THE LIST CAN GO ON!

CALL ME CYNICAL, BUT I STILL HAVEN'T DOWNLOADED THE APP AND STILL CALL A TAXI, A TAXI, I'LL ALSO CALL A HUMAN WHEN I NEED ONE.

AS I LISTED ABOVE, SOME OF THE REASONS ARE DUE TO CONVENIENCE, I WILL NOW LIST THE REASONS WHY IT MAY BE HARMFUL TO HUMANITY, BUT NOT IMMINENTLY DANGEROUS.

'PEOPLE TRACKING' FROM A DATABASE OF EVERYONE'S MOVEMENTS WHO ORDER A 'TAXI'. IS IT FAIR THAT THIS IS ALL STORED DATA? DO WE NEED WATCHED AND OUR DATA SOLD TO OTHER PARTS OF THE CORPORATION OR OTHER COMPANIES? WHY ARE PEOPLE SO EAGER TO SHOW THEIR MOVEMENTS JUST FOR CONVENIENCE?

I HAVE ALSO HEARD SEVERAL STALKING STORIES, AS THE DETAILS AND REAL NAME OF PASSENGER IS GIVEN TO THE DRIVER, WHICH IS UNFAIR IN MY BELIEF. I USED TO CALL 'TAXIS' FOR MY FEMALE FRIENDS SO THAT THEY WERE NOT AS VULNERABLE. NOW ALL DETAILS ARE SHOWN AND I DO NOT BELIEVE THE TAXI DRIVERS GO THROUGH ANY VETTING. IS IT REALLY SAFER? THERE HAVE BEEN MANY CASES OF STALKING IN THIS WAY OF WORKING AND IT IS ONLY GOING TO BECOME WORSE.

I ALSO HEARD THROUGH THE GRAPEVINE, AND A DRIVER, THAT YOU CAN WORK IN OTHER COUNTRIES WITHOUT HAVING TO PROPERLY REGISTER IN THE OTHER COUNTRY, AS IT'S AN INTERNATIONAL CORPORATION. IMAGINE YOU COULD GO ON HOLIDAY, HIRE A 'TAXI', WORK AND DO WHAT YOU LIKE, THEN LEAVE. SURELY THAT HAS TO RING ALARM BELLS AND BE A RED FLAG? JUST LIKE BEING ABLE TO GO ABROAD AND GET A TAXI ON

THE SAME APP YOU USE IN YOUR COUNTRY. IT'S ALL A BIT MAD. THE INTERNET OF THINGS IS DEFINITELY TAKING OVER AND PEOPLE ARE BEING PROGRAMMED LIKE ROBOTS, WHEN THEY ARE SO MUCH MORE! WILL YOU BE MORE INCLINED TO USE A STANDARD TAXI SERVICE?

CORPORATIONS HAVE FULL DETAILS OF ALL DRIVERS, THERE WHEREABOUTS AND IT MEANS THAT THEY CAN'T EARN EXTRA CASH FOR THEIR KIDS BIRTHDAY OR FAMILY HOLIDAY. COULD THIS HAVE BEEN CREATED TO MAKE THE GOVERNMENT MORE MONEY? EVERYTHING BEING DIGITALISED SO THAT EVERY PENNY AND HUMAN BEING IS TRACKED. IS THIS MOVING TOWARDS TOTAL CONTROL?

IT'S FUNNY, BECAUSE YOU ONLY HAVE TO PAY TAX IF YOU REGISTER TO PAY TAX. I HAVE ASKED SEVERAL LAWYERS AND PEOPLE WHO WORK IN THE TAX DEPARTMENT AND NOBODY CAN GIVE ME THE LAW THAT STATES 'YOU HAVE TO OR YOU WILL BE LOCKED UP'. IT'S ALL FEAR-BASED WITH THE BIG MACHINE AND EACH INDIVIDUAL HAS TO CONSENT TO PAY AND THEN IT IS A CONTRACT. THIS IS WHY THE BIG MACHINE DON'T LIKE THE TRAVELING COMMUNITY AS MUCH. THEY ARE SOVEREIGN.

THIS CORPORATION CONTROL STYLE IS NOT ALLOWING ANYONE TO BE SOVEREIGN IN THEIR EARNING CAPACITY. WHY IS THIS UNFAIR? DO YOU SEE A WAY OUT FOR YOURSELF? HOW WOULD YOU LIKE TO SEE YOUR EARNINGS PUT TO BETTER USE?

WE NOW HAVE SEVERAL OTHER CORPORATIONS CLASSED AS FOOD DELIVERY SERVICES AND ONLINE ORDER TAKERS... CONVENIENT, EH?! HAVE YOU USED ANY OF THESE SERVICES? DO YOU KNOW THE IMPLICATIONS TO THE ECONOMY? DO YOU KNOW THE IMPLICATIONS TO THE BUSINESS WHO USE THESE CORPORATIONS?

LET'S HAVE A LOOK...

THE SHOPS COULD BE POTENTIALLY BUSIER, BUT WITH THE ADVERTISING AND THE PERCENTAGE OF TAKINGS, ARE THEY REALLY MAKING MORE?

SO MANY PEOPLE CANNOT PUT THEIR PHONE DOWN, SO IT IS EASIER FOR MANY TO PLACE AN ORDER ON AN APP THAN IT IS TO CALL AND COMMUNICATE OR LEAVE HOME TO PLACE AN ORDER, WAIT AND COLLECT IT (LIKE WE USED TO DO). WHY DO PEOPLE TAKE THE EASY OPTION?

AS THE WORLD ECONOMIC FORUM HAS EXPLAINED, THERE WILL BE MORE LOCK-DOWNS, EITHER FOR COVID TYPE INSTANCES OR FOR CLIMATE CHANGE. WOULD THAT MEAN THESE CORPORATIONS HAVE BEEN ESTABLISHED BEFORE ALL OF THE LOCK-DOWNS SO THAT 'CERTAIN PEOPLE' CAN DELIVER FOOD, LIKE ON A LICENSE AS THEY ARE REGISTERED?

FEAR OF MISSING OUT HAS REALLY GOT MOST OF THE RESTAURANTS/TAKEAWAYS ON BOARD WITH THIS WAY OF WORKING. LIKE THE TAXI'S I MENTIONED EARLIER ON, EVERYONE AND EVERY PENNY TRACED AND THE PEOPLE IN THE SHOPS ARE GIVING THEIR SOVEREIGNTY AWAY FOR CONVENIENCE. ARE YOU STARTING TO SEE A PATTERN NOW? WHO DO YOU THINK IS GOING TO GAIN OUT OF ALL THIS? DO YOU THINK IT IS FOR CONVENIENCE OR CONTROL?

THE POWER OF INTERACTION IS HUGE, THE SMILE WHEN YOU MEET SOMEONE OR EVEN THE MOST BASIC OF ENERGY TRANSFER WHEN YOU PLACE AN ORDER FACE TO FACE. WHEN WAS THE LAST TIME YOU WENT AND PLACED AN ORDER FOR A TAKEAWAY IN THE SHOP AND WAITED FOR IT?

WHAT HAPPENS WHEN PEOPLE STOP COMMUNICATING? I BELIEVE THEY LOSE THE ABILITY TO COMMUNICATE PROPERLY, ALL BECAUSE INTERACTIONS TELL US A LOT ABOUT US AND IT KEEPS US SWITCHED ON AND LEARNING. I BELIEVE THIS LEADS TO PEOPLE LOSING THEIR MENTAL HEALTH.

YES, ORDERING TAKEAWAYS ISN'T THE BE ALL AND END ALL OF LIFE, BUT WHEN YOU THINK HOW MUCH PEOPLE ARE INTERACTING DIGITALLY ALREADY... IT'S MAKING A DETRIMENTAL CHANGE TO HUMANITY AND IT WILL ONLY CONTINUE TO GET WORSE.

SO MANY PEOPLE ACTUALLY THINK THEY HAVE FRIENDS WHEN THEY HAVEN'T EVEN MET THEM IN THE FLESH! IF HALF OF THE INTERACTIONS ONLINE WERE IN THE FLESH, DO YOU THINK THEY'D BE AS INTERESTING? AS GENUINE? WHO DO YOU INTERACT WITH MOST ONLINE? PEOPLE YOU HAVE MET OR PEOPLE YOU HAVEN'T? HOW OFTEN DO YOU ASK TO MEET PEOPLE?

SO BANK DETAILS CAPTURED, DATA CAPTURED... LIKE WHAT AREA YOU LIVE, ORDER FROM, WHAT YOU EAT, WHAT NIGHTS YOU USUALLY ORDER, LOCATION ALSO! ALL BECAUSE IT'S CONVENIENT? HAVE YOU GOT ANY OF THESE APPS? WILL YOU CONTINUE TO USE THEM?

THE SHOP OWNERS ARE PAYING UP TO 25% FROM THEIR TAKINGS AND GIVING THEIR SOVEREIGNTY AWAY. TECH COMPANIES ARE NOW IN CONTROL OF EVERY BUSINESS WHO HAS SIGNED UP AND CAN PULL THE PLUG IF THEY SO DESIRE. WHEN DO THE LITTLE PEOPLE JUST GET TO DO THEIR JOB OR RUN A BUSINESS WITHOUT THE BIG FISH WANTING TO CONTROL THEM OR TAKE FROM THEM?

IT'S NOW NOT A LOCAL DELIVERY DRIVER FROM THE AREA THAT PEOPLE KNOW, IS IT PEOPLE FROM OUTSIDE THE TOWN SIZING UP PROPERTIES? STALKING WOMEN OR CHILDREN? IT MIGHT SOUND FAR FETCHED, BUT IS IT? THINGS LIKE CHILDREN HAD TO PUT RAINBOWS ON THEIR WINDOWS DURING THE LOCK-DOWNS, THE HOUSE WAS AN EASY TARGET AS THEY KNOW KIDS ARE THERE. WHAT ABOUT IF THESE DELIVERY PEOPLE REPORT BACK AND IT WAS SOMETHING MORE SINISTER? YOU WATCH MOVIES AND THINK THEY ARE FAKE, SOMEONE HAD TO COME UP WITH THE IDEA THOUGH RIGHT???

THE LAST CONVENIENCE I'D LIKE TO LOOK AT IS THE CORPORATION THAT IS LITERALLY CONTROLLING THE HOUSING MARKET AND THE CRASH OF ALL CRASHES IN THE ECONOMY, THROUGH THE PROPERTY MARKET. OBVIOUSLY MOST PEOPLE PROBABLY WON'T BELIEVE THAT THE SO-CALLED WORLD LEADERS WOULD WISH TO CRASH AN ECONOMY ON PURPOSE!!! HOWEVER QUESTIONING EVERYTHING IS A MUST!

IN 2008, SOME MEN CAME TOGETHER AND STARTED A BUSINESS THAT

ADVERTISED PROPERTIES FOR PEOPLE TO STAY WITH OTHER PEOPLE. GREAT IDEA, RIGHT? THEY ARE VET CHECKED, ALL THEIR ID'S ARE KEPT ON FILE, AND THEIR PAYMENT DETAILS ARE ALSO KEPT SO THAT TRAVELLERS OR PEOPLE TAKING A SHORT BREAK CAN BE TRACED (IF NEED BE). IT SOUNDS TOO GOOD TO BE TRUE! CAN YOU SEE ANY ISSUES SO FAR?

PEOPLE THEN STARTED RENTING OUT THEIR ROOMS AND MAKING SOME EXTRA, BUT TRACEABLE MONEY. TO STAY IN SOMEONE'S HOUSE, WITH THE FAMILY, PEOPLE STARTED OFF PAYING LOW AMOUNTS, AND IT THEN STARTED TO GROW RAPIDLY! GREAT FOR PASSIVE INCOME, EH?

A WEEKEND AWAY IN A TOWN, IN A SHARED HOUSE WAS AFFORDABLE AND, YES YOU GOT IT... CONVENIENT! THE BUSINESS HEADS STARTED TO SEE POTENTIAL FOR SOME CASH AND JUMPED ON THIS. BUYING AND INVESTING IN PROPERTIES, DECORATING AND FURNISHING THEM TO RENT OUT ON A SHORT-BREAK BASIS. POTENTIALLY, YOU COULD COVER THE MORTGAGE IN A COUPLE OF WEEKENDS, THAT MEANS EVERY OTHER NIGHT RENTED IS A BONUS! IF YOU BOUGHT THE PROPERTY OUTRIGHT, WOULD TAKE LONGER TO SEE A RETURN ON THE INVESTMENT, AS IT WOULD TAKE MANY BOOKINGS TO PAY OFF THE PROPERTY IN FULL.

FAST FORWARD A FEW YEARS WHEN THIS METHOD BECOMES VERY POPULAR, WHAT ISSUES COULD THERE BE? THERE ARE MINIMAL RENTAL PROPERTIES ON THE MARKET IN COMPARISON TO A FEW YEARS PRIOR! WHY IS THIS? I BELIEVE THIS HAS STOPPED PEOPLE RENTING OUT PROPERTIES ON A MONTHLY BASIS BECAUSE THEIR POTENTIAL INCOME WITH THE NEW METHOD IS MORE LUCRATIVE. IS GREED TAKING PRESIDENCY OVER COMMUNITY?

IMAGINE I HAVE A PROPERTY WORTH 800 PER MONTH UNFURNISHED, BUT WITH THE NEW METHOD, I CAN GET 125 PER NIGHT FURNISHED AND IT WOULD MAKE GREAT BUSINESS AND GROW FINANCES. NOW MY PROPERTY WORTH 800 PER MONTH TO AN AVERAGE TENANT IS WORTH 3750 PER MONTH!!! I ONLY NEED TO RENT IT OUT 7 NIGHTS A MONTH TO MAKE A PROFIT.

ARE YOU NOW SEEING THE FIRST ISSUE? WHERE ARE THE PROPERTIES THAT ARE TO HOUSE FAMILIES AT REASONABLE PRICES? NOW THERE IS A HOUSING CRISIS BEGINNING NO? A SINGLE PARENT EARNING 1500 PER MONTH TO FEED 2 CHILDREN DOESN'T HAVE MUCH OPTION NOW.

IF I TAKE ON 5 BUY TO LET MORTGAGES, I COULD POTENTIALLY BE VERY FINANCIALLY WELL OFF, IF I GET THEM RENTED OUT OFTEN WITH THE NEW METHOD. IT IS NOT GUARANTEED THOUGH AND IS A GAMBLE ON LOCATION, DECOR AND OTHER FACTORS.

THE THING MANY PEOPLE AREN'T AWARE OF IS THAT SOCIETY SEEMS TO BE FOCUSING ON EARNING AND BEING WEALTHY AS THAT IS MEANT TO SHOW STATUS. WHAT SHOWS YOU SUCCESS? WOULD YOU DEFINE YOURSELF AS SUCCESSFUL? BACK TO THE HOUSING CRISIS... THERE IS MORE!

SO WE CAN'T GET HOUSES BECAUSE LANDLORDS WISH TO MAKE MORE MONEY, IN ESSENCE FACILITATED BY HOW THIS NEW SYSTEM WORKS AND THERE HAS BEEN A MASSIVE PUSH FOR INVESTING IN PROPERTY. THIS IS ALL FACTUAL, BANKS HAVE BEEN GRANTED POWERS TO BUY PROPERTIES, FURNISH THEM AND RENT THEM OUT... SHOCK HORROR!

THESE POWERS WERE GRANTED IN THE UK WHEN PEOPLE WERE LOCKED DOWN AND WAITING ON THEIR WONDERFUL GOVERNMENT TO GIVE THEM THEIR FREEDOM BACK THAT THEY CHOSE TO GIVE AWAY IN THE FIRST PLACE TO TELEVISED PUBLIC SERVANTS! ARE YOU STARTING TO FEEL HOW BAD THIS IS? IS IT FAIR THAT BANKS HAVE THE OPPORTUNITY TO BUY BEFORE SOMEONE WISHING TO GET ON TO THE PROPERTY MARKET? WHAT COULD THE IMPLICATIONS OF THIS BE?

SO... WHAT WOULD THE FUTURE LOOK LIKE?

WE ARE ANOTHER COUPLE YEARS DOWN THE LINE, THE PROPERTY MARKET COLLAPSES BECAUSE THE INTEREST RATES ARE CURRENTLY SO LOW, BUT BANKS CAN RAISE THE INTEREST RATES TO RECOUP FINANCES. THEN WHAT CAN HAPPEN? THE PEOPLE WITH ALL OF THESE PROPERTIES THAT ARE NOT FILLED WITH FULL-TIME TENANTS WILL HAVE TO PAY HIGHER RATES NO?

THIS COULD MEAN THEIR BUSINESSES COULD FOLD AND THE PROPERTIES REPOSSESSED IF THE BANKS DECIDE ON 7,8 OR EVEN 9% INTEREST ON THE MORTGAGES! WHAT HAPPENS NEXT?

THE BANKS BEGIN TO BUY THE PROPERTIES AND RENT THEM BACK TO PEOPLE? THIS WOULD MAKE GOOD BUSINESS AS WELL AS CONTROL FROM THE BANKS AND OTHER CORPORATIONS, WOULDN'T IT? WHAT ABOUT THE LITTLE GUY THAT WANTED TO MAKE A QUICK BUCK AND GOT GREEDY? HE ENDS UP WITH NOTHING AND BANKRUPT?

THE WORLD ECONOMIC FORUM STATES IN THEIR AGENDA 2030, WHICH ISN'T FAR AWAY... "THEY WILL OWN NOTHING AND BE HAPPY". HOW CAN THIS BE COUNTERED? ONE WAY IS LANDLORDS AND PROPERTY INVESTORS CAN PUT IN FULL-TIME TENANTS AND SAVE THEIR ASSETS FROM THE BANKS AND CORPORATIONS.

DO YOU THINK THIS SOUNDS LIKE A CONSPIRACY THEORY? CAN YOU NOT SEE THE TRUTH? DO YOU STILL THINK THAT CONVENIENCE IS HEALTHY? ARE YOU WILLING TO SUPPORT LOCAL BUSINESS BY GOING STRAIGHT TO THEM? ARE YOU WILLING TO TALK ABOUT WHAT YOU HAVE JUST READ TO LANDLORDS AND PROPERTY DEVELOPERS?

THE PEOPLE WHO CAME UP WITH THESE IDEAS ARE ALL BILLIONAIRES AND WILL CONTINUE TO BE, WHILE THE LITTLE PEOPLE OF SOCIETY BECOME POORER. WE CAN ONLY BUT TRY TO KEEP OURSELVES SOVEREIGN. THERE IS STILL TIME TO TURN THIS AROUND AND MAKE THE COLLATERAL DAMAGE MINIMAL.

CHAPTER 19: DISTRACTIONS

GIVE THEM BREAD AND CIRCUSES AND THEY WILL NEVER REVOLT-

JUVENAL 55AD.

WHAT IS A DISTRACTION? HOW EASILY DISTRACTED ARE YOU? DO YOU BELIEVE ENTERTAINMENT IS FOR YOU TO RELAX AND ENJOY OR TO PROGRAM AND DISTRACT YOU? IF YOU BELIEVE IT'S FOR YOU TO RELAX AND ENJOY, WHY DO YOU THINK THE PEOPLE WHO OWN THE MEDIA CHANNELS WANT YOU FOCUSED ON WHAT THEY SHOW YOU?

THIS CHAPTER IS TO SHOW HOW WE ARE LITERALLY CONTROLLED LIKE ROBOTS AND MOST DON'T EVEN KNOW IT WAS POSSIBLE, NEVER MIND TRUTH. THIS CHAPTER SHOWS THAT THE BEST THE WORLD CAN OFFER IS A DISTRACTION SO THAT WE DON'T RECOGNISE THAT WE AREN'T FULFILLED BY LIVING OUR PURPOSE. WHY WOULD ANYONE WANT TO DISTRACT THE MAJORITY OF HUMANITY FROM LIVING THEIR OWN SOVEREIGN LIFE?

I BELIEVE IT IS BECAUSE OF CONTROL, ALMOST LIKE A GAME OF SIMS. THE SO-CALLED RICH AND POWERFUL LIKE TO PULL THE STRINGS, SO THAT US MERE MORTALS ARE NOT ABLE TO BE FREE, THEREFORE WE MAKE THEM RICH AND POWERFUL BY BEING DISTRACTED FROM WHO WE ACTUALLY ARE AND CONSUMING THEIR PRODUCTS. MOST OF THESE PRODUCTS ARE NOT NECESSARY TO DAILY LIFE, BUT AS HUMAN BEINGS LIVING IN THIS TIME, WE ARE MADE TO FEEL WE NEED THINGS AND STUFF, WHEN IN FACT WE DON'T!

I STILL WATCH FOOTBALL GAMES. I STILL SOCIALISE AND USE SOCIAL MEDIA. I AM AWARE AND CONSCIOUS THAT I CAN LIVE MY LIFE WITHOUT IT. I FEEL THE MAJORITY OF PEOPLE WOULD BECOME ENERGETICALLY DRAINED IF THEY DIDN'T HAVE THEIR DISTRACTIONS, AS THEY WOULDN'T KNOW HOW TO LIVE A REAL LIFE. COULD YOU HANDLE NOT HAVING TV OR SMART PHONES? DO YOU KNOW YOU ARE THE PRODUCT OF ALL THE PROGRAMMING?

ALL WE HAVE TO LOOK AT IS THE WAY 'MENTAL HEALTH' TOOK A HUGE DOWNWARDS SPIRAL BETWEEN 2020 AND 2022 BECAUSE PEOPLE WERE LED TO BELIEVE THAT THERE WAS A GLOBAL CRISIS, SO HUMANITY WAS

FORCED INDOORS FOR THEIR SAFETY. WHAT'S YOUR THOUGHTS ON THE WAY THIS 'CRISIS' WAS HANDLED? DID YOU BECOME HEALTHIER DURING THAT TIME? DID YOUR LIFE STOP? DID YOU FEEL SCARED? DID YOU GET WORSE? DID YOU FIND ALL THE INFORMATION GIVEN BY THE MEDIA COVERAGE COMPLETELY TRUE?

IF YOU DID PUT EVERYTHING ON HOLD FOR TWO YEARS, WOULD YOU PUT YOUR LIFE ON HOLD AGAIN IF SOMETHING ELSE HAPPENED? DO YOU KNOW THAT YOU CANNOT GET TIME BACK ONCE IT'S GONE? WHO HAS CONTROL OVER YOU? WHY WOULD YOU LET ANYONE CONTROL YOU?

THOSE TWO YEARS WERE A BLUR FOR MOST PEOPLE; THERE WERE TOO MANY DISTRACTIONS THAT MANY WERE NOT CONCERNED ABOUT HOW BAD THE LIES AND CONTROL WAS. SO MANY PEOPLE CHASING DOPAMINE HITS BECAUSE THEIR DAILY LIFE WASN'T FULFILLED. THIS MEANS PEOPLE'S HABITS ARE GOING TO CHANGE AND SO THEY MAY NEVER BE LONG-TERM HAPPY, AS THEY WILL BE CHASING THE HIGHS FROM NOW ON, CHASING THE BUZZ LIKE AN ADDICT, IN ORDER TO FEEL HAPPY IN LIFE AND PRODUCE THE BRAIN CHEMICALS NEEDED FOR THAT QUICK FIX.

PEOPLE ARE NOT ADDICTED TO SUBSTANCES, SEX OR BEHAVIOUR THAT MAKES THEM FEEL GOOD! THE THING PEOPLE CHASE IS DOPAMINE, ENDORPHINS AND OTHER PLEASURE CHEMICALS. YET, HOW THEY GET THEM IS COMPLETELY DIFFERENT FOR THE INDIVIDUAL AND MOST PEOPLE ARE JUDGED ON THEIR BEHAVIOUR AND HAVE TO CONTROL THEIR BEHAVIOUR, WHEN IT IS KNOWN THAT THE HUMAN BRAIN GAINS ENERGY UNCONSCIOUSLY! WHAT DO YOU DO TO CHASE A HIGH? WHAT HABIT DO YOU HAVE THAT MAKES YOU FEEL BALANCED SHORT TERM, THAT YOU COULDN'T STOP? HAPPINESS IS A CHOICE, BY ACCEPTING WHAT IS AND LOOKING AT IT IN THE HEALTHIEST WAY POSSIBLE.

REMEMBER IN THE MEDICINE CHAPTER WHEN I SPOKE OF DIMETHYLTRYPTAMINE (DMT)? THIS IS THE ONE THAT IS ALMOST IDENTICAL TO SEROTONIN! WHY WOULD IT BE ILLEGAL IF IT WOULD STOP PEOPLE CHASING SHORT-TERM HAPPINESS AND HELP BE CONTENT WITH LIFE? THIS IS WHY YOU HEAR OF PEOPLE TRANSFORMING THEIR LIFE

AFTER AN AYAHUASCA EXPERIENCE! THEIR SEROTONIN RECEPTORS ARE FLOODED... IMAGINE THAT WITH ADDED PURPOSE... THERE WOULD BE NO STOPPING HUMAN BEINGS! MEANING WE WOULDN'T BE CHASING THE SHORT-TERM HIGHS OR THE PRODUCTS WE ARE MADE TO BELIEVE WE NEED, IN ORDER TO LIVE A FULFILLED LIFE.

LET'S LOOK AT WHAT THE MAIN DISTRACTIONS ARE AND HOW THEY ARE SOLD TO US.

THE GYM/FITNESS AND HOW ITS SOLD:

HEALTHY LIVING, GOOD FOR THE BODY AND THE MIND (IS IT REALLY GOOD FOR THE MIND?), MAKES US MORE AESTHETICALLY PLEASING, GREAT FOR SOCIAL INTERACTIONS, PUSH OUR OWN BOUNDARIES AND HELPS US GAIN ROUTINE. WHAT DO YOU AGREE/DISAGREE WITH HERE?

HERE IS THE TRUTH:

YES, FITNESS AND THE GYM WILL MAKE YOU HEALTHIER AND FITTER, WHICH ULTIMATELY ON PAPER COULD HELP YOU LIVE LONGER. NOW WHEN PEOPLE GO TO THE GYM, IT'S MORE TIMES THAN NOT, A DISTRACTION. (YEP! I SAID IT!) WHEN THE HUMAN BODY ENDURES A WORKOUT, IT RELEASES ENDORPHINS AND THIS GIVES THE MAN OR WOMAN DOING THE EXERCISE A SHORT-TERM TENSION RELEASE, WHICH MEANS THAT THEY CAN GET ON WITH THE REST OF THEIR DAY OR SWITCH OFF FROM WHAT IS BOTHERING THEM.

THE ISSUE HERE IS THAT NOW AFTER, THE WORKOUT AND FEELING BETTER WILL ONLY PROMPT ANOTHER WORKOUT... NOW WE ARE LOOKING AT A HABIT! HABITS ARE GOOD WHEN WE ARE IN FLOW AND BALANCE. IF WE WERE IN FLOW AND BALANCE, WE WOULD LIVE WITHOUT HABITS WOULDN'T WE?

SO, TO FIND A PHYSICALLY BENEFICIAL HABIT, THAT DOES NOT IMPROVE MINDSET... IS THIS THE WAY FORWARD? TO FLOOD YOUR RECEPTORS WITH SHORT-TERM RELEASE, IS THIS THE ANSWER? WHAT ABOUT LIVING

LIFE AS OURSELVES, FREELY AND REMOVING ANYTHING WE DON'T LIKE, OR LETTING GO OF THE PAST... WOULD THIS BE BETTER? ARE YOU FOCUSED ON THE TANGIBLE OR THE INTANGIBLE? WHAT DO YOU NEED TO DO IN ORDER TO LIVE A BETTER AND HAPPIER LIFE?

TV PROGRAMMES/BOX SETS AND HOW THEY ARE SOLD:

CAN'T MISS IT, BEST SERIES YET, GREAT FOR A COSY NIGHT IN, BEST TO SIT AND SWITCH OFF AFTER A LONG DAY VERY ENTERTAINING TOO! I MEAN, WHY WOULD YOU NOT WANT TO WATCH IT?

HERE IS THE TRUTH:

IT'S ALL DISTRACTION! WHAT DO YOU FEEL YOU BENEFIT FROM WATCHING TV AND BOX SETS? AS I EXPLAINED EARLIER, THEY WORK WITH THE AMYGDALAE IN YOUR BRAIN? YOUR AMYGDALAE ARE LIKE A DATA CENTRE WITH ALL THE INFORMATION ON EVERYTHING YOU HAVE EVER EXPERIENCED. SOME SHOWS YOU WATCH WILL TRIGGER YOU, SOME WILL CALM YOU, SOME MIGHT EVEN ENERGISE YOU. NONE OF IT IS REAL THOUGH... IT;S SCRIPTS PLAYED BY ACTORS AND THE TERM REALITY HAS CHANGED SINCE PEOPLE ARE BEING PROGRAMMED TO THINK REALITY TV IS REAL, WHEN IN FACT IT IS NOT. IT LOOKS MORE REAL NOW, BECAUSE SO MANY PEOPLE ARE TRYING TO COPY THE NONSENSE THAT THEY WATCH ON THE TV AND ONLINE... SO IT'S A VICIOUS CIRCLE THAT NEEDS TO BE BROKEN, WOULDN'T YOU AGREE?

WHAT ELSE IS WATCHING TV AND BOX SETS DOING? I BELIEVE IT IS KEEPING PEOPLE IN AND AT THE SAME TIME CAUSING THEM SOCIAL ANXIETY BECAUSE THEY ARE USED TO BEING ON THEIR OWN AND IN THEIR BUBBLE OF SAFETY! HOW MANY SIT SOMEWHERE IN NATURE, IN COMPARISON TO HOW MANY STAY IN TO WATCH THE LIGHT EMITTING DIODE BOX? WHY IS THE QUALITY OF LIFE DEPRECIATING IN THE WORLD WE LIVE IN? I BELIEVE IT IS PROGRAMMING IN EVERY SENSE OF THE WORD!

HOLIDAY/VACATIONS AND HOW THEY ARE SOLD:

GET AWAY, SWITCH OFF AND REALLY LET YOUR HAIR DOWN. GET OUT IN THE SUN, OR JUST SEE THE SITES IN A NEW PLACE... BECAUSE YOU WORK HARD OR TOO HARD, YOU DESERVE IT! PARTY ALL NIGHT AND SLEEP ALL DAY, OR JUST DO NOTHING AS YOU ARE TAKING A BREAK.

HERE IS THE TRUTH:

NOBODY 'NEEDS A BREAK AWAY'. IT IS USUALLY A WANT FOR SOMEONE WHO DOESN'T GET ENOUGH PLEASURE OR FREEDOM IN THEIR OWN LIVES. MAYBE SOMEONE WHO WORKS SO HARD IN A TRADE OR JOB TO MAKE ENDS MEET AND IT DOESN'T SUIT WHO THEY ARE SO THEY NEED TO SPEND TIME NOT LOSING AS MUCH ENERGY. MAYBE SOMEONE SHOWING OFF HOW MUCH MONEY THEY HAVE. DO YOU COME BACK FROM VACATION WITH MORE ENERGY OR DO YOU NEED TO TAKE ANOTHER VACATION BECAUSE YOU ARE EVEN MORE EXHAUSTED? ARE YOU HAPPY AND ENERGISED FROM WHAT YOU DO FROM A LIVING EACH DAY? WHAT WOULD YOU RATHER BE DOING?

HAVING A BREAK AWAY FOR A WEEK WILL USUALLY CONSIST OF A DAY OR TWO TO SETTLE IN AND GET YOUR BEARINGS, THREE TO FOUR DAYS DOING WHAT YOU FEEL IS GOING TO RELAX YOU, THEN A COUPLE OF DAYS PREPARING IN YOUR MIND TO LEAVE AND GO BACK HOME TO THE SAME LIFE, DOING THE SAME THINGS YOU TRIED TO ESCAPE FROM, THINKING A WEEK ISN'T LONG ENOUGH BECAUSE YOU HAVE LESS ENERGY THAN WHEN YOU WENT ON VACATION!

HAVING A TWO WEEK BREAK USUALLY STARTS OFF THE SAME... A DAY OR TWO TO SETTLE IN, MAYBE 7 DAYS HOLIDAY AND DOING WHAT YOU DO TO RELAX, BUT THEN FIND THERE IS NO ROUTINE AND THE LAST FOUR OR FIVE DAYS CAN BE BORING, THEN THERE IS THE MENTAL PREPARATION THAT YOU HAVE HAD A FORTNIGHT OFF AND THERE WILL BE A LOT MORE TO CATCH UP ON!

DO YOU GO AWAY ON HOLIDAY AND POST PICTURES AND STORIES WHILE YOU ARE AWAY? DOES THAT MAKE YOU FEEL PRESENT AND DISCONNECTED FROM WHERE YOU FELT YOU HAD TO GET A BREAK

FROM? DO YOU REMEMBER WHEN PEOPLE USED TO TAKE A DISPOSABLE CAMERA AND WAIT UNTIL THEY GOT BACK AND DEVELOPED THE PICTURES? DO YOU REMEMBER THEY USED TO PUT THEM ALL OVER THE WORLD SO EVERYONE COULD SEE? (ME NEITHER)

ALCOHOL/SUBSTANCES AND HOW THEY ARE SOLD:

HELPS YOU SWITCH OFF AND RELAX, ENHANCES THE ABILITY TO BE MORE YOURSELF, HELPS YOU HAVE FUN IN MODERATION (SOME EVEN THINK IT CAN MAKE THEM DANCE BETTER) BUT IF YOU TAKE TOO MUCH ITS SELF ABUSE. IT SLOWS THE BRAIN DOWN FROM OVER-THINKING AND CAN RELEASE HAPPY BRAIN CHEMICALS IN THE SHORT TERM.

HERE IS THE TRUTH:

ALCOHOL AND SUBSTANCES ARE MOSTLY POISON, YET THEY ARE SO NORMALISED THROUGH SOCIAL CHANNELS.

ALCOHOL IS A DEPRESSANT, MEANING IT CAN BE FUN WHILST ON IT, BUT AFTER THE EFFECTS WEAR OFF, THERE IS A GOOD CHANCE THAT THE FREQUENCY OF THE USER IS GOING TO BE LOWER (EVEN LOWER IN THOSE WHO ARE DRINKING ALCOHOL TO DISTRACT FROM ALREADY FEELING LOW ENERGY). DO YOU 'NEED' A GLASS OF WINE TO SWITCH OFF? DO YOU 'NEED ALCOHOL' TO HAVE FUN OR MORE FUN? IF IT MAKES YOU RELAX AND BE MORE YOURSELF, WOULD YOU NOT BE BETTER KNOWING WHO YOU ARE AND JUST BEING YOU?

SUBSTANCES CAN BE USED FOR HIGHS, LOWS OR EVEN TO TAKE YOU AWAY TO WHAT FEELS LIKE A WHOLE DIFFERENT REALITY. NATURAL AND SYNTHETIC HAVE VERY MUCH DIFFERENT EFFECTS ON THE BRAIN AND BODY. DO YOUR RESEARCH TO FIND OUT WHAT IS IN THEM AND THE EFFECTS THAT THEY HAVE LONG-TERM SHOULD YOU WANT TO USE THEM.

AGAIN... SUBSTANCES ARE USUALLY USED TO DISTRACT FROM FEELING OVERWHELMED, UNFULFILLED OR AN ARRAY OF OTHER REASONS. WHAT

IS THE AFTER EFFECT ON THE BRAIN OR ENERGY LEVELS? IF YOU ARE LOWER AFTER THE HIGH, THIS IS NOT THE WAY TO GO AS THE CHASE WILL BE ON?

MANY PEOPLE ARE DEMONISED FOR USING THESE AND THE TRUTH IS, THEY JUST AREN'T HAPPY WITHOUT THEM AND DON'T SEE ANOTHER WAY TO FEEL ENERGIZED. HOW MANY TIMES HAVE YOU DONE THIS? DID YOU KNOW YOU CAN CHANGE IT BY NOT RELYING ON THEM AND LISTENING TO WHAT YOUR LIFE NEEDS FROM YOUR HIGHER SELF? WHAT WOULD YOU SAY IS A HEALTHY AMOUNT?

PORN AND HOW IT'S SOLD:

IT IS USUALLY FREE ON TV PACKAGES AND THE INTERNET, AIDS RELAXATION WHEN THE VIEWER MASTURBATES WHILE OR AFTER WATCHING AND CAN CAUSE A RUSH OF BLOOD, HORMONES AND BRAIN CHEMICALS WHEN WATCHED. SOUNDS GREAT!

HERE IS THE TRUTH:

IF SOMETHING IS FREE, YOU ARE THE PRODUCT AND THE CURRENCY YOU PAY IS YOUR ENERGY! HAVE YOU EVER WATCHED PORN? HOW DO YOU FEEL ABOUT IT?

I'M GOING TO GO THROUGH THE MAIN PARTS OF PORN AND WHAT IT IS DOING TO SOCIETY (UNKNOWN TO MOST).

FIRSTLY, I'LL START WITH THE PERFORMANCE! DO YOU WANT TO PERFORM LIKE A PORN STAR? HAVE YOU BEEN WITH ANYONE WHO WAS ALL ABOUT PERFORMANCE? THIS USUALLY TAKES THE INTIMACY OUT OF SEX. THESE PEOPLE ON CAMERA ARE BEING PAID SO THEIR PERFORMANCE IS EXAGGERATED AND SO ARE THEIR VOCALS, IF THEY ARE NOT DUBBED. THIS MEANS THERE WILL BE A CONNECTION OF TWO PEOPLE TOGETHER, BUT ON THE SHALLOW LEVEL, MEANING IT WILL USUALLY BE MEANINGLESS, NOT NECESSARILY INTENTIONALLY, BUT UNCONSCIOUSLY.

MANY PEOPLE USE PORN TO GET TIPS FOR HOW THEY PERFORM OR DETERMINE WHAT THEY 'THINK' THEY LIKE. WHEN WAS THE LAST TIME YOU WERE WITH SOMEONE, FELT NO AWKWARDNESS AND WERE ABLE TO LET GO FROM THE BEGINNING AND THE FIRST INTERACTION? DID THEY PUT YOUR NEEDS FIRST?

THE STORY LINES IN PORN NOWADAYS ARE LITERALLY NORMALISING INCEST, UNDERAGE SEX, GANG SEX, MISOGYNISM AGAINST WOMEN, WHILE LAWS AND SOCIETY 'IN THE REAL WORLD' ARE AGAINST IT! THE TABOO EXERTS IN THE STORIES CREATE AN UNCOMFORTABLE FEELING IN THE BRAIN OF THE VIEWER AND THEY MUST CHANGE THEIR PERCEPTION IN ORDER TO MAKE IT COMFORTABLE, SO THEIR BRAIN CAN PROCESS IT AND THEY CAN GET TO CLIMAX OR WHATEVER SAFELY.

HAVE YOU WATCHED ANYTHING TABOO AND FELT YOU HAD TO NORMALISE IT BEFORE GOING THROUGH WITH IT? EVEN A HEADING SUCH AS 'TEENS', IS THIS HEALTHY? IN THE UK YOU HAVE TO BE SIXTEEN TO HAVE SEX LEGALLY, EVEN THOUGH A SIXTEEN YEAR OLD IS STILL EXTREMELY YOUNG. UNDER THE HEADING 'TEENS', IT COULD INCLUDE THIRTEEN, FOURTEEN AND FIFTEEN YEAR OLDS... IS THIS ACCEPTABLE? HAVE YOU EVER CONSIDERED THAT THERE COULD BE VIDEOS OR PICTURES WITH YOUNGSTERS... 13,14,15 IN THERE AND PEOPLE AUTOMATICALLY JUST THINK IT IS OK BECAUSE THE CATEGORY DOESN'T SPECIFY? OR THAT BECAUSE IT IS AN OVER 18 WEBSITE, THAT IT'S ALL ABOVE BOARD?

WHAT ABOUT THE STORIES OF THE BROTHER AND SISTER, OR THE STEP PARENTS AND THE CHILDREN... IS THIS ACCEPTABLE, ESPECIALLY WHEN YOUNG KIDS CAN ACCESS THIS SO EASILY AND THINK THIS IS NORMAL LIFE? GROUPS OF MEN, SPITTING AND SLAPPING A YOUNG WOMAN IN THE NAME OF 'PLEASURE'? IS THIS REALLY ACCEPTABLE? THE HUMAN BODY IS LOOKED UPON AS A COMMODITY AND NOT A LIVING SOUL CAN CHALLENGE IT, AS THE BIG SYSTEM IS REALLY PROGRAMMING ALL SORTS OF ABUSE, ILLEGAL ACTS AND DESENSITISING THE MOST SACRED HUMAN INTERACTIONS. WANTING WOMEN TO FEEL EMPOWERED IN SOCIETY, WHILE ALLOWING THESE VIDEOS TO BE AIRED? IS THAT A

CONTRADICTION?

LET'S LOOK AT PORN AND SEX/MASTURBATING AND THE BRAIN... PLEASURE IS WHERE IT'S AT NOWADAYS AND SO MANY PEOPLE THINK THAT THEY AREN'T HAPPY IF THEY ARE NOT FEELING PLEASURE, SO THEY MAKE A HABIT OF DOING THE THING THEY THINK IS THE PLEASURE, WHEN ALL IT REALLY IS, IS THE BRAIN RELEASING THE CHEMICALS AND NOT THE ACT ITSELF!

DO YOU CHASE THE PLEASURE TO THINK YOU FEEL HAPPY? IF YOU AREN'T HAPPY, IS IT APPROPRIATE AND GROWTH IF YOU MASTURBATE YOUR LIFE AWAY? MASTURBATION IS THE EASIEST WAY IN MY BELIEF TO RELEASE THESE PLEASURE CHEMICALS, WITHOUT HAVING TO USE SOMEONE ELSE OR PUTTING A FOOD, DRINK OR SUBSTANCE IN TO YOUR BODY, THEREFORE, PROBABLY ONE OF THE MOST USED DISTRACTIONS. WHAT COULD YOU USE INSTEAD OF PORN? MAYBE SELF DEVELOPMENT? WHAT DO YOU NEED TO DEVELOP?

FOOD, MUSIC, PUBS, CLUBS, SPORTS, TV AND SO MANY MORE DISTRACTIONS ARE AVAILABLE. I'M NOT SAYING DON'T USE THEM, I'M ASKING YOU TO REALISE WHY YOU ARE USING THEM, THINK WHAT YOU ARE DISTRACTING YOURSELF FROM, ASK YOURSELF WHY YOU CAN'T STAND BEING ON YOUR OWN OR EVEN TRYING TO DETERMINE WHO YOU ARE AND GROWING YOURSELF TO THE POINT. YOU COULD USE ANY DISTRACTION AS A TAKE IT OR LEAVE IT OPTION. WE ARE ALL HUMAN!

DISTRACTIONS ARE THE CONVENIENT WAYS TO ACHIEVE SHORT-TERM PLEASURE CHEMICALS, HOWEVER, THEY REWIRE OUR BRAIN AWAY FROM THE ABILITY TO EXPERIENCE AND ATTAIN LONG-TERM PLEASURE AND FULFILMENT. WHAT IS YOUR GOAL? HOW MANY PEOPLE DO YOU THINK REALISE THAT THEY ARE SPENDING THE TIME THEY COULD BE USING TOWARDS HEALTHY HAPPINESS FOCUSED ON SHORT-TERM PLEASURE BECAUSE IT IS CONVENIENT?

WHAT'S YOUR NEXT STEP? WOULD YOU WRITE DOWN ALL OF YOUR DISTRACTIONS AND WHY YOU ARE DOING THEM? WELL THEN DO IT AND

START UNDERSTANDING YOU AND YOUR BEHAVIOURS/HABITS. ACCEPTANCE IS THE BEGINNING OF THE JOURNEY!

CHAPTER 20: THE DISSOLVE

SO MANY PEOPLE TRYING TO SOLVE THE PUZZLE OF LIFE OR TRYING TO RESOLVE THINGS THAT HAVE HAPPENED IN THE SAME MINDSET THAT THE ISSUE WAS RAISED IN THE FIRST PLACE. DEFINITIONS OF WORDS BEING THROWN AROUND WITHOUT UNDERSTANDING THE EFFECT THEY HAVE ON US AND OTHER PEOPLE. WHAT'S WORSE IS THAT PEOPLE DON'T UNDERSTAND THAT OTHER PEOPLE DON'T ALWAYS HAVE THE SAME DEFINITIONS FOR WORDS, MEANING EXPECTATION WILL BE DIFFERENT.

WE ARE CURRENTLY GOING THROUGH (WHAT I BELIEVE IS) THE MOST DETRIMENTAL TIME FOR HUMANITY. WHILE GENERATIONS BEFORE US HAVE BEEN THROUGH WORLD WARS WITH BOMBS AND RATIONS, THE WORLD IS NOW GOING THROUGH WARS ON THE MIND AND YOU NEVER KNOW WHEN THE RATIONS MIGHT COME INTO PLAY WITH THE GAMES THAT ARE BEING PLAYED.

THE SYSTEM THAT CONTROLS THE WORLD AS IT IS, THE RULES, THE REGULATIONS, THE LEARNING, THE TRENDS... IT CANNOT BE CHANGED OR FOUGHT, IT'S TOO BIG! A SMALL GROUP OF PEOPLE GOING AGAINST BANKERS, GOVERNMENT, SECRET SOCIETIES, BILLIONAIRE INVESTMENT COMPANIES AND MARKETING FIRMS MAY HAVE A SLIGHT IMPACT, BUT THEY WILL BE SILENCED AND OR BE INVOLVED IN A TRAGIC ACCIDENT, AS WE'VE SEEN THROUGHOUT TIME. I'M VERY AWARE AND NOT VERY ACCIDENT PRONE (JUST IN CASE SOMETHING HAPPENS, HAHA).

WHAT I BELIEVE IS NEEDED, IS FOR ALL PEOPLE TO COME TOGETHER AND CREATE A NEW LIFE FOR THEMSELVES AND OTHERS OUTSIDE OF WHAT IS GOING ON JUST NOW. LEARNING HOW TO BE BALANCED MENTALLY,

EMOTIONALLY, PHYSICALLY AND SPIRITUALLY, WHILE BRINGING THE PEOPLE TOGETHER AS HUMAN BEINGS UNDER THE UMBRELLA OF ACCEPTANCE AND LOVE, WITHOUT FORCING AGENDA OR BELIEFS. HOW CAN WE DO THIS WHEN THE WORLD IS SO DIVIDED WITH OPINIONS AND BELIEFS WITH NO SUBSTANCE?

HOW CAN WE DO THIS WHEN THE PEOPLE THAT CONTROL THE NARRATIVE ARE POWER HUNGRY AND CORRUPT?

IF YOU HAVE ANSWERS TO THESE, WHY AREN'T YOU TRYING? WHAT CAN YOU DO TO MAKE CHANGE?

IT'S WILD HOW PEOPLE ARE BEING HURT AND DAMAGED WITH SO MANY UNTRUTHS AND WRONG DEFINITIONS OF WORDS, THAT IT;S BECOMING HARDER TO BRING PEOPLE TOGETHER AS THEY SELF SABOTAGE THEMSELVES INTO A PLACE OF SELF PITY AND WEAKNESS, WATCHING BILLIONS OF AMAZING AND STRONG HUMAN BEINGS BEING DUPED INTO BELIEVING THAT THERE IS SOMETHING WRONG WITH THEM OR THAT THEY ARE NOT GOOD ENOUGH WHEN EVERY INDIVIDUAL SOUL IS HERE TO GROW AND EXPERIENCE A LIFE OF CHOICE AND FREEDOM OVER CONTROL AND LIMITATIONS.

DO YOU SEE YOURSELF AS FREE? ARE YOU TOLD WHAT YOU CAN AND CANNOT DO BY A GROUP OF FINANCIALLY WELL OFF PEOPLE WHO DO NOT HAVE YOUR BEST INTERESTS AT HEART? ARE THE SAME PEOPLE MAKING BAD DECISIONS FOR THE ECONOMY AND THE DAY TO DAY RUNNING OF THE WORLD THAT IS DETERIORATING? WHY HAVE YOU NOT REALISED THAT THIS WILL NEVER CHANGE UNTIL WE COME TOGETHER AND CHANGE IT FOR OURSELVES?

THROUGH MUCH OF THE SECOND HALF OF THIS BOOK, I HAVE MENTIONED A MAN CALLED JOHN LENHART. WE MET RANDOMLY ON A BUSINESS PLATFORM AND TOTALLY HIT IT OFF BECAUSE OF OUR DESIRE FOR TRUTH AND BOTH WANTING TO HELP PEOPLE LIVE THEIR BEST LIVES, THEREFORE MAKING THE WORLD A BETTER PLACE WHEN LOTS OF PEOPLE HAVE THE SAME VISION.

WHEN I MET JOHN, THERE WAS AN INSTANT CONNECTION. IT ALMOST

FELT LIKE ALL THE INFORMATION JOHN WAS GIVING ME, I KNEW, BUT DIDN'T HAVE THE WORDS FOR, LIKE WE HAD THESE CONVERSATIONS BEFORE (IT FELT RIGHT). I HAVE ALWAYS SEEN AND FELT TRUTH DEEPLY. IT WAS DIFFICULT WHEN I WAS YOUNGER AND WASN'T ABLE TO HANDLE TENSION OR WAS SCARED OF CONFLICT SO I KEPT QUIET. NOW I SEE IT MORE, BUT DON'T MIND BEING SHOT DOWN AS THE ONES THAT WANT TO SILENCE US OR SHOOT US DOWN USUALLY HAVE THE BIGGEST ISSUES OR THE MOST TO LOSE WHEN THE TRUTH COMES OUT.

JOHN HAS QUITE THE RESUME AND HAS WON NUMEROUS AWARDS FOR WHAT HE HAS DONE FOR 'REAL SCIENCE'. HE IS A REAL SCIENTIST WHO TRIES TO PROVE HIMSELF WRONG, NOT THE FINDINGS OF OTHER PEOPLE! JOHN HAS WORKED WITH SOME OF THE BIGGEST COMPANIES IN THE WORLD AND HAS HELPED ESTABLISH PRODUCTS THAT WE USE IN OUR DAILY LIFE... FRAGRANCE, DETERGENTS AND MORE! JOHN HAS A DEGREE IN CHEMISTRY AND CHEMICAL ENGINEERING, THAT HE STUDIED AT THE SAME TIME, THAT IS BOTH HEMISPHERES OF THE BRAIN!!

JOHN IS A WORLD CLASS PROBLEM SOLVER BECAUSE HE INTENTIONALLY USES FOUR PRINCIPLES THAT DETERMINE TRUTH, WHICH EVEN LED TO HIM SOLVING A ONE IN A MILLION PROBLEM. HE ALSO USED THESE PRINCIPLES TO CREATE THE ONLY NON CONTRADICTORY MODEL FOR THE MIND AND BRAIN.

WHILE YOU MAY THINK THAT THIS IS WHAT MAKES JOHN BETTER THAN ANY OTHER PROBLEM SOLVER, IT IS ACTUALLY BECAUSE HE REALISED THAT WHEN PROBLEM SOLVING TOOLS ARE APPLIED TO PEOPLE, THEY MAKE THE PERSON WORSE! JOHN EXPLAINS IT THIS WAY:

THERE ARE FOUR APPROACHES TO A PROBLEM.

-ABSOLVE: IGNORE IT, MAYBE IT WILL GO AWAY. (IT WON'T)

-RESOLVE: FOCUS ON THE TANGIBLE EFFECTS AND RESPOND WITH REWARD OR PUNISHMENT.

-SOLVE: FOCUS ON THE TANGIBLE CAUSES AND RESPOND WITH A PROGRAM.

SOLVE WORKS FOR EQUIPMENT, HOWEVER, WHEN IT IS APPLIED TO PEOPLE IT CREATES AT LEAST THREE MORE PROBLEMS FOR THE PERSON ("LAW OF UNINTENDED CONSEQUENCES") AND THE OVERALL STRESS FROM THE SOLUTION IS WORSE THAN THE STRESS FROM THE ORIGINAL PROBLEM. THIS IS WHY THE WORLD IS GETTING WORSE. HUMANS THINK THE ANSWER IS TO SOLVE OUR PROBLEMS AND WE MAKE EVERYTHING THREE TIMES WORSE! LOOK NO FURTHER THAN THE PANDEMIC!

THIS IS THE APPROACH THAT IS USED BY PSYCHOLOGY AND PSYCHIATRY! THE PATIENT IS TREATED LIKE A ROBOT, NOT A HUMAN. THE PERSON PROVIDING THE TREATMENT IS REQUIRED TO ACT LIKE A ROBOT, NOT A HUMAN. IF ALL YOU HAVE IS SOLVE, THEN YOU WILL SPEND YOUR LIFE GETTING OUT OF HOLES YOU FELL INTO, ONLY TO FALL INTO ANOTHER HOLE! IS THAT YOUR PLAN FOR HAPPINESS?

WHEN JOHN WORKED WITH THREE PSYCHOLOGY STUDENTS FROM THREE DIFFERENT COLLEGES TWENTY YEARS AGO, HE TOLD EACH STUDENT TO ASK THEIR PROFESSORS, "HOW DO WE HELP PEOPLE BE HAPPY?" THE ANSWER WAS ALWAYS THE SAME, "OUR JOB IS NOT TO HELP PEOPLE BE HAPPY. IT'S TO HELP PEOPLE STOP DOING BAD BEHAVIOUR." RESOLVE AND SOLVE!

JOHN REGULARLY ASKS PEOPLE, "WHO OUGHT TO BE THE HAPPIEST PEOPLE IN THE WORLD?" THE COUNSELLORS! YOU CAN'T GIVE SOMETHING YOU DON'T HAVE, SO IF YOUR COUNSELLORS AREN'T HAPPY, THE BEST THAT THEY CAN DO IS HELP PEOPLE NOT KILL THEMSELVES, AND SOMETIMES THEY CAN'T EVEN DO THAT.

WHAT IS THE RIGHT APPROACH TO A HUMAN PROBLEM?

DISSOLVE: FOCUS ON THE INTANGIBLE CAUSES! THIS IS THE UNIQUENESS OF THE PERSON! THE INTANGIBLE DRIVER!

I DON'T HAVE ROOM TO EXPLAIN EVERYTHING, THAT WOULD TAKE ANOTHER BOOK. HERE IS MY OVERVIEW OF JOHN'S APPROACH...

RATHER THAN FOCUS ON THE BAD BEHAVIOUR AND EVENTUALLY GET DRAINED FROM THE PROGRAM'S DAILY REMINDER OF YOUR PROBLEMS, IF YOU FOCUS ON YOUR UNIQUENESS, WHICH IS YOUR SOURCE OF ENERGY, YOU WON'T EVEN HAVE TO DEAL WITH THE BAD BEHAVIOUR. THE ISSUE WILL BE DISSOLVED!

SO WHAT THE INTANGIBLE DRIVERS WITH FLOWCESS OFFERS IS... A UNIVERSAL WAY OF TALKING TO ALL HUMAN BEINGS, REGARDLESS OF RACE, RELIGION, GENDER, SEXUAL ORIENTATION, AGE OR SHOE SIZE! WHAT WE DO IS ENERGISE EACH OTHER IN EVERY INTERACTION, AS IT'S DONE ON PURPOSE. HOW WOULD THIS MAKE YOU FEEL IF EVERYONE CHOSE TO IMPLEMENT THIS AND WE WERE ABLE TO CREATE A NEW WAY OF LIVING? MORE INTERACTION AS IT WAS ALL GIVING... SOUNDS IDEAL RIGHT?

I WILL GIVE YOU THE QR CODE AT THE END OF THIS CHAPTER TO DO YOUR QUIZ AND WORK OUT YOUR INTANGIBLE DRIVER AND HOW YOUR BRAIN FUNCTIONS! WHO WOULDN'T WISH TO KNOW THEMSELVES BETTER? HOW WOULD YOU FEEL KNOWING WHAT ENERGISES YOU AND WHAT DRAINS YOU ENERGETICALLY? WOULD YOU NOT LIKE TO BE ABLE TO BE SPECIFIC TO OTHERS IN HOW TO INTERACT WITH YOU?

YOUR INTANGIBLE DRIVER IS YOUR ID, YOUR IDENTIFICATION... NOT A PASSPORT OR A DRIVING LICENCE, THESE ARE JUST METHODS OF CONTROL AND TRACKING. WHO YOU ARE IS INSIDE AND NOT WHAT YOU LOOK LIKE ON THE OUTSIDE. THERE HAVE BEEN MANY PEOPLE SAY THIS OVER CENTURIES AND NOT BEEN ABLE TO PROVE IT! JOHN AND FLOWCESS HAVE THIS DOWN AND I HAVE 4 YEARS OF HELPING PEOPLE UNDER MY BELT TO PROVE THAT THIS METHOD WORKS!

YOUR ID INCLUDES YOUR WHY (THE EFFECT YOU WISH TO HAVE ON OTHERS) AND YOUR HOW (HOW YOU APPROACH A SITUATION). FOR EXAMPLE, I AM A COMPASSION-SERVER. I GAIN ENERGY DOING WHATEVER IT TAKES (SERVER) TO HELP PEOPLE HAVE THEIR PAIN BEARED

(COMPASSION).

THE INTANGIBLE DRIVERS ARE, IN ORDER: PERCEIVER, TEACHER, COMPASSION, GIVER, SERVER, ADMINISTRATOR, EXHORTER. YOUR WHY AND HOW CAN BE ANY MIX OF THESE, WHEN YOU DO THE QUIZ AT THE END OF THE CHAPTER, YOU WILL BE SENT VIDEOS TO WATCH TO YOUR EMAIL AND THIS WILL HELP EXPLAIN THEM.

THE TENSION SCALE IS IN ORDER OF THE INTANGIBLE DRIVER WHYS, SO PERCEIVER WHY AND EXHORTER WHY WILL FEEL THE MOST NATURAL TENSION BETWEEN EACH OTHER BECAUSE THE PERCEIVER WANTS TO POINT OUT THE OBVIOUS FACTS, WHILE THE EXHORTER IS ALL ABOUT THE SHOW/EMOTION. THAT IS 6 STAGES OF TENSION BETWEEN THEM BOTH AND IF THEY DON'T HAVE THIS INFORMATION, THEY COULD LITERALLY RUIN EACH OTHER IS THIS FAIR? HOW WOULD IT BE IF PEOPLE WERE ABLE TO SEE PAST THE LOOKS AND BEHAVIOUR OF OTHERS AND UNDERSTAND WHERE THIS CAME FROM? WOULD THE WORLD BE A MORE BALANCED PLACE TO LIVE IN?

WHAT JOHN DOES IS BASICALLY A TWO STEP PROCESS. REMEMBER SYNAPTIC PRUNING? AROUND 13 YEARS OLD, YOU GOT STUCK DRIVING A CAR (BRAIN) THAT DOESN'T FIT YOU (INTANGIBLE DRIVER). JOHN HELPS PEOPLE GET THEIR UNIQUE CAR BACK IN TWO STEPS!

THE FIRST STEP IS TO HELP YOU DRIVE YOUR CURRENT CAR, THAT IS A MISMATCH, IN A SAFE MANNER. HE WANTS TO MAKE SURE YOU ARE AROUND FOR THE SECOND STEP WHEN YOU GET YOUR CAR BACK. THIS INVOLVES LEARNING AND USING THE COMMUNICATION GUIDELINES AND REHEARSING YOUR TRIGGERS AWAY...LEARNING HOW TO THINK! IF YOU DON'T REHEARSE YOUR TRIGGERS AWAY, THEN YOU ARE SUSCEPTIBLE TO LOSING CONTROL FOR SECONDS THAT COULD IMPACT YOUR LIFE FOR WEEKS, MONTHS, YEARS, EVEN DECADES.

THE SECOND STEP IS TO EMBRACE YOUR UNIQUENESS AND COMMUNICATE IT TO OTHERS, WHILE LEARNING THE NON CONTRADICTORY DEFINITIONS FOR TEN WORDS THAT CAUSE PEOPLE THE

MOST CONFUSION AND ANXIETY IN THEIR LIVES. WHILE THE DEFINITIONS REPAIR THE BRAIN, PEOPLE INTERACTING WITH YOU IN YOUR UNIQUENESS CAUSES YOUR BRAIN TO REWIRE TO THE CAR THAT FITS YOUR DRIVER! AS YOU CONTINUE IN THAT, YOU WILL GROW TO HIGH SELF-ESTEEM AND HEALTHY HAPPINESS.

JOHN OPENED THIS INFORMATION UP TO THE PUBLIC DURING THE PANDEMIC. IT WAS EXTRAORDINARY TO SEE THE NUMBER OF PEOPLE WHO SAID THEY HAD THEIR BEST YEAR EVER DURING THE PANDEMIC!

WOULD YOU LIKE TO DETERMINE HOW YOUR BRAIN IS WIRED FOR HAPPINESS?

IF SO, WRITE DOWN YOUR ANSWERS TO THIS QUESTION: WHAT DO YOU THINK YOU NEED TO DO OR HAVE IN ORDER TO BE HAPPY?

WARNING: IF YOU WRITE SOMETHING DOWN THAT IS DIFFERENT THAN YOUR BEHAVIOUR, YOU MAY BECOME DEPRESSED. YOUR UNCONSCIOUS WILL SEE WHAT YOU WRITE AND IT WILL DEPRESS YOUR ENERGY IF IT IS DIFFERENT THAN YOUR BEHAVIOUR. FOR INSTANCE, IF YOU DON'T WRITE DOWN YOU NEED MONEY TO BE HAPPY, YET YOU SACRIFICE THINGS IN YOUR LIFE IN THE PURSUIT OF MAKING MORE MONEY, YOUR UNCONSCIOUS WILL DEPRESS YOUR ENERGY.

YOU DON'T HAVE TO SHOW ME YOUR ANSWERS BECAUSE EVERYONE'S ANSWERS FALL IN ONE OF FOUR CATEGORIES!

NO SELF-ESTEEM: SOMETHING BAD TO HAPPEN TO A PERSON OR A GROUP OF PEOPLE. ENEMY DIE, COMPETITOR GO BANKRUPT.

LOW SELF-ESTEEM: NO TENSION. WIN THE LOTTERY, RETIREMENT, SPEND ALL DAY DRINKING MAI TAI'S UNDER A CABANA.

MID SELF-ESTEEM: ACHIEVEMENT. WIN AN AWARD, GET A PROMOTION, EARN AN ADVANCED DEGREE.

NOTICE, ALL OF THESE ARE TANGIBLE AND OUTSIDE YOURSELF. JOHN'S

BIG DISCOVERY WAS THAT OUR BRAIN GETS USED TO ALL THESE THINGS SO THAT WE WILL NEED MORE OF THEM TO GET THE SAME EFFECT. THIS IS CALLED HABITUATION. THIS MEANS THAT NONE OF THESE WILL RESULT IN LONG-TERM HAPPINESS AND FULFILLMENT!

CAN YOU SEE HOW WE'VE ALL BEEN PROGRAMMED TO PURSUE THESE THINGS OR HAVE BEEN LED TO BELIEVE THAT MORE OF THESE THINGS WILL MAKE US HAPPY? WHAT IS THE ONLY WAY TO BE HAPPY AND FULFILLED?

HIGH SELF-ESTEEM: RESPOND TO EVERYTHING BY BEING MORE YOURSELF!

THE KEY TO MENTAL HEALTH, HAPPINESS, AND FULFILLMENT IS VALUING THE INTANGIBLE AND THE QUALITATIVE. THE KEY TO BEING CONTROLLED AND GETTING FURTHER AWAY FROM MENTAL HEALTH, HAPPINESS, AND FULFILLMENT IS VALUING THE TANGIBLE AND THE QUANTITATIVE BECAUSE YOU CAN NEVER HAVE ENOUGH. WHICH ONE ARE WE BEING PROGRAMMED TO VALUE? NOTICE, RESPONDING TO OUR PROGRAMMING BY WISHING THE PROGRAMMERS ILL ONLY CAUSES US TO GO TO NO SELF-ESTEEM. THEY WIN!

SELF-ESTEEM IS CONFIDENCE IN YOUR UNIQUENESS. NO SELF-ESTEEM PEOPLE DON'T KNOW HOW TO GET CONFIDENCE, SO THEY FOCUS ON WRECKING OTHER PEOPLE'S CONFIDENCE. LOW SELF-ESTEEM PEOPLE JUST WANT CONFIDENCE WITHOUT KNOWING WHO THEY ARE. MID SELF-ESTEEM PEOPLE ARE FIGURING OUT WHO THEY ARE, BUT THEY AREN'T CONFIDENT THAT THEY KNOW HOW. THE FIRST STEP TOWARDS INTENTIONALLY DETERMINING WHO YOU ARE IS THE INTANGIBLE DRIVERS! WHO DO YOU THINK OUGHT TO KNOW THIS INFORMATION AND BE TEACHING IT TO ALL OF US?
THE BIGGEST SYSTEM THAT CONTROLS THE POPULOUS IS PSYCHOLOGY: CONTROL PEOPLE'S MINDS BY DAMAGING THEIR BRAINS, YOU WILL CONTROL THEIR BEHAVIOUR. IF YOU WERE WANTING TO KEEP EVERYONE'S BRAINS FROM DEVELOPING FURTHER, HOW WOULD YOU DO IT? IF PEOPLE ARE ALWAYS LOOKING UP TO LEARN FROM TEACHERS, WHO

MAKES UP THE CURRICULUM FOR THE TEACHERS? IF THE SYSTEM THAT TEACHES THE TEACHERS TO REGURGITATE INFORMATION, IT MEANS THE TEACHERS WILL THINK THAT THEY ARE RIGHT BASED-ON WHAT THEY HAVE BEEN TAUGHT, NOT NECESSARILY ON THE TRUTH THAT IS. WHAT WOULD IT LOOK LIKE IF THERE WERE LEARNINGS OUTSIDE OF THE SO-CALLED EDUCATION SYSTEM? DEBUNKED? NOT CREDIBLE? YOU ABSOLUTELY MUST LEARN FROM ONE SOURCE FOR IT TO BE TRUTH, RIGHT? WHAT ABOUT ALL THE INVENTORS WHO ARE SILENCED? THE SCIENTISTS WHO ARE PAID HUSH MONEY OR HAVE BEEN INVOLVED IN ACCIDENTS AND THEIR FINDINGS DON'T COME OUT? IS THIS BECAUSE THE BIG SYSTEM IS IN CONTROL? IF YOU HEAR OF ME BEING INVOLVED IN AN ACCIDENT... JUST REMEMBER THIS BOOK WAS PROBABLY THE CAUSE AND THE NEXT BOOK WILL BLOW YOUR MIND COMPLETELY!

IMAGINE KNOWING WHY YOU TRIGGER OR HOW OTHERS ARE TRIGGERED BY YOU WITHOUT KNOWING? THIS INFORMATION IS HUGE! IT IS NOT A FACADE OR SOMETHING THAT CAN BE OUT DONE, AS ALL OF THAT WORK HAS BEEN DONE, BETWEEN JOHN AND I, PLUS THE TEAM AT FLOWCESS. WE CAN GUARANTEE THAT THE INFORMATION WILL BE DELIVERED IN A WAY IT CAN BE FULLY UNDERSTOOD AND INTEGRATED TO LIFE.

IMAGINE YOUR LIFE BEING CONTROLLED SO MUCH THAT YOU HAD TO LEARN TO COMMUNICATE AGAIN. MOST PEOPLE CAN SPEAK, BUT HARDLY ANY CAN COMMUNICATE! HOW WOULD YOU LIKE INTRODUCING YOURSELF AND PEOPLE ALREADY KNOW HOW YOU WOULD LIKE TO BE SPOKEN TO OR HOW TO GET THE BEST OUT OF YOU BY MAKING YOU FEEL WELCOME AND COMFORTABLE! SOUNDS LIKE THE LIFE EVERYONE CRAVES!

WE ALL KNOW PEOPLE WHO HAVE BEEN THROUGH TRAUMA OF SOME DESCRIPTION. WHAT I HAVE FOUND OUT IS IT'S THE WAY OUR BRAINS PROCESS THE TRAUMA THAT CAUSES MOST DAMAGE. IMAGINE UNDERSTANDING HOW TO PROCESS AND MOVE ON FROM LESS ENJOYABLE SITUATIONS ON PURPOSE! WOULD YOU NOT LIKE TO KNOW HOW TO THINK? IMAGINE KNOWING HOW TO ENERGISE A NEW SUITOR IN A RELATIONSHIP OR UNDERSTANDING HOW MUCH NATURAL TENSION THERE IS BETWEEN YOU BOTH BEFORE YOU EVEN GO ON A DATE! SHOULD

THIS INFORMATION NOT BE OUT THERE? IMAGINE KNOWING HOW YOUR CHILDREN'S BRAIN PROCESSES INFORMATION AND HELP THEM IN THEIR DEVELOPMENT, RATHER THAN JUST TEACH THEM WHAT YOU THINK IS RIGHT! IMAGINE BEING ABLE TO TEACH THEM HOW TO THINK BECAUSE YOU KNOW HOW TO THINK. SHOULD THIS INFORMATION NOT BE OUT THERE?

IMAGINE BEING ABLE TO TEACH TEACHERS HOW TO TEACH CHILDREN WITHIN THE EDUCATION SYSTEM IN THEIR OWN WAY, SO THAT IT'S NOT A ONE SIZE FITS ALL METHOD AND STUDENTS ARE SINGLED OUT. SHOULD THIS INFORMATION NOT BE OUT THERE? IMAGINE HAVING BUSINESSES AND COMPANIES THAT THE STAFF AND MANAGEMENT INTERACT AND WORK WELL WITH EACH OTHER. SHOULD THIS INFORMATION NOT BE OUT THERE? IMAGINE SPORTS TEAMS INTERACTING WELL TO GEL AND WORK TOGETHER AS ONE UNIT WITHOUT IT AFFECTING THE MENTAL HEALTH OF THE ATHLETES! SHOULD THIS INFORMATION NOT BE OUT THERE?

I COULD GO ON ALL DAY ABOUT THE BENEFITS OF WHAT CAN BE DONE IF WE ALL WISH TO LEARN AND GROW OUTSIDE THE SYSTEM WHICH CONTAINS US FROM BEING MORE! WHO IS WITH ME IN THE BELIEF WE CAN CREATE A NEW ONE? OTHERWISE, WE GIVE THE RICH AND POWERFUL MORE POWER BY DESIRING THE AMOUNT OF TANGIBLE THINGS THAT THEY HAVE.

IT STARTS WITH SMALL CHANGES IN AND AROUND US, THEN WHEN WE ALL START TO MAKE THE CHANGES, WE CAN ALL JOIN TOGETHER WITH STRENGTH IN NUMBERS AND MAKE THE CHANGES NEEDED. NOBODY IS IN CHARGE OF YOU, HOWEVER YOU WILL ONLY BE ABLE TO FULLY FUNCTION WHEN YOU KNOW YOU! THIS IS NOT BASED ON PSYCHOLOGY OR THE 16 PERSONALITY TYPES, WE'VE FOUND AND CAN PROVE THEM TO BE DAMAGING. HOW YOU FUNCTION IS THE MOST IMPORTANT THING TO UNDERSTAND!

HERE IS YOUR QR CODE TO FINDING OUT YOUR INTANGIBLE DRIVER AND BEGIN THE PROCESS OF GETTING YOUR CAR BACK SO THAT YOU CAN LIVE YOUR LIFE BY IT AND IT WILL KEEP YOU ENERGISED. WE HAVE OVER 100

FREE VIDEOS ON MY YOUTUBE CHANNEL "TRUTH IN THE 2020S". WE WILL HAVE APPS AND WEBSITES COMING SOON TOO! NO MORE WILL PEOPLE BE IN THE DARK WHEN THE LIGHT IS SUCH A BEAUTIFUL PLACE TO BE!

THIS IS THE QR CODE TO UNDERSTAND YOUR CAR AND DRIVER!

GET YOUR CAR BACK, REREAD THIS BOOK, AND REWRITE YOUR STORY!

EPILOGUE:

NOW YOU HAVE WRITTEN YOUR TRUTH- IN THE 2020s, LOOK OUT FOR MY NEXT BOOK WHICH IS ENTITLED TRUTH- BIGGEST SYSTEMS AND INSTITUTIONS TO UNDERSTAND THROUGH YOURSELF, WHY ALL OF WHAT WE HAVE JUST DONE TOGETHER HAPPENS IN THE FIRST PLACE!

REMEMBER... BEING CLEVER IS NOT ABOUT BEING EDUCATED, IT'S THE ABILITY TO SEE THROUGH SYSTEMS AND VEILS THAT HAVE BEEN USED TO PROGRAM US AND HIDE TRUTH.

I WILL SHOW YOU TRUTH, THROUGH YOUR OWN EYES, THIS JOURNEY HAS JUST BEGUN AND THE 2ND INSTALLMENT OF THIS SERIES WILL BE OUT 2025.

ARE YOU READY?

BE WELL AND LIVE WELL.

Printed in Great Britain
by Amazon